Why GM Matters

Why GM Matters

*Inside the Race to Transform
an American Icon*

WILLIAM J. HOLSTEIN

WALKER & COMPANY
NEW YORK

Published by Walker Publishing Company, Inc., New York

Photos used by permission of General Motors.

All papers used by Walker & Company are natural, recyclable products made from wood grown in well-managed forests. The manufacturing processes conform to the environmental regulations of the country of origin.

LIBRARY OF CONGRESS CATALOGING-IN-PUBLICATION DATA HAS BEEN APPLIED FOR.

ISBN-10: 0-8027-1718-7
ISBN-13: 978-0-8027-1718-4

First U.S. Edition 2009

1 3 5 7 9 10 8 6 4 2

Typeset by Westchester Book Group
Printed in the United States of America by Quebecor World Fairfield

To Rita, my new and enduring love

Contents

Preface

In 1953, General Motors President Charles E. Wilson testified before
Congress and spoke the words that for decades defined his company's
place at the center of American commerce and, indeed, defined its
national identity. It was a time of unparalleled optimism in America.
World War II was over, thanks in part to GM's contribution to America's superior war manufacturing effort (and to Wilson's leadership of
the War Production Board, which put him in charge of procuring all
matériel for the military). Cadillacs sported tail fins like those of rocket
ships. The American love affair with cars was exploding in movies and
music, but was also being woven into the very fabric of society. With the
new mobility afforded by autos, suburbs started sprouting up and an
interstate highway system was born. Americans were literally building
their lives around the automobile.

Wilson was in Congress that day because President Dwight D. Eisen-
hower had asked him to become his secretary of defense. The request
shocked the country. GM was incredibly powerful at the time, as the *Detroit Free Press* noted; its employees outnumbered the populations of
Delaware and Nevada combined. Didn't placing him in a senior government position represent a danger to the country?

Asked by a hostile Senate Armed Services Committee whether he
faced a conflict of interest between GM and the United States, Wilson
made the resonant statement that is often taken out of context: "For
years, I thought what was good for our country was good for General
Motors and vice versa. The difference did not exist. Our company is too
big. It goes with the welfare of the country."

A little more than half a century later, under radically different circumstances, General Motors chief executive officer Rick Wagoner appeared again before Congress. Toyota Motor, which had been derided as a pathetic maker of "Toyopets" when it first entered the U.S. market four years after Wilson's testimony, had pulled neck and neck with GM as the world's largest automaker and appeared poised to dethrone GM. The American economy was in crisis as it started to dig itself out from under a mountain of debt. GM's sales of sport-utility vehicles and pickup trucks, the segments of the market where it had made most of its profit, were in deep trouble. After spiking above $4 a gallon, gasoline was still selling for more than $2, despite wild swings in the price of oil. Even though the price of gasoline had gone down, consumers appeared to have concluded that it would soon go back up.

The indicators were undeniably grim. GM's stock hit an all-time low of around $3 a share, down from recent highs above $40. The company's share of the U.S. vehicle market, at 22.4 percent, was down from almost 51 percent at the height of the company's power in 1962. Nineteen thousand unionized workers were taking buyouts, and the company was closing factories that made larger vehicles, while rapidly gearing up production of newer, more fuel-efficient models. The company was burning cash from its reserves every month, and capital markets were reluctant to lend it fresh money. Newspapers hammered away at GM, assuming that it would have to either merge with the troubled Chrysler or declare Chapter 11 bankruptcy. In the *New York Times*, Bill Vlasic wrote, "Mr. Wagoner, 55, faces the prospect of cutting a deal for Chrysler or perhaps another automaker—or possibly going down in history as the executive who presided over GM's demise." An overstatement, but shocking nonetheless.

So when Wagoner went to the U.S. Senate Banking Committee in November 2008 to argue for a federal bridge loan of $25 billion for the Big Three, the contrast with Charlie Wilson's appearance could not have been starker. Rather than commanding a position of strength, Wagoner was on the defensive, warning that the government needed to take action to "save the U.S. economy from a catastrophic collapse." If GM did not receive the loans it was requesting—what the company's critics called a bailout—"the societal costs would be catastrophic," Wagoner warned. "Three million jobs lost within the first year, U.S. personal income reduced by $150 billion, and a government tax loss of more than $156 billion over three years, not to mention the broader blow to consumer and business confidence."

Wagoner's testimony was met with hostility from senators such as Richard C. Shelby (a Republican from Alabama). With Congress dead-locked on the issue, the Bush administration in its final days threw a temporary lifeline to GM in the form of loan guarantees. But a lasting solution would be possible only after the inauguration of President-elect Barack Obama, the former Illinois senator, who was more sympa-thetic to the manufacturing sector. In what became the first real test of his leadership, even before he was sworn in, Obama called the U.S. auto industry the "backbone" of the nation's economy. Some sort of federal help was in the offing.

But in stark contrast with 1953, the prevailing conviction among many American opinion leaders, including the senators who grilled Wagoner and the heads of Ford, Chrysler, and the United Auto Work-ers, was that GM doesn't matter at all. Because GM had lost so much ground to Toyota and other Japanese manufacturers, decision makers in New York and Washington seemed to have concluded that a Toyota job in Texas was the same as a GM job in Michigan.

Many average Americans also seemed to have turned against GM, judging not only from their purchasing patterns but also from the burst of letters from readers in major business publications. "While the GM corporate types were hauling their truckloads full of salary, stock op-tions and bonuses to their banks, realtors and brokers year after year, Japan's automakers were quietly feeling our nation's pulse, watching world events unfold, adjusting their corporate strategies and building our automotive future," wrote Mark Nickels of Manitowoc, Wisconsin, to the *Wall Street Journal* in early 2008. "What does GM stand for? Vi-sionless pathetic leadership, master blame gamers, out of touch with American consumers, laggards—I could go on."

Or as a blogger, williambanzai7, put it on *BusinessWeek* online in June 2008, "This company is a giant quagmire of mismanagement, intractabil-ity, intellectual laziness and competitive stupidity. I don't know anyone who would buy one of their gas guzzlers, and I predict that after a long drawn out process of denial, this hulk will be extinct. Labor, if you want to build cars, tell your members to go work for Toyota."

Some of the criticism was on target. For decades GM was slow to respond to external pressures and seemed completely out of touch with its customers. In the blogosphere, GM was portrayed as being part of the problem of deep economic insecurity, not as part of the solution.

But does globalization mean that a company in the Far East is the same as a company in the Midwest—and that it is acceptable to allow GM to slide into oblivion because Toyota is ready to fill the vacuum? The answer is no. What globalization means is that the United States has opened its market to major competition from foreign companies that wish to do business here—which forces American companies to become stronger and offer more choices to consumers. The right response to globalization is for industry, government, and society in general to create a climate in which America retains vibrant leadership in key industrial and technological sectors. Automobile manufacturing is certainly one of those sectors. Wagoner's effort to transform GM into a leaner, profitable competitor is thus a test case of how American manufacturing is to fare in a new global order.

No industrial nation in the world, with the exception of Britain, would even debate the importance of owning a large portion of its own automotive industry rather than allowing others to dominate it; indeed, Japan, Germany, France, South Korea, China, India, and others are making the development and expansion of their auto industries major priorities. Why? Because they recognize that the industry is a crucial generator of national wealth and, more, a guarantor of self-determination. As the collapse of the financial-services sector reminds us, the way to build wealth in the long term is by building things—and by accruing the knowledge that comes from the process of building them.

Simply put, if America is to remain a First World nation, with the sort of standard of living that it implies, it must maintain an American-owned auto industry. The skills that are necessary to design and engineer vehicles, along with the vast measure of parts and technology that GM buys from other American companies, including those in Silicon

Valley, help create wealth and innovation that flow far beyond the confines of the automotive business. These skills and new technologies are at the heart of maintaining America's ability to compete in the world.

Thus the battle to transform and indeed save General Motors in 2009 and 2010 is arguably the largest, most dramatic, and most difficult corporate turnaround effort in American economic history, on par with what Louis V. Gerstner Jr. accomplished at IBM or what Jack Welch did at General Electric. Some insiders call it the equivalent of rewiring a Boeing 747—in flight. Wagoner does not believe he has been attempting a "turnaround," in which the company would simply bounce back to what it once was. He has used the word "transformation"; in his thinking, for GM to survive, it has to be a dramatically different company.

Although GM boasted $178 billion in automotive sales in 2007, the company now is an underdog in many ways against the mighty Toyota, which has enough cash on hand to simply buy GM outright, if the American political environment was to allow it. The acid tests for Wagoner, now that he has almost certainly secured financial support from Washington, are whether he can return the company to profitability in North America and can improve the negative perception that entire generations of Americans have toward his company's products. Charlie Wilson would find it ironic indeed that GM's worst problems today are in its home market.

Inevitably, Wagoner's personality and style have been central to his efforts toward the transformation. Wagoner, six feet four, is a former Duke University basketball player, and the language of sports permeates his conversations. He calls himself a "player-coach," someone who is on the floor with his team, rather than someone who merely sits on the sidelines.

Wagoner has already moved to dramatically reduce GM's retiree health care and pension expenses, which had traditionally given his vehicles a $1,500 cost disadvantage. Starting in 2000, he closed eight U.S. assembly plants and one in Canada. Incredibly, from the start of 2006 to mid-2008, about 53,000 workers, roughly half GM's hourly workforce, had agreed to leave the company, accepting early-retirement packages. Other workers earning a fraction of their salaries will be hired as tier 2 employees, bringing GM's cost structure much closer to that of Toyota. To raise extra cash, he has spun off assets such as General Motors Acceptance Corporation and Delphi, GM's largest parts supplier.

While Wagoner has taken these painful steps that dominate the headlines, he has also been pushing a complete reinvention of GM. Perhaps his most significant bet is on the extended range electric vehicle, the Chevrolet Volt, due to go into production in November 2010, which would reestablish GM's technological leadership and repair its image. Under Wagoner, GM has transformed the way it assembles vehicles, copying wholeheartedly from Toyota's lean manufacturing techniques. It has revitalized its design studios, after years of dormancy. It is opening up the valves of its research and development efforts. And GM is thoroughly globalizing business on every front—design, engineering, purchasing, manufacturing, and other functions—to finally take advantage of its size and scale.

The wrenching—some would say brutal—cost-cutting, combined with huge bets on the future, give new meaning to the phrase *creative destruction*. One of Wagoner's problems is that his destruction has been much more visible to the outside world than what he is trying to create. In the debate that raged about GM's future, most critics argued that Wagoner and management had essentially sat on their hands for years. But the reality is that they had been striving mightily to transform GM into a company that could survive in a new era.

Wagoner is very much a product of GM's traditional culture, but he does not display the arrogance that some of his predecessors have. When I asked him in 2005 how it felt to be closing factories and losing money, he said, "Is it more fun to play in a game that you won by forty points or to play in one that your backs were up against the wall and you really had to use all of your capabilities and assets and your teammates' capabilities and get the game moving in the right direction? The latter is clearly more satisfying when you get it done."

So the debate about GM can be boiled down to a few simple questions: Should anybody care if GM survives? Do Rick Wagoner and his eventual successor understand what's at stake? Do they have the character and intelligence to repair the damage that decades of mismanagement have inflicted upon a hundred-year-old company? Is it too late?

Will the sheer weight of GM's baggage—the costs of pensions and medical benefits for retirees, plus the deep troubles at its finance subsidiary GMAC and its biggest parts supplier, Delphi—prevent it from transforming itself? And will deep economic woes in the U.S. market torpedo the GM transformation effort, no matter how effective Wagoner and his team can be?

PART I

The Stakes

CHAPTER 1

What Went Wrong

It used to be that GM executives denied anything had gone wrong at their company. That denial was part and parcel of the problem. But today top executives from Wagoner on down are candid in acknowledging that GM ran off the rails. "Obviously, something went wrong because the company went, over about a fifteen-year period, from the midseventies until the early nineties, from being in a very strong position to being in a very different position and quite a bit weaker financially," Wagoner says in his office high in the Renaissance Center in downtown Detroit. "The model that had served the company unbelievably well for years no longer did."

That's an astonishing but true statement. An organization with many decades of experience and many hundreds of thousands of employees simply became outmoded. GM didn't stop working overnight, of course. A company that big is something more like an aircraft carrier. Even if it takes a torpedo hit below the waterline, it still has forward momentum. For a while. The reasons this happened are complex—a perfect storm of new competition, bad decisions, radical market shifts, and plain bad luck. But the answer to what went wrong begins in the history of how GM was created.

In the briefest possible fashion, the story goes like this: Billy Durant, a swashbuckling iconoclast who loved the art of the deal, created General Motors in 1908 by smashing together different auto companies headquartered in different cities—Cadillac in Detroit, Pontiac in Pontiac, and Oldsmobile in Lansing. It was at a time of enormous flux in the auto industry, much like today, and it wasn't at all clear which type of auto and which brand name would prevail. "I was getting every kind of car in sight, playing it safe along the way," Durant once said.

Altogether, Durant bought twenty-five companies, including parts makers, between 1908 and 1910 and put them under the General Motors umbrella. Between 1916 and 1920 he bought another fourteen, including Chevrolet and Fisher Body. He bought the companies with stock and never attempted to consolidate their operations into a single cohesive whole. Each vehicle and component division handled its own purchasing, set its own prices, and managed its own accounting. Although the field was fragmented at the time, and GM was by no means the dominant player, Durant's prospects seemed reasonably secure.

But an unexpected recession hit the U.S. economy in 1920, and GM's sales plunged. With the company on the verge of bankruptcy, Durant was forced out. (He died in 1947 managing an eighteen-lane bowling alley in Flint, having squandered a personal fortune of $120 million, an incredible sum for that era. Wagoner wisecracked in a 2003 speech that the prospect of ending one's career that way "has haunted GM chairmen ever since.")

In 1923, the company was taken over by Alfred P. Sloan Jr., whose roller and ball bearing company had been acquired and eventually assimilated into General Motors. Out of the chaotic assembly of companies Durant had put together, Sloan created a system with greater controls, particularly financial controls. It was Sloan, for instance, who figured out a price ladder for GM cars; whereas Durant had allowed his various companies to compete against one another with similarly priced cars, Sloan sought to differentiate their products, so that a buyer in a given price bracket would have only one GM option. He positioned Cadillac at the top, a car for the wealthy or the aspiring, followed in descending order by Buick, Oldsmobile, Pontiac, and Chevrolet. He also introduced the concept of annual style changes, replacing the haphazard introduction of new models with a schedule that buyers could predict—and anticipate.

But even as Sloan brought a measure of order to GM, it was still not really a unified company with a centralized management. Within divisions there were separate fiefdoms, which managers guarded against meddling from headquarters. And the company kept adding pieces, reaching out into the world. Between 1923 and 1928, it opened nineteen assembly plants in fifteen countries in Europe, South America, Asia, Australia, New Zealand, and South Africa. It made outright purchases of other automotive manufacturers, such as Britain's Vauxhall in 1925, Germany's Opel in 1929 (at the start of the Great Depression), and Australia's Holden in 1931. The new companies added to the group kept operating largely independently.

This fragmented model worked well for many decades. It worked so well that between 1948 and 1950, management started agreeing to a compact with the United Auto Workers that over coming years would pour unprecedented wealth into the hands of workers. In 1948 it agreed to the concept of annual cost of living pay increases. Then in 1950 it agreed to provide its workers full pensions and free health care coverage for life. These were the origins of how the UAW became so powerful that GM's cost structure was essentially uncontrollable.

But none of that mattered because GM kept gaining ground through the 1950s and 1960s. In 1962, at the high-water mark, it controlled 50.7 percent of the U.S. automotive market. "Back in 1963 when I joined, GM was without question and by a wide margin the dominant automotive producer in the world," recalls Robert Lutz, who is now vice chairman of global product development and the oldest member of Wagoner's management team. "We actually had a concern in the U.S., as our market share was heading over fifty percent. There was noise from the Justice Department that GM would be split up. So it was almost a disincentive to achieve greater growth and efficiency. We had a structure that worked very well for us back then, which was a great deal of divisional autonomy." By that model, once a division had its budget approved, it could design and develop and manufacture its own cars without oversight from the top.

That model helped the company make each of its brands distinct, which the market wanted. But it also made the process of making decisions at GM enormously complex and convoluted. "GM organization charts out of the sixties were published in these huge light-green foldout things," Lutz says. "It looked like a gigantic inverted oak tree. There were so many little boxes and so many divisions—and we still had all the nonautomotive."

By "nonautomotive," he means all sorts of businesses that were not even remotely related to the making of vehicles—like, for instance, the Inland Ice Cube Tray Division, which sold parts to Frigidaire for use in refrigerators. Indeed, when Lutz first arrived at GM in 1963, very little had changed in decades in the way the company was run. "It was very much into the dictates of Alfred P. Sloan—there was a degree of central coordination but decision making was decentralized," Lutz adds. "It was unbelievably slow, complex, and bureaucratic." But in an era with precious little competition from outside the United States, inefficiency could run unchecked, and the company was still "totally competitive, because we had such enormous power that we could always steamroller everybody else," Lutz says. "Even if we were late coming out with something, once GM geared up to do it, whoever started it would get crowded to the sidelines."

Nor had much changed by the time Rick Wagoner joined the company in 1977. GM was still divided and subdivided. "Our tradition was separate brands," he says. "Chevy was a pretty integrated auto company itself. Pontiac was, and so was Buick. To their credit, I think the leaders in the late seventies and early eighties saw that that needed to change. But that was hard to do, changing fifty years of history."

At about this time, in 1973 and 1974, the first major oil shock hit the United States, and the game started to change. Toyota had entered the U.S. market in 1957, but by the early seventies had gained only a very small toehold. Their first model, the Toyopet, had been derided by consumers and the automotive press, and the company's image hadn't entirely recovered. But with the new thirst for fuel-efficient cars, Toyota became a much more significant player.

Part of Toyota's advantage was in its totally different management model and manufacturing system. Toyota and other Japanese manufacturers had learned a great deal from W. Edwards Deming and Joseph M. Juran, two early pioneers of quality and efficient manufacturing who had been involved in helping the American war machine improve the quality and output of ordnance and armaments. But American manufacturers, confident in their superiority following World War II and basking in postwar prosperity, largely ignored these statistics gurus. The Japanese, however, had been stung by the manufacturing power of the United States during the war. They were open to learning. Their goal after the war was to "catch up and surpass the West."

So Deming and Juran lectured, consulted, and urged Japanese manufacturers to embrace concepts such as quality assurance and total quality control. If war-torn Japan committed to continuously improving its industrial processes, it could lead the world within a single generation, Deming suggested in 1951.

The Japanese, partly as a result of the war's devastation, also were prepared to do more with less. They had a fundamental understanding of the need for efficiency; in their model, it made a difference that each worker on the line took fewer steps to get a part and made fewer turns of the screw to attach a part. And as countless books have revealed, Toyota had a different philosophy about labor-management relations. There was very little of the hostility that characterized relations between American managements and labor forces, including GM's. In Japan, management and labor were in the battle against the enemy together; they had little or no time to fight each other. And unlike GM, Toyota had a clearly centralized management system, with the Toyoda family at its heart. (The product name had been altered slightly to Toyota to make it more appealing to American customers.)

All this gave birth to what was called the lean manufacturing system, built on several signal principles: there was *kanban*, in which parts were delivered to the assembly line just as they were needed, rather than being stockpiled; *kaizen*, a philosophy of constant improvement; and a team-based approach to manufacturing, in which a small group of workers would be responsible for each phase of building an entire car, unlike the Henry Ford system of long, depersonalized assembly lines, where few workers could be held accountable for the quality of their performance.

7

Whereas GM and the Americans in general had "mass," Toyota and the Japanese in general had "lean"—and lean, in the new era, was clearly better. Their vehicles were cheaper and more efficient, and did not break down nearly as often. The lean model also allowed for quicker decision making and much more efficient use of materials and energy, not to mention manpower. GM and other American manufacturers, in contrast, had not changed their fundamental approach since the days of Henry Ford's Model T.

Jack Smith, who became CEO in 1992, is the GM executive who is given credit for recognizing that there was a serious competitive imbalance. "The first indication that something was different in the auto industry was in the midseventies, when we had an overseas team that happened to be in Japan," he recalls. "They witnessed a fast die change by Nissan."

It was an unusual place for an epiphany. A die is one of the massive steel forms that shape the large metal panels of a car; massive, earth-shaking stamping presses hold these dies and pound out thousands of identical parts a day. American companies would use a single die set to stamp a warehouse full of parts, then laboriously change dies before starting on another part. At the Nissan plant, the Americans saw a die that would take GM hours to change get swapped in fifteen minutes flat. They were astonished.

Such are the things that manufacturing advantages are built on. With a shorter changeover time, the Japanese company could use each press more efficiently, doing a short run of each part before switching dies and stamping another part. This required less downtime, fewer presses, and less warehouse space, all of which offered potentially huge cost savings. It was clearly a better model.

The GM team brought their observation back to headquarters, where committees reigned supreme. "At that time, we had policy groups. One was the overseas policy group, and I was working with that group," Smith explains. "If this is really true what they're doing, changing dies in fifteen minutes, it had huge implications. You have the capability to really reduce the investment [needed to manufacture cars]."

Smith was impressed, and he took the team's findings to his bosses. But his message, Wagoner recalls, went over "like a lead balloon." Top

GM management wouldn't hear it and continued to deny that the Japanese had any advantage. Many executives suspected the Japanese had production technology secrets, like a specialized piece of equipment, that GM would eventually learn about. They could not accept that the Japanese had devised a superior manufacturing or management method.

Smith, however, persisted in trying to learn more about the Japanese system. In the early 1980s, he traveled to Japan and met senior members of the Toyoda family. He wanted to learn more about how they did what they did. The Toyodas, in turn, wanted to have political cover to expand their operations in the United States. What better way to protect themselves from political backlash than to have a joint venture with America's largest car manufacturer? "They weren't real comfortable with the culture and a joint venture would be a great place to start," Smith recalls.

In 1982, Toyota and GM began discussions about creating just such a joint venture: New United Motor Manufacturing Incorporated (NUMMI), which would be housed in a shuttered GM plant in Fremont, California. It was to be a collaborative effort that would manufacture cars that GM and Toyota could each sell under its own brand name. In the two years it took to negotiate the deal, Smith, then head of product planning, learned even more that alarmed him. "We had an opportunity to review our manpower versus Toyota's at a Toyota assembly plant that was making a relatively small car," he explains. "Toyota said it had two thousand people" at work on the project. "We had fifty-five hundred people doing comparable work in the United States. I lugged that information back to Detroit and it was very unwelcome news. The people responsible for manufacturing were in denial."

To be sure, Toyota was learning a lot about GM as well. "We took them to a couple of our plants and they were scared by the way we operated. They were really leery," Smith says. "They couldn't believe that not everyone came to work every day and that there were alcohol and drug problems."

The bad news continued as the two archrivals geared up to start manufacturing together in 1984. At NUMMI, the two companies had created a unified management team empowered to make its own purchasing decisions. But the members of the team—even the GM personnel—weren't impressed with GM's quality. In quality and in cost, the vast majority of GM's parts just weren't competitive. "We only won three or four parts" in the competition at NUMMI, Smith says. "We won seats," he says, and "wiring harnesses, but that came from Mexico. We won front drive axles, but that was because Toyota was out of capacity. The message coming back was that our components were out of line. This was a tough recognition for the organization. We were grossly uncompetitive in everything."

This was a very dark period in GM's modern history. The company was completely adrift without any clear and coherent strategy. Its cars weren't nearly as good or as reliable as those of a new set of competitors. Its manufacturing processes were antiquated. A new CEO, Roger B. Smith (no relation to Jack Smith), had started in 1981, and he was clearly not up to the job. He could not articulate a strategy for GM to respond to Toyota and others. Thus, when Toyota came along, GM had a ripe underbelly—a corporate structure that put it at risk to a much more centralized, focused organization like Toyota—yet its arrogance prevented it from responding.

GM wasn't even sure what business it was in. In 1984, it purchased Electronic Data Systems (EDS) from Ross Perot and Hughes Aircraft. It launched disastrous forays into front-wheel drive, and Roger Smith, who was deservedly pilloried in Michael Moore's 1989 film, *Roger and Me*, spent heavily on robots, which he hoped could replace human labor. Billions of dollars were squandered.

The company attempted one major reorganization in 1984 that resulted in the Buick-Oldsmobile-Cadillac/Chevrolet-Pontiac-Canada/Truck & Bus group. The company was trying to break down the divisions between its separate brand names and its separate geographic and functional subsidiaries. It was trying to get its various arms and legs to dance together as part of one cohesive management structure. But the acronym used to describe the reorganization, BOC/CPC/T&B, said it all; the company was mired in complexity. "GM is a giant that is sick in bed," one Toyota executive told *BusinessWeek* in 1985.

"We were still running the Sloan model of a decentralized organization," Jack Smith explains. "At the time, we had twenty purchasing operations—all the component divisions, car and truck divisions—and on the auto side, we had seven manufacturing units. You had Truck, Buick-Olds, Cadillac, and others. They all had separate engineering systems. It was just unbelievable. Why did you have that? GM came together by acquisition. Sloan had invented the model that worked remarkably well and people were reluctant to change. Even when they tried to change, there were very powerful people running the divisions and they resisted."

Lutz was a competitor at Chrysler during the late 1980s and early 1990s—and he knew that GM had a complete mess on its hands when it came to purchasing its parts. "Every important supplier, I'd try to have lunch with him once a year," Lutz explains. "One time I was having lunch with Federal Mogul. One of my questions was always, 'How are we to do business with?'"

After comparing different companies, the Federal Mogul lunch partner said, "Our favorite customer is GM by far."

Lutz said he was surprised.

The supplier responded, "Oh, I'll tell you why. They have so many purchasing departments and so many various groups that buy engine parts that we sell the same ball bearing set to eleven different organizations at GM under seventeen different part numbers and under prices that vary widely, and nobody in GM knows that somebody else in GM is getting exactly the same Federal Mogul part for vastly less money than they are paying." That was the picture of utter dysfunction.

After Jack Smith became CEO in 1992, he started his drive to have GM "run common." What that meant was that Smith wanted to start consolidating operations to have units around the world use common parts, processes, and systems—to make sure that everyone was using the same ball bearings and paying the same price. Although very few people inside or outside of GM recognized it at the time, this was the equivalent of Mao Zedong or Vladimir Lenin attempting to destroy the old order and create a new one. This was the beginning of GM's response to Toyota, but it was at least a critical decade late.

In the A111 conference room in the Design Building at GM's Technical Center in Warren, Michigan, there is what amounts to a shrine to the glory years of beautiful American cars. On the wall are images of Cadillacs from over the course of nearly a century. From the 1920s to the 1960s, Cadillacs captured the imaginations of Americans, and no wonder. There's the Aero-Dynamic coupe of the early 1930s, a gorgeous old top hat of a car. There's the Sixty Special from the early 1940s, whose front end looks like a submarine surfacing. There's the 1959 Eldorado, with its huge tail fins swept back like a cruise missile, or two scarves streaming in the wind. Then there's the single vehicle that represents the entirety of the 1970s and 1980s. This is a car best—or most charitably— described as *nondescript*. After fifty years of romance and magic, GM produced a box on wheels.

"This is what we lost from the late seventies through the nineties," Lutz explains, sitting in his office in the Design Building. And the problem wasn't just the Cadillac. For too long, GM's cars were not visually appealing, inside or out. Today, GM leaders understand that. But looking at the sequence of photos on the wall in A111, it isn't until the 1990s that the images once again become visually striking.

"Beginning with Harley Earl and then later especially with Bill Mitchell," the heads of design from the 1930s through the mid-1970s, "there was a tremendous enthusiasm and belief in the power of design and sex appeal of the cars to win the hearts and minds of the American public. Design basically drove the company. Design had Eero Saarinen do this whole complex," Lutz says, gesturing out his window at the series of low-slung buildings that make up the Tech Center. The Tech Center is stunning, even though it is located in the drab industrial suburb of Warren, about thirty minutes north of Detroit's Renaissance Center (Ren Cen). An enormous dome, a series of striking water towers, and large pools of water are placed between the dozens of buildings in the complex. "The first big design dome in the world, and even these ultramodern water towers were not designed by a water tower company. They were done by GM Design.

"Design basically was the face of the company and Design was constantly and enthusiastically coming up with new design concepts. They were driven to always do the most beautiful cars in the world."

The problem was, they went about designing cars with scarcely any regard for how they would actually sell. Pete Estes, then president of the company, could merely react to some of what the designers did. "They would do them in clay models and then they'd bring senior management in and say, 'Pete, listen. We've got something that's really hot. We have to show it to you.' And Pete would go into design and he'd look at this clay model and he'd say, 'Whoa. Holy mackerel! What *division* are you thinking of?'"

There were other excesses. Designers were having their own personal cars restored in back rooms of Design and taking liberties with the cars they built. "One famous excursion was when Bill Mitchell didn't like the way the Camaro and Firebird sounded," Lutz remembers. "He thought the thumping sound of the big V-8s, which everybody kind of reveres today, sounded unrefined and cheap. He decided he would modify a Firebird to show the engineers what a good sports car is supposed to sound like. So he ordered a 12-cylinder Ferrari engine, which today would cost about $55,000, if not $60,000—more than most cars—and that was dutifully installed in a Pontiac Firebird." In its warehouses, GM still has the car, which was called a Pegasus.

Mitchell, a designer, summoned the engineers. He said, "Drive this. This is what a good sports car is supposed to sound like."

The engineers were less than charmed. And over time, the rest of the company turned against the designers, too. "When the last of these flamboyant designers left," Lutz explains, "the empire struck back and said, 'We're not having any more of these prima donnas who think they're running the company. All they are is a bunch of artists.' Design was relegated downward. Everyone else said, 'We don't want you people creating any more. The rest of the organization, through methods that are as scientific as possible, will determine what the right cars are. We will define them, we will determine the dimensions and the power trains by analyzing market trends. And then we will tell you at the right time what it is we want, and you'll put a wrapper on it.'"

Wagoner, who arrived later at GM with an entirely different background, sees Design's loss of stature within the company as a reflection of GM's determination to improve its quality to compete against Toyota.

"I'm not sure [design] got lost in the shuffle," he says. "I think the priorities of the company changed a little bit." GM at that time was reeling in disbelief that the Japanese could make cars that were better built than its own. Addressing that became the burning priority. "Do I want to do this outstanding design or is there maybe a less interesting design that will yield higher quality?" Wagoner says. "The quality was needed, and that somewhat carried the day. I think maybe we got a little bit carried away by manufacturing efficiency and things of that sort. Nobody was running around saying, 'Let's *not* do great designs.' Among the competing priorities, the voice of quality was so important in the late eighties and nineties. We weren't in the competitive range. We had to get lean in manufacturing. Those voices just got a little bit louder relative to the design voice."

Gradually, the design sensibility was corroded. From year to year, "it wasn't one car to the next," Wagoner continues. "It was, 'You're not quite where you want to be. Then *you're* not quite where you want to be.' Then all of a sudden you wake up and say, 'Hey, we're kinda in a crowd here. We're not distinguishing ourselves.'"

It was a long, agonizing near-death spiral. Aside from the fact that the cars were not exciting, GM's brands started blurring into each other. "How did we find ourselves over time with products—Buicks, Pontiacs, Chevrolets—that weren't that distinguished looking?" the CEO asks. "We lost the separateness and character of our brands. They kind of melded." A famous *Fortune* magazine cover in 1985 showed how the comparable Oldsmobile, Chevrolet, and Buick looked just alike. Wagoner still remembers that cover story.

Predictably, the people who controlled the purse strings bear some responsibility for those decisions. "I think it's fair to say that Finance had some ownership [of the problem]," Wagoner says. "We began to lose some of the competitive position because of the fuel economy, because we converted radically over to front-wheel drive," Wagoner continues. "We didn't quite meet the quality standards, so we began to lose some pricing because our quality wasn't good. So, gee, we're losing pricing, so we had to get tougher on costs. Okay, one way to get more efficiency is to share more panels across cars." Sharing panels across cars means that a Chevrolet shares a common metal panel with a Pontiac, for example.

Listening to Wagoner describe the past is like watching a slow-motion train wreck. "Profitability is still under pressure, so, gee, maybe we'll put in a little bit less expensive carpet. Nobody will notice it this time. Pretty soon, not only does the interior not look rich, it begins to look subpar. That begins to affect your brand. The need to meet cost targets was one of the culprits. It wasn't the only one. But it basically got driven as we began to lose competitiveness. Year by year, you crank down, crank down."

Design was obviously compromised as engineers and product planners took charge. A "design by committee" mentality set in, one that was heavily influenced by market research. The company would ask consumer focus groups (in what were called "clinics") what they found attractive and valuable. That meant GM could not produce breakthrough designs. It could only muddle through with what the potential customers wanted. And a room full of focus group volunteers is hard-pressed to imagine what had not yet been created. They wanted design features that they were already familiar with. All of which made for a poisonous environment for designers.

One last strand of what went wrong that bears mentioning is research and development, which is the lifeblood of any manufacturing company. Simply put, GM did not invest enough for many years, partly because it was straining to pay an average of $7 billion a year on health care. The paucity of research is one reason GM was surprised by Toyota's introduction of the Prius hybrid; GM wasn't pushing the edge of the envelope in alternative propulsion systems. One or two years of trimming back on R&D spending isn't a problem, says Wagoner. "But you wake up ten years later and you go, 'Geez, we really eroded some of the fundamentals of the company,' " he adds. "Design would have been number one. Technology leadership would be number two. We really slipped off. Not because it was a strategy or people weren't watching it, but because it was this year-by-year thing—driven by an uncompetitive cost structure and revenue pressures. It was not an irrational response year to year. But then one day you wake up."

The most burning questions about what went wrong at GM are these: Why did the company take so long to respond? And if some people in top management knew something was wrong, why didn't they fix it?

Wagoner's argument is that even the best captains cannot make an aircraft carrier turn on a dime. "I don't think it's surprising that it takes time to change the paradigm," he says. "Obviously, when oil prices went up a second time, the competitors and particularly the Japanese competitors really got a foothold in the market," which radically changed the dynamics of the car business in the United States. "When that happens, it's usually the biggest guy who comes under pressure for losing market share. We began a long period of share loss that put pressure on the whole business model." At the same time, GM was struggling to accommodate expensive union contracts in an age of lower sales. Profits started to dip, and "that led to a series of actions which didn't necessarily hurt us from one day to the next but over time began to hurt our brands, our products, our technological prowess."

To respond, GM had to transform its corporate structure. It had to completely attack its cost structure, and that would require attacking a sense of entitlement that was deeply established throughout the company, among both salaried and hourly employees. Many jobs on the shop floor had been handed down from grandfather to father to son. The temptation for management was to just keep pumping out the metal to maintain labor peace and to earn enough cash to pay all those people, plus their medical benefits and pensions. If GM didn't play its hand just right, the union could shut down production and the company would be hemorrhaging even more money. Thus the company's primary focus was not truly on the marketplace. To a great extent, it was on its internal constituencies, but that mentality had to be shattered.

And the challenge was even bigger than that. GM had to learn how to manufacture all over again. It had to learn how to design again. It had to learn how to allow innovation to flow again. All those qualities had been lost or rendered obsolete. The rapid gains of Toyota and other Japanese manufacturers required a reversal of decades of established practices, forcing GM to learn how to compete as a single global entity, a most painful undertaking for such a sprawling assembly of different organizations. All this would force the company to change fundamentally. It's one thing to create a new company to take advantage of deep technological or competitive shifts in the marketplace. But it is infinitely more challenging to guide a large, highly complex company that had a long history of success through a period of gut-wrenching change. If GM was to survive, that's what Rick Wagoner would have to do.

CHAPTER 2

People on the Front Line

The state of GM can be explained in terms of market share won and lost, units sold, debts incurred, and earnings projected. But the story of General Motors is first and foremost a story about people. Yes, GM is a huge corporation with a board of directors and an imposing headquarters. But one of the most important factors in whether this company can revitalize itself is its people. Who are they and what are they trying to achieve? Some of GM's people are energized and attempting to fulfill their dreams; others have been left behind or are dangling, just waiting to see whether they will survive. Not all are Americans, and certainly not all are white men in their fifties, as the common stereotype presupposes. The vast majority have passionate connections to the automobile. In one way or another, Rick Wagoner is depending on them to deliver in design, in manufacturing, in product planning, in engineering, and certainly on the assembly line. GM has 96,000 employees in the United States and more abroad. If the company continues to struggle, these are the people whose lives may be affected. If GM is to prosper, it is their skills and their passion that will save the company.

Ed Welburn grew up in Berwyn, Pennsylvania, out on the Main Line from Philadelphia. His African American family was well educated—he is a third-generation college graduate—but the Welburns considered themselves working class, partly because Ed's father ran a "bump shop," an auto body repair place. Because of that, Welburn grew up in a strong car culture, but also a culture that encouraged the young boy to dream big dreams. "I felt wealthy growing up," Welburn, now fifty-seven, recalls. "I didn't come from a wealthy family but in many ways I felt wealthy. My parents always wanted to expose us to interesting things, to museums. We traveled the country by car. There was no interstate highway system. We took Route 66, which was just two lanes, and it passed through the Southwest. We saw the Grand Canyon, Yellowstone Park."

Back in Philadelphia, the young Welburn fell in love with a General Motors car that his father owned. "He had this Riviera that just blew me away. He'd bring it home every day, and I'd want to wash the car for him. I just loved the car. I'd wash it, I'd check the oil. At age eleven, I wrote General Motors and told them I wanted to be a car designer and wanted to know what classes to take in school."

Relatives told Welburn that GM would never hire him because he was black, but he persisted. "My parents knew that's what I wanted to do, and they just supported me in every way they could."

After attending Howard University, he was in fact hired as a GM designer, the first ever African American in his job. "It wasn't until I started to work at GM that I realized GM didn't have any other African American designers at the time. I don't dwell on that. Why should I be excited about the fact that GM didn't have any others?"

Today, Welburn is vice president of design, in charge of all of GM's design activity around the world, overseeing 2,075 people in all. Most people have an idea what traits a car designer should display—flashy clothes and a boisterous personality. Welburn isn't that sort of guy; he's a soft-spoken, buttoned-down executive who seems at home in a dark suit and tie. But while Lutz, with his flashy lifestyle and provocative pronouncements, attracts more media attention and acts as an ambassador for design within GM, it's Welburn who runs GM's design operations on a day-to-day basis.

It's Welburn, for example, who plays host at the design studios in Warren, Michigan, when Wagoner, Lutz, and other top brass descend on most Friday mornings to see what designers are doing. "Ed Welburn takes us into his virtual reality studio," Wagoner explains. "We look at clinical results and renderings and have somebody from Germany or Korea or China or sometimes all three places on the phone."

Then they look at the latest designs, often in the form of full-size clay models. "It's a great way to stay on top of the business, and it's actually a fun thing for us all to do," says Wagoner. "It's a reward I get for making it through to the end of the week."

So it is that the son of an auto mechanic from Philadelphia is in charge of design operations on five continents, all aimed at helping General Motors regain its leadership in automotive design—and indeed to survive.

When Mary Barra was graduating from the Waterford Mott High School, just west of Pontiac, in 1980, she made a choice not many of her girlfriends were making. "A lot of my friends were working at the local Dairy Queen and places like that," she recalls. "But I was walking into an assembly plant."

Barra had started at General Motors Institute (now called Kettering University), a college that allows students to alternate between academic study and hands-on experience in GM plants. It's a route that thousands of young people have taken to enter GM. Like others, Barra rotated between classroom work and temporary assignments in the company's Pontiac Division, which back in those days was a fully integrated, stand-alone car company, with its own foundry, engine plants, and assembly plants.

After two years of rotations, she was asked to identify her career choice. "I chose the plant because I thought it was energizing," she says. "I just loved the fact that every day you build X amount of cars and you knew you had a scorecard you were measured to regarding safety. Did I meet my schedule? Did I meet my quality? Did I achieve my costs? My father was a diemaker at Pontiac Motor Division for thirty-nine years.

He retired in December. I started working at Pontiac the next July. It was a little bit in my blood."

It was still relatively early in American women's campaign for greater recognition and power in the workplace, and Barra was entering environments that were all-male or very nearly so. "Women got noticed, especially as a young student walking in," she recalls. "But very quickly, you started working with the people, whether engineers or team members on the line. We got to know each other and we worked together. My strategy was to get past, 'Hello, how are you? My name is Mary.' Once you did that, it was no different than it is today. But you had to make the introduction and make sure people knew who you were and what you were doing there."

Barra graduated in 1985 and began working her way up the GM management ladder. In the late 1980s, she went to Stanford Business School on a GM scholarship, but was frustrated at how professors spoke about her company. "It was very disheartening because many of the classes used General Motors as a case study, and GM would get mentioned in a negative tone."

She also had some explaining to do back home. "One low point was when you had to go to family and friends and explain why the company lost twenty-two or twenty-three billion dollars. That was in the nineties. That was probably the period when it was difficult. People said, 'Oh, you work for *GM*.'"

Barra, at age forty-six, has been with GM for twenty-seven years and was recently promoted to a job at headquarters. Now she's responsible for global manufacturing engineering, with 7,100 people reporting to her. Her group decides what equipment and work processes a factory needs to make vehicles that have been designed and engineered by other units within GM. "We are the bridge between manufacturing and product," Barra explains. "We are responsible for machinery and equipment. We deliver machinery to a plant and it has to be integrated with material flow and the people. It's man, machine, material integration. We can put equipment in a plant, but if it's not integrated with how we design the jobs for employees, we haven't done our whole job."

Her job puts Barra at the center of Wagoner's effort to improve GM's global manufacturing to compete toe-to-toe with Toyota. Because she works with GM employees in dozens of countries, Barra rushes home most evenings to spend some time with her nine-year-old daughter, Rachel, and her ten-year-old son, Nick, before getting back to work. After getting the kids off to bed, she sits on the couch with her husband, also an engineer, and calls and e-mails factories around the world.

She finds the work rewarding. "I love to talk about our products with friends and family. There was a point when you'd hear every little story about 'this went wrong' and 'that went wrong,' but I'm driving an Enclave right now. I have people coming up to me and asking, 'Is that an Enclave? Can I sit in it?'" That didn't happen very often in the days when GM was putting out lackluster products. "It's fun because people approach you. It's rewarding to have that external recognition. We can have the best vehicles on the road. By any measure, that's rewarding."

There are also profound rewards for women in manufacturing, she feels.

"One of the things I've been involved in is our affinity group for women," she says. "I think it's very important that we continue to encourage girls and young women to study math and science. From a woman's perspective, it's very important. We've all read articles about what girls think in shying away from math and science. And I think it's important for General Motors because we want the diversity of thought. Whether it's gender or what culture we're from or what our hobbies are, we look at a vehicle differently because of those factors. If we get diversity of thought into our vehicle design and how we do our work, we're going to have better products. In the United States, eighty percent of the buying decisions are influenced by women. I think it's important for us as a company to have that voice."

Barra is clear about what she's trying to achieve at GM. "I want to be part of the team that helps GM regain its indisputable number one status. I grew up with my father having great pride in Pontiac Motor Division and General Motors. I want to be part of that."

When John F. Smith was growing up, his father was a journalist at the *Kansas City Star* and *Kansas City Journal*, which helps account for his easygoing manner with a visiting journalist. One of the sharpest memories of his youth was provided by his mother's side of the family. It came when he was nine years old. "Aunt May pulled up in my driveway with a pea-green two-door Eldorado, with black walls and four-foot wings on the back," he recalls. "I said to myself, 'This car is the *berries.*' I decided I wanted to do this. I am living the dream."

Of course, the dream went sour for many of the years after Smith joined General Motors in 1968. By the late 1990s, the enormous scale of GM's losses to Toyota and other manufacturers had become clear to Smith. His frustration was building. "We all wanted to stop apologizing at cocktail parties for our products," he recalls.

Starting in 1997, he had a chance to respond. As general manager of Cadillac, he began working with design chief Wayne Cherry (now retired) to improve the appearance of Cadillacs, which had become grandpa cars, fit only for snowbirds traveling to their winter homes in Florida and back. "We knew we could do better," the soft-spoken Smith says.

"Wayne and I spent the better part of a year with other support folks thinking, just what does the restoration of Cadillac entail? We spent hours talking about it and decided it boiled down for us to one word: *attitude.*"

It was the fourth quarter of 1997 at Cadillac Headquarters in the Technical Center in Warren. "We were having our teams work on what makes for a relevant Cadillac. And I came around this corner at Cadillac Headquarters around six P.M. and out of the corner of my eye I caught a graphic. It was the top half of a 1960 black Cadillac Eldorado convertible, and the top is down. There is a lovely woman wearing sunglasses with a bright yellow scarf that is wafting out over the entire rear length of the car. That Cadillac was all about attitude, and confidence about styling, and self-confidence." A lot like Aunt May's car.

"It was an aha moment. We pretty much realized that we were going to get back in the business of doing confident, leading-edge design. If our new look had a polarizing reaction from consumers, and that had been an important navigational aid to us for fifteen years, we were determined to listen to our inner voice."

In February 1998, Cherry and Smith laid out their vision of edgy

Cadillac design to Rick Wagoner, then president of GM North America. He liked it. The next step was a presentation to the entire top management team, which was considering what to do with the Cadillac Catera. The Catera was billed as the "Caddy that zigs," even if consumers found its styling nondescript and its handling only slightly less so. The management team, called the Automotive Strategy Board, was contemplating continuing with a new version of the Catera—until it saw Smith's new angular design treatment. "Everybody at the strategy board said, 'That's it,' " Smith recalls.

It was the beginning of GM's design turnaround. Now fifty-seven, Smith is two years older than Rick Wagoner, whom he met when both attended Harvard Business School. After forty years with the company, he has the title of group vice president, global product planning, meaning he is responsible for deciding which vehicles the company should design in each market around the world.

The first vehicle to get the revamped Cadillac design was the Escalade sport utility, but in Smith's mind, that was just a placeholder until the company could design a Cadillac car that would fully represent the new design direction. That was the Evoq concept car, presented at the January 1999 Detroit Auto Show. Smith recalls the moment well. "When the drapes came off, there was spontaneous applause."

Sylke Rosenplaenter was born in East Berlin, within sight of the Berlin Wall. After the wall fell in 1989, she was among the first waves of young East Germans to come to what was then called West Germany. Today she is the manager of concept validation and data management, in the Advanced and Concept Engineering Unit of General Motors Europe, based in Rüsselsheim, in a unified Germany. This is where Opel, owned by General Motors, is based, and it is where Wagoner's team decided to locate its global "homeroom" for the development of mid-size cars.

It's unusual to find a woman at her level and in her field. "We have not so many women in engineering management," says Rosenplaenter, thirty-nine. In a red blouse and gray checked pantsuit, she has cropped blond hair, penetrating hazel eyes, and a ruddy complexion. Her English—her third language, after German and Russian—is nearly flawless.

Her key job is "validating" designs of vehicles, which means checking on the work of others to make sure that the bodies, engines, and parts all function as expected. Because so much of that design and engineering work is done on computers, GM has to proof designs and specifications—down to the hoses and clamps—to make sure that a project is on track. She oversees three concept validation teams of about ten people each. In most cases, she does not know with absolute certainty that a vehicle can be assembled until it is rolled out on a pilot line, which is the step just before full-fledged production.

Rosenplaenter, a mechanical engineer, grew up in one of the harshest dictatorships of the twentieth century. The combination of a Soviet-style socialist system with German efficiency thoroughly discouraged individual initiative or risk taking. Not surprisingly, Rosenplaenter discovered when she arrived in the West that she lacked "soft skills"—handling the emotional dynamics of a team, persuading colleagues without fighting. Her West German husband, also an engineer, helped her make the transition from a Communist system, in which people were not encouraged to argue for what they wanted or to attempt to influence the actions of others. "One of the things I hadn't learned before was to make a personal network," she recalls. "You can't be successful without it. I also learned how to convince someone who was taking a different position from me. I had not learned this." She also had to adapt to a more outspoken environment. "No one can know what you would like. You have to tell them. So I started to tell. And you cannot be everyone's friend. Sometimes you have to stand behind your decision."

Now she works every day with Korean and Chinese engineers at GM facilities in Asia and with her American counterparts in the United States. GM has design and engineering people all over the world, so Rosenplaenter has to figure out how to get the different nationalities to function together. Part of the challenge is that the Koreans and Chinese typically don't speak English as well as the Germans do. And there are also big cultural differences when it comes to resolving conflicts. "If you want to express feelings, it is more difficult to get those across in a foreign language." One technique that helps is sending e-mails in English ahead of the meetings to give everyone time to understand the issues "so they don't feel under pressure." Many Asians understand written English better than spoken English.

For someone born into Communism, she takes a decidedly capitalistic view. Some people in GM Europe see themselves as Saab employees or as Opel employees only. "But we all should feel connected to the bigger umbrella called GM," she says.

Does she believe she is fighting for the German economy? "I don't think so much about the Germany economy," she says. "When I'm on the pilot line and can see that a vehicle can be manufactured, it has nothing to do with Germany. It means that the team has performed well and can be very proud of this."

In the new global GM, people like Rosenplaenter will do well. The GM of the future is going to demand more technical skills from people who are comfortable engaging across cultural boundaries; employees who cannot upgrade their skills or travel and make long-distance phone calls at odd hours will face distinctly limited futures.

One of the most important constituencies that Wagoner has to convince to come along for the ride is organized labor. Yet within the United Auto Workers, there are many different voices, divided by age, seniority, geography, and a hundred other personal factors. At one point on the continuum is Walt Wedow, who started working on the line at GM's Leeds plant, near his native Kansas City, Missouri, in the late 1970s. Back then, the atmosphere between management and labor was downright poisonous. As he recalls, "If I had a suggestion—maybe something with the car was wrong or some parts were wrong—the standard response from management was, 'Hey, we didn't hire you for your brains. We hired ya from the neck down.' "

Partly as a result of that climate of hostility, the company laid off the second shift in 1987, and that threw Wedow out of work. That same week, Wedow's new wife was laid off after eighteen years at Western Electric and was given only six months in severance. The following week they found out she was pregnant.

They struggled for several years. Wedow was out of work for four years before he agreed to move his young family to Lordstown, Ohio, to work at the GM plant there. The move was disruptive, but it held his family together, which isn't always the case when GM workers are redeployed to other factories. Many marriages so affected end in divorce. "I wanted a job. I wanted to keep my pay and pension and health care going," he recalls. "I didn't like moving, but it's just a fact of life." He speaks with a soft Kansas City accent, dropping *g*'s on the end of verbs and pronouncing the name of his home state as *miz-oor-a*.

After two and a half years in Lordstown, located sixty miles southeast of Cleveland and seventy-five miles northwest of Pittsburgh ("kind of in the middle of nowhere," he says), he received an offer to return to the Fairfax assembly plant in Kansas City, Kansas, across the river from Kansas City, Missouri. He's been there since.

Today, Wedow is fifty-seven and has long silver hair and a gray mustache. He's a zone committee person for the United Auto Workers, Local 31, which means he's the chief negotiator for the second and third shifts, and also a sort of resident philosopher. The Fairfax plant, which produces the hot-selling Chevrolet Malibu and Saturn Aura, has had a reputation for better management-labor relations than plants in Michigan and Ohio. One reason is that workers in Kansas City recognize that if GM stumbles, the company will close the plant. They can see a clear connection.

In his life, Wedow has seen dramatic changes in how management and labor get along. "Now we have a suggestion program where they actually pay you to come up with ideas—monetary rewards," he says. "That's how dramatic the change has been in my career."

And he has had the opportunity to look the CEO of the company in the eye and tell Wagoner what he thinks, which would never have happened in the bad old days. "When Rick Wagoner came here six or seven years ago, he toured the plant, and I met him," Wedow recalls. "I talked to him and said, 'I really appreciate the job that you guys are doing.' Because I could see then that things were starting to turn around. At a Q&A session, I told him, 'You really need to do something about the interior of these cars. You get in and they just feel cheap.'

"He agreed with me. He came straight out and told me, 'You're right, and we're addressing that issue.' I think management has done that—not as quickly as I would have liked. The first car I saw that had a dramatic turnaround in the interior was the Saturn Aura. In fact, I bought one for my wife. That's what we need to do."

Wedow, holding forth at a roundtable in the plant manager's office, can comment on global economic issues, partly because unlike most other workers, he went back and got a bachelor's degree in business administration when he was laid off. So I ask him: Does GM matter? Would it make a difference to anybody if GM simply went out of business and Toyota picked up the slack? "That's pretty shortsighted thinking," Wedow responds. "General Motors has contributed an enormous amount to the United States of America. The fact that it became the greatest country in the world was driven in large part by the United States auto industry because of the jobs it provided and the opportunity it provided to people to lift themselves up to the middle class.

"I had a huge argument when I was laid off and I returned to college to get my degree, with a classmate of mine who was a salesman from Toyota," Wedow continues. "He tried to tell me that Toyota had done more for America than the Big Three combined. I said, 'Have you ever heard of the Ford Foundation or the Alfred Sloan Foundation?' All these things that the car companies have done, the charitable contributions they've made, the things they did during World War II to save our country, to keep our freedom and also that of Europe. Yes, I think it's important."

Younger UAW workers don't necessarily share Wedow's sentiments. Harry Clay, thirty-four, and his wife have had a baby in recent months, which has the often-noted effect of wonderfully concentrating the mind on making a living. The wiry African American Clay, wearing safety glasses and sporting a Nike shirt and a thin goatee, is sitting at a table in the team meeting area, just beside the trim line at the new Delta Township factory. This three-million-square-foot facility, on the outskirts of Lansing, Michigan, is the newest, most modern plant that GM has built in the United States. The first shift started at six in the morning; now it's about nine in the morning, and the first work break is ending. Unlike

Wedow, who is in the final phase of his working life, Clay needs to work for many more years.

Clay, whose father and uncle worked in the car industry and who has two cousins also working at Delta Township, has been with GM for thirteen years. First, he was at Fisher Body in downtown Lansing before the company closed it, so he has tasted economic dislocation, and he has also seen some GM suppliers in the area go out of business. At Delta Township, where he's worked for the past two and a half years, he was recently promoted to team leader, supervising four mostly older men and women (Phyllis, Maggie, Barb, and Kevin) who install lining inside rear wheels of the Buick Enclaves, Saturn Outlooks, and GMC Acadias to protect against weather and foreign objects. When he became team leader, his hourly wage was raised fifty cents to about twenty-eight dollars an hour.

Clay sees some worrisome signs. One is that GM seems to be building a lot of factories in other countries while closing them in the United States. "Some people are skeptical about how long GM will be willing to keep their operations in Lansing and in the United States," Clay says. "I'm not worried as long as the cars are coming out and they're selling. But I guess management is looking for cheaper labor. And they're not getting it here. That's what people are scared of."

Who do you blame for the tough economic pressures on GM? "I can't blame it on the managers. I can't blame it on another company for running their business," says Clay. He keeps glancing over at the line to see if his team members are having any problems. "I think it's a set of circumstances lined up like the perfect storm—the economy, weakened dollar, a global system. And I blame the lawmakers. I think it's the laws that create the freedom for a company to leave without actually investing any money here. It's like an inducement to leave instead of to stay."

The Delta Township plant had been shut down by a strike for four weeks earlier in 2008, and Clay, as a member of the United Auto Workers, went out with his coworkers. Some analysts thought the UAW was trying to use a strike at Delta Township, makers of the popular Buick Enclave, to bring pressure to bear on GM to intervene in a strike at another company called American Axle; others saw the strike as centered on local issues, particularly the fact that five hundred workers at Delta Township had taken early buyout offers from the company. The burning question was how, and whether, they would be replaced. But in either case, in light of the tremendous challenges that GM is facing, I ask Clay, "Wasn't that a destructive strike?"

"I don't think it was destructive. It was necessary," Clay argues. "It was like a necessary evil. We haven't had a raise in six to eight years here. None of us have had a raise. When you have five hundred people set to retire, of course the union and membership here would like to see those people all replaced with new workers. But the company would like to see the people who are here picking up the slack of those people who retire and taking on a larger workload. So it might save the corporation some pennies on the cars. But right now, we're working nine-and-a-half-hour days, six days a week, and that makes it hard to have time with our families. We're doing three shifts worth of cars in two shifts. You're going to have a lot of burned-out people here."

I keep pressing him for a sense of who he blames for the fact that, although he's making good money, he's working long and hard. "The management here, I think, is great," he says. "Their jobs are affected too, just like ours are. We're all pretty much in the same boat. The only way to survive is to work together.

"But I don't feel the same way about the people sitting down at headquarters," he adds. "I think it's hard to tell people to take a pay cut or put in a two-tier pay system and then watch the CEO get a twenty-million-dollar bonus at the end of the year. To tell us we're making too much, but twenty million dollars a year isn't enough for one person. You say the company hasn't made a profit in five or six years but you deserve a raise for leading this company?"

Wagoner's transformation effort depends on tens of thousands of Harry Clays, who obviously don't trust top management. They're being asked to work hard, particularly in factories that are producing cars or vehicles in demand, yet the chance that they will be getting pay increases is slim to nonexistent. If anything, pressures on wages and overall benefits is going to continue to intensify, particularly in view of the economic crisis gripping America. Cost pressures are going to continue to be intense. Bringing the Harry Clays along for the ride is one of Wagoner's greatest challenges.

CHAPTER 3

Does GM Matter?

In May 2006, Thomas L. Friedman, author of *The World Is Flat* and a star columnist for the *New York Times*, wrote in a column, "Is there a company more dangerous to America's future than General Motors? Surely, the sooner this company gets taken over by Toyota, the better off our country will be." Friedman went on to equate GM to a "crack dealer" because it has addicted Americans to fuel consumption.

GM was outraged by what Friedman said, but it was even more shocked that other intellectual, political, and media elites did not quarrel with him. It was like a holy man on top of the mountain had made a booming pronouncement—and no one dared to disagree. In many ways, Friedman had laid the intellectual foundations for the argument that exploded into public view in late 2008—just let GM and other U.S. automakers fail. They are irrelevant to the U.S. economy.

That point of view really rankles Ralph Szygenda, GM's chief information officer. At age sixty, the white-haired Szygenda (pronounced shuh-GEN-da) has spent forty years working in information technology; after all that time, he's earned the seniority to speak frankly. Born in Pittsburgh to Polish immigrants (his father was a municipal engineer for Alleghany County), he spent twenty years in Texas at Texas

Instruments and many more years in Atlanta working for Bell South, and the hint of a southern accent pops up in his speech.

Having started at GM in 1996, Szygenda now spends $3 billion of GM's money a year on computers, telecommunications equipment, and related gear. This huge expenditure helps support AT&T, Cisco, Hewlett-Packard, IBM, Microsoft, and Oracle, among others, and each of those companies is invested enough in GM to station R&D people in Detroit to stay in touch with what Ralph Szygenda wants to buy.

One consistent refrain from the GM-doesn't-matter school is that manufacturing is "the old economy." We lost shoes and textiles and steel, the argument goes, so why not autos? After all, the future of the economy is services, don't you know? At a conference table in his office high up in the Renaissance Center, Szygenda disagrees: "I think we're learning real fast that the service sector only goes so far in sustaining a national economy," he argues.

The credit crunch created by the subprime mortgage lending mess has slammed into the economy, destroying jobs and pushing the unemployment rate higher. It is becoming evident that having investment banks and hedge funds on Wall Street slice and dice mortgages and sell them to other investors is not really the way to create wealth. "Today, of all those service businesses, the only one that's really flourishing is health care," Szygenda says. "I think your manufacturing sector is where you really innovate, whether you like it or not. You can say Google is an innovator. Yes, but you have to have airplanes, you have to have automobiles, you have to build houses, you have to build bridges. A society needs to have engineering, mathematics, and science know-how. Many other countries in the world are investing in that know-how."

His point that much innovation springs from the manufacturing sector isn't a popular one in Silicon Valley. But having come from Pittsburgh, once the home of America's steel industry, Szygenda is a big believer in the need for manufacturing leadership. "You need that knowledge base," he argues. "Sooner or later, you cannot survive just as a services provider. It's not just that we need automobiles. It's what comes next—something not invented yet. You have to have that manufacturing knowledge. We've gotten to the point where people believe that you can get a marketing job or an IT job and solve everything. But that is a short-term mindset that's dangerous."

Manufacturing has been the bedrock of American living standards in many ways. The equipment that U.S. companies make creates better air and water quality. New medical devices and biotech-based drugs make health care better. And faster and better airplanes improve mobility. Manufacturing power helped send a man to the moon, and it has supported America's ability to project military power to such distant places as Iraq and Afghanistan, where Humvees equipped with special armor have been essential.

What many Americans don't understand is that even the U.S. technology sector depends on manufacturers to buy their wares. GM is America's largest private sector buyer of information technology (second only to the federal government), which it uses to automate its factories, to connect designers and engineers around the world with massive telecommunications and computer-aided design links, to manage its sales and finances, and much more. "It's not just building a car or a truck," Szygenda argues. "It is all the other technologies. These satellites of innovation spin off from manufacturing. In the services industry, innovation is usually feeding off something else.

"Who is going to innovate the most?" Szygenda continues. "Everyone uses Microsoft as an example of an innovator, but who's going to push Microsoft to other levels? Who's going to push Google to other levels? GM has a history of doing that and it still is."

Szygenda is articulating beliefs that are deeply held at GM and throughout the U.S. manufacturing sector. Manufacturing represents less than 20 percent of the U.S. economy, but the people involved in making things still believe such activities are critically important. A dollar spent on goods or services doesn't simply stop where it's spent; it gets spent again, and where and how it's spent can creak a dramatic ripple effect. To measure the size of the ripple, economists talk about "multiplier" or "knock-on" effects. The rule of thumb is that for every dollar GM pays to one of its workers or one of its suppliers, $5 to $7 of spending is generated in the broader economy.

Yet when American ownership of the steel industry largely disappeared, many Americans thought it just didn't matter.

"Steel was a raw material," Szygenda says. "It's different. It isn't as much about building a system, which is what we do in the auto industry." It's true that the auto industry sits astride a pyramid of suppliers in many different fields, from glass to fabrics, from metals to rubber, and from semiconductors to sensors. Tier 1 suppliers with names like Dana, Johnson Controls, and Lear buy from tier 2 and 3 suppliers and pre-assemble the components. When a dashboard and all the controls swing onto the assembly line to be installed into a car, that subassembly includes materials and components from dozens or hundreds of subsuppliers.

Szygenda says the loss of an industry—any industry—matters over time. "In ten or twenty years, is the U.S. going to be in the same position globally as it is today? It isn't whether you lost the steel industry or the electronics industry or the television industry. If you're a U.S. political figure, ask yourself, Will the United States have the same stature in the world? Twenty years from now, who is going to be the technology leader of the world? Nobody wants to answer that question. It's too hard. So people say, 'It doesn't hurt me. I'll go buy something from somebody else.'"

Like Szygenda, many GM executives are shocked to hear the argument that it doesn't matter whether an American works for GM in Michigan or for Toyota in Kentucky. A factory job is just a factory job, they say. Admittedly, GM is no longer the GM it was in the 1950s because it has closed so many factories and shed so many people—some 60 percent of its sales are outside the United States and more than half its people are offshore. But it's still true that GM makes a significantly deeper contribution to the American economy than Toyota does.

To understand, pause for a moment to consider the steps involved in designing and producing one vehicle. Each vehicle has a different history, of course, and the process—thousands of parts, hundreds of steps executed by scores of workers—is far too complex to explain in a few paragraphs. But a simple answer to the complicated question, Where does a car come from? goes something like this:

A new model starts with the type of car planning John Smith does. Executives get together to try to understand where the market is headed.

Do Americans want two-seat convertibles, four-door sedans, crossover hybrids, or large pickup trucks? That takes market research and deep experience.

Once top management agrees on what new products will be most profitable, and in the case of GM that may involve fifty different programs at any one time, they let the designers loose. To get the best design, top brass encourage competition among different teams of designers around the world. Massive amounts of data are transmitted over Szygenda's telecommunications connections as full-scale computerized mockups are moved around the world. This design task is what Ed Welburn is in charge of.

It may be that designers in the United States came up with the best body shape; designers at GM's Opel facility in Germany came up with the best chassis, including the engine and transmission; and other designers at GM DAT, or Daewoo Automotive, in Korea, came up with the best interior. Those efforts are blended into one "package," and that package has to be "verified," which is what Rosenplaenter does.

Verification occurs at each major stage of a vehicle's birthing process. That means teams of people rely heavily on computer-aided design and algorithms to make sure that the vehicle, as it is evolving, makes sense. Obviously, parts should not collide with one another and destroy themselves. The tolerances, or distances between pieces of metal, must be acceptable, and so forth. This process is heavily computerized because it is much cheaper to verify each part through virtual three-dimensional imaging than it is to physically build the parts.

After the design is approved, a vehicle moves to engineering, where each part is physically designed so that the vehicle can be manufactured. In some cases, engineers can use parts from previous iterations of the vehicle, but if the car is completely new, they have to make sure that each part is designed just right. Manufacturing people often push back against the designers and engineers who want a particular part made in a particular way, either because it's too technically difficult to make or too expensive. Those issues must be hashed out.

Purchasing people get involved to make sure that each of the four thousand parts can be acquired on a certain date, at a certain price, and in a certain volume. About a thousand of those are moving parts, meaning they move in relation to each other (obviously, all four thousand parts move down the highway). Finance people set pricing to make sure that the vehicle will make money. Marketing gurus and salespeople are involved in deciding how to promote the vehicle.

Then factories have to get ready to make the cars. That requires establishing what practices and tools the workers will use, and the UAW is now deeply involved in helping GM make those decisions. Obviously, the workers need a huge amount of equipment, so a separate set of engineers, called manufacturing engineers, like Mary Barra, make sure that factories have the right robots, conveyor belts, communications systems, and all other equipment. GM wants the equipment and the processes to be equivalent around the world.

When everything is finally set, the vehicle comes together in an amazing ballet of precision and grace. Sheet metal enters a stamping plant, and the steel parts of the body—the side panels, the roof, the hoods—are created. (In the old days, the presses that stamped parts were three stories high and came down with such force that the noise would reverberate for miles; dishes would fall off shelves in nearby homes. Today, at the most modern plants, stamping is done underground, and the only sound is a deep muffled thud. Workers don't even need to wear ear protection.)

Engine and transmissions, items that make up the chassis of the vehicle, are all made in other GM plants. The sheet metal body parts enter the factory on conveyor belts and have to be welded together. This is a heavily robotized and computerized process. Sparks fly.

Painting is next. The raw metal bodies, still on conveyor belts, are rotated into paint shops, hermetically sealed like the clean rooms in semiconductor factories. This process is also highly automated. Big robots, twisting and turning at angles that would break a human arm, do the work.

At this point, in most GM plants I visited, the painted and welded bodies are "married" to the chassis. (In Germany, the "marriage" happened later in the process.) The bodies come down from conveyor belts overhead, and the chassis are lifted up into the bodies. This is one of the toughest physical jobs in the plant. In more modern plants, Automatic Guided Vehicles (AGVs) bring the chassis to the line.

The last stop is General Assembly. The doors are taken off the vehicle so that operators can get inside to install dashboards, steering wheels, seats, rearview and side-view mirrors—most of the things that the consumer sees inside the car. Another reason the doors are taken off is so they don't get dinged—or "mutilated," in the parlance. (They're reattached near the end of the line.) Most of the parts like dashboards come in subassemblies, as described above. Suppliers typically get four hours of notice before they have to deliver these parts to the right place in the plant. Workers check the tolerances and visually inspect the car for imperfections.

Vehicles leave the plants and are transported to dealerships across the country, and some are exported as well. There is a whole industry of logistics and transportation involved in getting the vehicles to the dealers. Then dealers, who employ hundreds of thousands of people, sell the vehicles. Of course, GM and the dealers cooperate to spend hundreds of millions of dollar for advertising and marketing, which is another industry that depends heavily on autos.

From beginning to end, it's a job of enormous complexity. It's not unlike getting the different branches of the U.S. armed forces to cooperate, while providing them with all the material support they need to win a war.

The point of describing all this is to illustrate that the assembly jobs are but a tiny piece of the overall process. For every job on the line, there are ten other jobs in design, engineering, finance, and management, inside GM and throughout the whole chain of suppliers, estimates David Cole, head of the Center for Automotive Research in Ann Arbor, Michigan. (By contrast, he estimates that an investment banking position creates only two or two and a half jobs.) The actual assembly of the automobile thus is a relatively minor part of the total cost of designing and developing vehicles.

One way to think of the importance of the auto industry to the U.S. economy is to liken it to a body's central nervous system. Many of the large suppliers to GM have business relationships with Ford and Chrysler, and possibly the transplants as well. They are knit together in a mesh that extends to all fifty states. They are bound by contracts. If this vast infrastructure were suddenly to be thrown into bankruptcy or worse, it could take years to reassemble.

Another important distinction between what GM does in the United States versus what, say, Toyota does is that the quality of GM's economic activity is higher. Economists often overlook what the quality of economic activity means, but I take it to mean that activity's impact on living standards and the technological and management skills it engenders in a population. GM makes all top decisions in the United States, meaning the mix of its employment is richer than Toyota's is in the United States because Toyota makes many more decisions in Japan. It's true that Toyota has design centers in the United States, but they are quite modest compared to GM's. If one of the hallmarks of an advanced economy is a large body of managerial, finance, and design jobs, then there's little question that the profile of GM's workforce is significantly more sophisticated than that of Toyota, at least on American soil.

If you want to understand GM's impact on the economy, take a trip to Kansas City, Kansas. Existing in a separate orbit from the rest of the Midwestern industrial economy, it's a microcosm of car manufacturing in America. There used to be four auto-related plants in the area, but three of them, including the GM plant in Leeds, Missouri, have closed down. Now there is just the one where Wedow works, located in the Fairfax section of downtown, on an old airfield near the Missouri River. The old-fashioned set of aspirations that has come to be called the American dream—good pay and health care for workers, decent housing, better education for the kids—has been realized in places like this.

Kansas City, Kansas, is located across the river from Kansas City, Missouri. Whoever decided to give the same name to two cities in different states on opposite sides of a river had a sick sense of humor; it creates constant confusion between two cities of very different character. Kansas City, Missouri, is a city of about 450,000 souls, and the other Kansas City has about 150,000. The Missouri city has a downtown with a skyline and fine restaurants; the city in Kansas has grain elevators, warehouses, and railroads close to the river. The city in Kansas has traditionally been a city of immigrants, many of them originally drawn to the cattle packing plants that used to be here. It is still a magnet for immigrants. There's a Croatian neighborhood called Strawberry Hill, and also Russian and Irish communities. There's also a large black population. (Kansas City, Kansas, was a stop on the Underground Railroad for slaves trying to escape from the South.) About 50 percent of its population is made up of people of color; its public schools are 75 percent non-white. Reflecting the immigrants' presence, forty-one languages are spoken in the school district.

As president of the local chamber of commerce, Cindy Cash is in a unique position to understand the economics of Kansas City, Kansas. In her fifties, Cash is bright and irreverent. And the fact that she's not working at the plant, for either management or the UAW, gives her a certain detachment, although she obviously tilts more in management's direction than labor's because the Chamber of Commerce represents companies, not unions. She's sitting in her very modest office on the very modest main street of downtown Kansas City.

Although she's been here for twenty years, she's originally from Michigan—and lived for a time in Flint, which is one of the cities most devastated by the long and bitter decline of GM in Michigan. So she has extensive experience with the interconnections between the auto industry and the lives of people who depend on it for their living. "In Flint, a good year was having fifteen percent unemployment," she recalls.

She explains that the Fairfax plant, with 2,600 workers (and currently ramping up to 2,900 because of demand for its cars), is the largest private employer in Wyandotte County, which surrounds Kansas City. The University of Kansas Hospital and Medical Center employs more people, as does the public school system, but GM is the largest private sector company. It's also the largest taxpayer, paying about $10 million a year, out of a total city-county combined budget of about $240 million.

People who work on the line at the GM plant can make $90,000 to $100,000 a year, and the skilled trades—the electricians and plumbers who keep the plant running—can make more if they get overtime. As a result, Wyandotte County has the highest average hourly wage of all the 105 counties in the state of Kansas, Cash says. There is 4.5 to 5 percent unemployment in the county, slightly better than the national statistics.

"These are good-paying jobs," she says. "If you take them away, you cut into the standard of living."

This is a handy indicator of the multiplier effect of GM's payroll dollars. If a worker at GM gets a dollar, he or she spends that dollar at a retail establishment, and the retail establishment spends the dollar, perhaps by paying a person who works there. That person then spends the dollar at a restaurant. And so forth. That's how she and others estimate that the multiplier effect for each dollar paid to a worker at the plant is between five to one and seven to one.

The fact that Fairfax had back-to-back winners with the Saturn Aura and Chevrolet Malibu suggests that the plant will survive, and with it an important bulwark of the local economy. "If something happened to GM in this community, you're looking at losing ten million dollars in property taxes. And you can't put a price tag on what the employees do in this community," she says. She notes that GM employees are the number one source of funding for the local United Way; both the company management and the UAW Local 31 support the Soap Box Derby and other charity events. "There are dollars and cents that have trickle-down effects, but there are many other things they bring to the community," she adds.

The Fairfax plant is known for being one where management and labor have a relatively good relationship. Part of the reason is that everyone in Kansas City can see that other plants in the area—indeed, across the country—have closed down. Bitterness between management and labor was certainly one of the factors that accelerated Flint's decline. In general, plants that have poisonous labor relations are less productive and therefore more vulnerable to closings. Whenever Wagoner makes a round of plant closings, "we always breathe a sigh of relief when it doesn't happen here," says Cash.

Add it all up and a clear pattern emerges—factories that make products that Americans want hire more people. They offer good wages. Positive relations between management and labor are directly related to the plant's productivity and efficiency, and hence its survival. The plant also pays taxes that support governments and charitable causes. And the jobs support the people and their dreams for better lives, whether they are immigrants or African Americans or anyone else. Is the GM plant contributing to the American dream here? "Hell, yes," says Cash. "They're great jobs."

On a national scale, there are other multipliers to consider. If GM spends a dollar to buy a particular part, that dollar is then used to buy a subpart or to pay workers at the parts supplier, who go into their communities to buy food or housing. Overall, GM buys a higher percentage of its parts and components from U.S. manufacturers than does Toyota. Just how much higher isn't completely clear; though Toyota's factories in the United States buy a significant quantity of parts from Toyota suppliers that have set up assembly plants in the United States, the actual numbers are carefully kept secret. What's certain is that much of their core technology is still designed, engineered, and manufactured in Japan and shipped into the U.S. for final assembly.

Based on information that Toyota provides to comply with auto U.S. labeling laws, Mustafa Mohatarem, GM's chief economist, estimates that Toyota's U.S. content is about 50 percent compared with 75 percent for GM. Most of Toyota's non-American content is from Japan, while most of GM's non-American content is from GM-affiliated factories in Mexico, he adds.

The argument is not that GM is a purely American company and Toyota is a purely foreign interloper. The world has become more complex than that. "Both are global companies," says Mohatarem. "The difference is that GM is much more integrated into the U.S. economy, while Toyota still depends more on imported components. There is more leakage from the United States." By leakage, he means that the dollars spent on a Toyota may benefit certain American constituencies but many dollars are taken back to Japan in the form of profit. He estimates that the average cost of producing a vehicle is $22,500, so the difference between 50 percent and 75 percent American content is $5,625. That's the average difference between the wealth created by a GM car and that generated by a Toyota car for the U.S. economy. Multiply that by millions of cars per year, and it amounts to a colossal figure. Because of GM's sheer scale, Mohatarem estimates that it accounts for a full 1 percent of U.S. gross domestic product, if one includes all its suppliers and dealers.

In addition, GM spends roughly $6 billion on research and development, including product development, and that effort is coordinated from the Technical Center in Warren. Toyota has some R&D in the United States, but its efforts are concentrated in Japan.

The same is true of how GM and Toyota spend on capital equipment, such as the conveyors and automated equipment they use to operate their manufacturing lines. And the pattern holds when it comes to not only steel, tires, and glass, but also semiconductors. The U.S. auto industry is one of the largest buyers of semiconductors, which is why Intel has an office in Detroit. Contrary to the perception in some quarters, the buying patterns of a company like GM do not touch only Michigan and Ohio and Indiana. It has a national footprint, and even California's Silicon Valley depends to some extent on selling to GM. Toyota buys its semiconductors elsewhere.

In sum, for each vehicle manufactured, the two companies make very different contributions to the U.S. economy and technology base. The critics can argue that GM has stumbled and hasn't adapted fast enough to global economic pressures, which may be true, but the fact remains that GM is at the heart of America's manufacturing economy, and that sector supports both high tech and many service sectors, such as logistics and advertising. In the final analysis, Mohatarem is much less emotional than Szygenda, but he is also irritated by the argument that GM's survival simply doesn't matter. "It's easy, sitting in New York," he says, "to ignore what's happening in the American economy."

CHAPTER 4

Who Is Rick Wagoner?

To reach the office of George Richard Wagoner Jr., you take an elevator to the thirty-eighth floor of the Renaissance Center, a Byzantine complex with multiple towers soaring to the sky. If you're a reporter, you'll always be accompanied by at least one public relations person. When the door opens, there's a single person behind a security desk in a big room that seems Scandinavian in inspiration—lots of metal and blond wood. From the windows, there are sweeping views of the Detroit River, from Belle Isle down to the big Ford facilities at River Rouge. Across the Detroit River is Canada (some parts of which are actually south of this part of Detroit). You hover here while hushed phone calls are made to Wagoner's secretary. When the word is given, you proceed up a sweeping semicircular staircase to the thirty-ninth floor, where Wagoner's office is adorned with colorful automotive and basketball memorabilia.

But in all the times I have ascended those stairs to speak with Wagoner, he has never appeared to be an imperial CEO, however grand his trappings. His personality, operating style, and values are those of a humbler man, serious and focused on his business. Many people find that he actually listens when they talk to him. These values explain why he was tapped to sit in this office, and they are also at the heart of the debate about whether he is part of GM's problem—or part of the solution.

Born in February 1953, Wagoner was raised in what he calls an "extremely middle class" setting in the West End section of Richmond, Virginia. Historically, this area of pine trees and rolling hills was where the First Families of Virginia lived, but by the time Wagoner came along, it had become somewhat less rarefied. Wagoner's father, a graduate of Duke University in North Carolina, held a relatively modest position as a cost accountant for the Eskimo Pie ice cream company. Wagoner says his father was "very smart" but that his first priority in life was his family, not his career. "I remember a few times he came in and said, 'I got a job offer. Let's move,' and we said, 'We're not moving. Are you kidding?'"

His mother stayed at home with Rick and his younger sister. Originally from South Carolina, Mrs. Wagoner was "always busy, very active," her son recalls. "If someone down the street, somebody's grandfather died, she'd be the first one with all the food, this and that. All my friends would hang around our house because we always had enough food to feed the Russian army. It was a fun upbringing."

Inevitably, certain values were inculcated in the boy, who was an only son and the eldest child. Sports were an important part of his life, particularly basketball, because he was thin but tall. "Nothing was organized as it is today," Wagoner told the *New York Times* in 2002. "Kids just got together and played."

And family values, in the best sense of the term, were strong. "From the fairly early days, my parents were always supportive," he says. "They were the first people to sporting events. It might have been an inconvenience to them, but the kids were the top priority."

His parents seem to have drilled a strong work ethic into Wagoner. He mowed lawns for two dollars apiece. And his parents urged him to achieve at school as well. He recalls them saying: "It's your responsibility to do the best you can. If you're no good in Latin and you do your best and you get a C, then OK. But don't get a C because you didn't do your best. You grow confidence over time in your ability and you work hard and you get benefits from it and it goes toward life. Hey, you were put here for a reason, and if you have the capability to do something, your responsibility is to do your best."

English class obviously was not his strongest; Wagoner had a difficult relationship with the English language as a child, and still does. Structure shifts in the middle of the sentence. Indefinite antecedents abound. Conversations start and stop in the middle of other conversations. His meaning is usually clear, however, even if his prose isn't perfect.

He also didn't grow up in a particularly strong automotive culture. But the young Wagoner was exposed to at least one hot car that left an impression—a Jaguar XKE. "When I was a kid, some guy up the street— he was in the Navy—used to come up from Norfolk every weekend with a Jaguar XKE," Wagoner recalls. "His girlfriend was living up the street."

During that era, Jaguars may have been beautiful, but they were also notorious for having mechanical and electronic glitches. "I remember that he was always parked in the street. He was always working on the car. I thought it was because he loved to work on cars. I later found out he had to fix the car so he could get it back to Norfolk, so he could be back for duty. But it was a stunning car." The fact that a Navy man, of whatever rank, was visiting his neighborhood from the naval base at Norfolk and had to park a Jaguar on the street is also a useful indicator that this was not a terribly posh neighborhood at this point in its history.

Nor was Wagoner's high school an elite one. Less than half his graduating class went to college. "It was mid-range, but perfect," he says. In basketball, he was something of a star; he made all-district his junior and senior years and averaged about eighteen points and fourteen rebounds a game during his senior year on his school team. He was also developing into a leader; he became captain of the basketball team and student body president.

After graduating, he went on to Duke, his father's alma mater, where he played freshman basketball. He had aspired to play pro ball, but competing at the college level was tougher than he expected. "I learned pretty quickly I would not be pursuing a career in the NBA," he later told Duke's daily newspaper, the *Chronicle*. In particular, he recalls one game against North Carolina State. He was assigned to cover David

Thompson, one of the game's great talents. "I remember him taking a jump shot from the corner, and I was looking at his *waist*," Wagoner recalls.

In 1973, while enrolled at Duke, Wagoner was able to put together enough money to buy his first car, a 1973 Chevrolet Camaro—a far cry from a Jaguar XKE, but at least it was his. It cost $3,500, and he paid for it with his savings, some of which came from cutting lawns.

Wagoner also met Kathleen Kaylor, who was two years behind him, and who would later become his wife. During this era, Wagoner was elected president of his fraternity and graduated summa cum laude and Phi Beta Kappa. He took his bachelor's degree in economics.

Nothing at this point suggests that Wagoner was destined to become the leader of the world's largest industrial corporation. He wasn't elite; he wasn't glamorous; he was "a money guy," a bean counter, as critics would later argue. But he did have a strong work ethic and was a team builder, with his athletics and fraternity life. He had people skills; he listened and knew how to persuade.

After Duke, Wagoner earned an M.B.A. from Harvard Business School. Even with that credential, though, he never thought he would be the CEO of a company, any company, and he told friends he didn't want to ever work in New York or go overseas. Yet in 1977 he took a job in the GM treasurer's office in New York. Rick and Kathy were married in 1979, and in 1981 Wagoner went to work for GM's Brazilian operations, the first of four international assignments. This was in an era when, reflecting the Sloan philosophy of allowing GM's international units to operate with great independence, GM do Brasil was largely a self-contained entity, not truly knit into the rest of the corporation.

Once in Brazil, Wagoner won a quick promotion to CFO when the person who held that position left unexpectedly. "It was a big step and an unbelievable opportunity to go from being a money guy to being in the middle of running the business," Wagoner told *Fortune* in 2002. He spent six years in Brazil and learned to speak Portuguese. (Surprisingly, Wagoner speaks English with no trace of a southern accent. "I just think over the years moving around, I lost a little of my accent," he says.)

In 1987, he and the family, which by now included three sons, moved to Canada but didn't stay there long. He left for a finance job at GM

Europe in Zurich. In that capacity, he helped GM buy 50 percent of Sweden's Saab. Then it was back to Brazil in 1991, this time as managing director. When the market began opening to foreign automakers, he devised a cheaper way to bend sheet metal on older GM cars to freshen their look. "We changed the economics," he told *Fortune*, "and it paid big dividends," to the tune of a 20 percent return on investment.

This Brazilian assignment lasted only thirteen months; in 1992, Jack Smith became CEO and asked Wagoner to come back to Detroit and become his chief financial officer.

"I'm not sure this is what I want to do," Wagoner recalls telling Smith.

Smith's response was "I understand, but we would really like you to do this." Wagoner took the job.

What was it about Wagoner, at the tender age of thirty-nine, that merited such a promotion? He wasn't a flashy designer. He didn't run with a jet-set crowd. He wasn't a charismatic visionary. His track record had been on the financial and procurement side of the house; he was never a car guy who came up with an actual product.

I put the question, Why Wagoner? to the man who elevated him to CFO—in effect, setting him up to run GM. "He's a terrific guy," says Jack Smith, who is now retired and living in Cape Cod, Massachusetts. "He's very smart, hardworking. He's a great guy, a great family man. He had done an exceptional job in all his assignments."

Note the sequence of attributes: Terrific guy. Smart. Hardworking. Family man. Done an exceptional job in his assignments. Job performance is fifth on the list.

As difficult as it may be to believe, in an era of great cynicism about CEOs and large corporations (some of it thoroughly justified), Wagoner appears to have been elevated at least partly, perhaps even mostly, on the basis of his values and character. Certainly, he was competent with financial statements, and this was part of a long tradition at GM. CEOs came from the money side of the house, to make sure that the business was run well. A car designer couldn't be trusted to do that. But there was something else about Wagoner that appealed to Smith.

The company was in crisis, Smith felt, and he was looking for people who could lead well after he was gone. After a decade of denial, the full significance of Toyota's superior manufacturing method, organizational model, and labor management all were sinking in. This was when Smith proclaimed that it was time for GM to "run common and run global." He felt he needed a successor who had deep international experience. Even at his young age, Wagoner had worked for GM on three continents. And at a time when sweeping change was necessary, he seemed to have the capacity to inspire and build loyalty. Wagoner seemed to be the right kind of change agent.

As CFO, Wagoner started working behind the scenes to unify the company's duplicative engineering, purchasing, and manufacturing systems. Soon Smith gave Wagoner the added responsibility of running the purchasing department. This was the beginning of GM's transformation dream. "Jack sort of started that process in the early nineties," Wagoner says today. "To be honest, there have been some twists in the road, but basically we built the strategy consistently from there. We added some pieces in as we went along. I think that really signified the beginning of the turnaround and the re-creation of General Motors in the United States."

In October 1998, Wagoner was named president and chief operating officer, and he began to consolidate control of all the company's far-flung and competing divisions by creating the Automotive Strategy Board. It consisted of about eighteen members, most of whom Wagoner had inherited from the Smith era. It emerged as the central structure that Wagoner still uses to run the company. Every key function and geography was represented on the ASB.

This move started to heal the schism between GM North America and GM International. The management consolidation was by no means complete. It was still what Wagoner calls a "soft matrix" because the process leaders, such as Gary Cowger, the head of manufacturing, were not given absolute control over how manufacturing was done in every geography, just an added measure of influence.

As this management model took hold, some executives on the ASB wore multiple hats; Cowger, for instance, was responsible for global manufacturing, a functional position, but also for the entire territory of North America. It wasn't perfect, but it was a big step toward a rational management system. In effect, Wagoner was beginning the process of unifying the company's warring tribes. All this was important because Wagoner was creating a single cohesive body with a single management culture to make all key decisions. Decision making in the past had been characterized by powerful heads of divisions or heads of geographies jockeying for the ear of the CEO and top management in a decidedly competitive, nontransparent manner, almost like the intrigue in a medieval kingdom. Not everyone understood how or why decisions were made.

It's always dangerous to ask people who work for a CEO, any CEO, about that person's personality; no employee is objective about his boss. But Ralph Szygenda, the CIO, is a veteran with little left to fear in his professional life, and he has an interesting take. "Rick has a magnetic characteristic about him," says Szygenda. "He pulls you into the mission. He's very team oriented. But he's an individual who can disagree with you, and you still like him."

Szygenda has decades of experience, which often leads to a certain cynicism, yet he feels it would be disloyal to abandon the mission. "Why am I still here after twelve years? You have this terrible feeling that you can't leave until after the mission is done. We're bringing this icon back."

After all the bloodshed that GM has been through, and all the headlines about the impending end of the company, Wagoner has been able to help people still believe in the future. "He keeps people engaged," Szygenda says. "He keeps people believing, and that's pretty hard." That may sound like boilerplate from the annual report, but not all CEOs attempt to persuade their people to believe in a mission; they create a climate of command and control—and fear.

The sports metaphor, held over from his youth, is central to Wagoner's approach to his management challenge. "Rick is such a sports addict, and it's all one sport, basketball," says Szygenda. "He says, 'You may not be the best team, but you could still win.' He tends to coach as opposed to direct. If you're changing a culture, coaching isn't all that bad. A dictator may not work in a cultural transformation."

Wagoner indeed sees himself as a "player-coach," as he told me in 2003. He didn't like to be considered purely a coach on the sidelines. "I definitely like to play," he told me. "I like to keep my hands in the game because I don't think you can really feel it if you get too far away from it."

Whatever the precise model, Szygenda thinks it works. "I don't think I've seen anybody who develops teams better," he says.

Wagoner has loaded up his team—the Automotive Strategy Board—with very strong players. His decision to hire the legendary Bob Lutz in 2001 as vice chairman sent a particularly strong message: Wagoner was confident enough to bring in an executive who was much older and much more experienced and put him in a position of real power. He also installed James E. Queen as group vice president of global engineering—like Lutz a former combat aviator, and a plain speaker from the backwoods of Ohio. Ed Welburn, the voice president of design, considers Queen his best friend, and their relationship helps bridge the traditional divide between design and engineering.

Frederick "Fritz" A. Henderson was brought in from running GM Europe to become vice chairman and chief financial officer; he was quickly promoted to president and chief operating officer, putting him in position to succeed Wagoner. Henderson, fifty, a mustachioed, fast-talking native of Detroit, is very different from Wagoner in some respects, but their styles and backgrounds overlap nonetheless. Henderson earned a business degree with an emphasis on accounting and finance from the University of Michigan, where he was a pitcher on the varsity baseball team. He is a known sports fanatic, even though his sport of choice is baseball, not basketball. Like Wagoner, Henderson received an M.B.A. from Harvard and started his career in the treasurer's office in New York. And like Wagoner, he served in Brazil. His next assignment took him to Singapore (where Wagoner never served); but immediately thereafter, Henderson headed to GM Europe's offices in Zurich, where Wagoner had also spent time. Although Henderson is known as being more aggressive than Wagoner on making tough business decisions, the two of them are cut from very similar cloth. Indeed, most of the men with whom Wagoner has surrounded himself (and the majority of them are men) are big guys, with either sports of military backgrounds. The echoes from organizing neighborhood basketball games back him in Richmond are obvious.

Of the powerful personalities on the ASB, one of the most compelling is that of fifty-two-year-old Bo Andersson, the head of purchasing. Andersson served in the Swedish military for twelve years, from 1975 to 1986, at the height of the cold war, rising to the position of major. He doesn't talk about it much, but he saw some extreme conditions in the far north of Sweden when the United States and its NATO allies tried to monitor and impede the movement of Soviet nuclear-armed submarines into the Atlantic Ocean. He faced life-and-death conditions many times, particularly because of the Arctic cold. "Yeah, I did everything," he says flatly.

Today, Andersson is in charge of buying $121 billion worth of goods and services for GM each year. He first met Wagoner in 1993. "He's confident in himself. He's a big guy," says Andersson. "He understands most of the stuff and knows what he's looking for." Wagoner and Andersson have a particularly complex relationship because Wagoner held the procurement job briefly in the early 1990s, while also serving as CFO, and knows how to keep the heat on Andersson, whose main mission is to control and reduce how much GM pays for its components and materials. (GM is the world's largest purchaser of steel, for example, some ten million tons a year. Andersson personally negotiates those purchases.)

At one point in Andersson's tenure, Wagoner made a remark publicly about the need for the Swede to keep striving to reduce costs. Andersson didn't like being called out publicly; "it didn't feel that good," he said. So, privately, he sought an explanation from Wagoner.

Wagoner told him, "Bo, I understand your view. But if you were me, would you want to beat the faster horse or the slowest horse?"

Andersson responded drily, "I understand your point. Now I feel better."

Andersson says he respects Wagoner partly because of how he has drawn on Lutz's experience. "It's a very strong characteristic of Rick to have people around him who are experts and listening to them and getting the best out of them," he says. And it also made an impression on him that Wagoner put his own career on the line in 2006, after the crisis of 2005, by taking on the added responsibility of running North American operations. Another CEO could have fired the executive in charge—Cowger—and blamed him for failure. But instead, Wagoner eased Cowger into his manufacturing role and personally took the heat. "He took a very, very clear leadership position," Andersson says.

What Andersson and other top executives particularly admire is Wagoner's work ethic. "Every Wednesday morning at seven A.M., eastern standard time, we have our corporate management calls—three times a month," Andersson says. "Then once a month, we have a meeting that is two days long. I think it tells you a lot that one of the highest leaders in America is getting up at six A.M. to take the call from his office, because we're not allowed to take the call on our cell phones for security reasons." (When I later mention to Wagoner that he has to be at seven A.M. meetings on Wednesdays and at the design studios on Fridays, he replies, "Those are the easy days.")

The engineering chief, Queen, puts it this way: "I don't want to go on a plane ride anywhere with Rick because I'll walk off that plane with two million additional assignments. I don't know if the guy ever sleeps. He's right there, just busting his ass with everybody else. There's nothing he asks me to do that he wouldn't do himself."

It may seem trite to say that Wagoner is trying to create a team spirit at the top of GM, but at a company that never had truly unified management, it borders on radical.

"Today," says Ed Welburn, "the enemy isn't another division within General Motors. The competition isn't another brand within General Motors. It's someone else. And everyone recognizes that. I tell you, it feels good to sit in those meetings and to witness the kind of dialogue, the kind of push that occurs, the kind of roll-up-your-sleeves-and-get-the-work-done attitude that is there."

Cowger, a forty-year veteran of GM, says Wagoner "looks at the ASB as the team that's strategically setting the vision and guidance for the company, and also running the plays."

Wagoner's goal is to force GM to greatly accelerate its notoriously slow decision making. When Lutz worked at Chrysler, he used to tweak Wagoner by saying that smaller, faster auto companies would always beat the big and the slow. "Fair point," Wagoner came back. "But the big and the fast beat the small and the fast. If you check out the NBA today, the players are big AND fast."

Part of the challenge of making any team perform is resisting the personality cult that sweeps up many chief executive officers—particularly in the auto industry. I've interviewed Ford Motor CEO Jacques Nasser, DaimlerChrysler CEO Jürgen Schrempp, Chrysler CEO Robert Eaton, and Chrysler CEO Dieter Zetsche, and I've covered other CEOs over the years, including Roger Smith. The trap that tempts them all is what you might call the "great man syndrome." A CEO becomes convinced that his judgment is superior to anyone else's, and he screens out opinions that are at odds with his own. He limits his personal contacts to people who support him, cutting himself off from crucial insights into what the broader marketplace is thinking about him or his company. Although I was a fan of Nasser, for example, he cut himself off from others by turning his office in Ford's Dearborn headquarters into a sanctuary filled with New Age music, Brazilian art, and a whole wall of television monitors. In the back room, he installed a shower, which attracted many brickbats at the time.

But Wagoner has resisted allowing his status as CEO to shape his entire personality and lifestyle. "I don't think it's the right thing for a company like this," Wagoner says. "Obviously, Durant was quite a character." But since then, CEOs "have been very much focused on their responsibility as head of the company, and it's all about doing what's right for GM. That's very much a model that Jack Smith exhibited and lived. And I think it's the right model for a company like GM. And hey, you can't run this company or be in a senior position like Bob or Fritz without being out there yourself some. If you don't like that, you shouldn't take the job. Personally, I've felt more comfortable that way, too. But I think this is about growing the future of GM, and we have to take responsibility for those roles. There will be a GM after we go, and nothing would make me happier than for it to be more successful."

He's also intensely private about his personal life. It's known, though, that he remains married to his first wife and is a devoted father of three sons, now about twenty-four, twenty-two, and seventeen. He once built an indoor court at his home in an undisclosed suburb of Detroit so that he could play basketball with his sons. And lately he's gradually been expanding his home garage to make room for more cars, including a new Camaro.

The fact that he's married and has a home life may not seem important, but management experts such as Bill George, the former CEO of Medtronic and now a professor at Harvard Business School who coined the term "authentic leadership," say that CEOs who maintain their marriages and families are more balanced than those who become attracted to glitzy lifestyles. Automotive CEOs seem particularly susceptible to turbulent marriages and home lives. (Take Schrempp of Daimler, who ran off with his secretary.) But Wagoner is never seen hobnobbing on golf courses with tony investment bankers; he's not in the society pages with Hollywood personalities. He does not seem to socialize with GM people on the weekends. He does answer e-mails on the weekends and works on piles of mail and correspondence, but otherwise he seems to spend time with his family.

Communicating is another key to Wagoner's style. He's known for seeking out views from people who might be considered critics. He meets once a year, for example, with David Champion, the head of testing for *Consumers Reports*, which has been very tough in comparing GM products with Japanese cars, to hear how GM products are shaping up.

Within the company, he spends hours in town hall meetings with employees and in "diagonals," or meetings with employees at various levels, who talk to Wagoner without their superiors present. Wherever you go inside GM there are television screens and Wagoner is often there explaining to the troops what is happening inside the company and in the industry.

Humor is never very far beneath the surface. When asked in 2003 what it felt like to turn fifty, he said, "I feel like I'm moving up here lately. I notice when I get in meetings that I'm not the young guy anymore."

And when a photographer who was taking his picture for the cover of *Chief Executive* magazine joked that she had only two employees in her company, compared with 349,000 at GM at the time, Wagoner wisecracked, "I'll bet you have more control over your organization than I have over mine."

If it's dangerous to talk to a CEO's direct reports about him, it may be even more dangerous to talk to his board members. But it's instructive how George Fisher, the co-lead director and therefore the closest person that Wagoner has to a "boss," feels about him. Fisher is one of the best-known personalities in American business, having served as CEO of both Motorola and Eastman Kodak.

Fisher has been on GM's board since 1995 and therefore has witnessed Wagoner's rise and supported it. "He is one of the most wonderful human beings I have met in American business or worldwide business," Fisher says. "He is a caring, sensitive person who at the same time can be very tough in his decisions and who's very, very analytical in the way he goes about it, probably coming from his finance background. He is dedicated to his family and to his work family called GM. GM is a wonderful company in that sense. It's both a strength and a weakness. I prefer the strength. I'll take the weakness. Rick has a tremendous loyalty, which drives him to want General Motors to be a successful company. He is driven by that in a selfless way. What he says is, 'I don't want the headlines for Rick Wagoner. I want General Motors to be healthy.' "

Fisher, who is now sixty-seven and living in semiretirement in Arizona, notes that running a company with sales of nearly $200 billion a year is spectacularly complex. "It requires a lot of work on the part of a CEO who really is trying to transform the company rather than just babysit it," he says. "That's what Rick is all about. He's going to change the company. He's already changed it significantly."

Again, it's instructive to note what factors Fisher lists—wonderful human being, caring, sensitive, and, oh yes, makes tough decisions. Fisher's evident loyalty is to Wagoner as a person as much as it is to a CEO.

Fisher has a lot at stake in the relationship—he was not an unqualified success at either Motorola or Kodak. Motorola began to stumble after Fisher left, which inevitably he bears some responsibility for, and in his tenure at Kodak, he was unable to force the company to move quickly into the digital era. If history records that he backed the right CEO at GM, leading to a successful business transformation, Fisher will be judged in a more favorable light. If, however, he backed the wrong horse, he will be seen as foolish. To force out Wagoner, as some speculate the board should do, it would also have to dismiss Fisher. Such is the intensity of the bond between the two men.

The critics, like the ones who pop up at GM's annual shareholder meetings, argue that Wagoner's relationship with his board is too cozy. They would like to see a tougher tone between the board and Wagoner, assuming that would improve GM's performance.

The counterargument is that if there were major irritants in Wagoner's relationships with his board or his management team, he would be less effective in managing the company. "The board has a great deal of confidence in Rick," says David Cole, whose father ran GM at one point and who has emerged as the top outside commentator on GM. "I've seen very few leaders in the industry who have had almost universal support from their entire team. Rick is one of those people. From the management team and board on down through the organization, it's absolutely amazing to see the level of support that he has."

How did that happen? "He really acts like a coach, rather than a king," says Cole. "One of the recent kings at Ford, Jacques Nasser, got into the details of the business and everybody knew that. He really lost his people. Rick is a demanding CEO but a very fair one. He basically knows what he doesn't know. That's key. He has strong people around him who do know, and he listens to them."

No matter how appealing a personality Wagoner may be, at some point, he has to start delivering consistent profitability for GM, particularly in North America. The first decisive test of his ability to do that began in 2005.

CHAPTER 5

2005

The Crisis Begins

In 2005, the strategy that top management had pursued for many years started to come unstuck. For decades, management had watched almost helplessly from the sidelines as the company's wage, health care, and pension costs steadily mounted. The UAW achieved advances almost every time it negotiated a contract, creating hundreds of thousands of relatively affluent workers and more than one million retirees. The creation of the Jobs Bank program, which guaranteed workers 95 percent of their pay even when they weren't working because their jobs had been eliminated, was unique. Their health care packages were particularly rich; union workers and retirees had "first dollar" medical coverage, meaning they and their families did not pay a penny for medical care. Some wags joked that GM was actually a health care company, not a car company. In theory, well-paid and well-cared-for workers are a wonderful thing; they demonstrated how GM had been good for America. In practice, however, with the market slipping away, the costs were becoming more than the company could handle and remain competitive against not only imports but the increasing number of foreign manufacturers that were building plants mostly in southern states.

Since the 1950s, GM had never made a serious effort to alter the benefits equation, partly out of fear that the United Auto Workers would cripple the company with strikes if management challenged the status quo. As Lutz says, "The language from the union was that if you touch health care, we're going to shut the place down forever."

As a result, the company's philosophy was to keep pumping out the metal and to try to achieve enough sales so that it could afford its wage, health care, and pension costs and still invest in the business and make a profit. On one hand, that may have been shortsighted management; on the other, it represented a continuation of the policies that had in many ways helped create the American middle class. Starting in the 1920s, when Henry Ford offered the vast sum of five dollars a day to his workers, the auto industry had lifted countless people to a higher living standard. Over the years, hundreds of thousands of workers, many with only high school degrees, were able to buy homes, send children to college, and (in the best cases) have enough left over for a cabin at the lake.

But the economics were getting kicked out from under their feet, and in 2005 GM had to recognize it. "I wouldn't want to relive 2005," recalls Gary Cowger. "With double-digit inflation in health care, we could no longer outrun [the mounting costs]."

This is more than management propaganda; American health care costs really were soaring (and continue to do so). The tab for GM was averaging more than $7 billion a year. In management's view, these costs were cutting into how much the company could spend on designing cars and investing in new technology—a slow form of economic suicide. The $7 billion, for example, was only slightly less than GM's global engineering budget. After a profitable year in 2004, the company disclosed in April 2005 that it had lost $839 million in the first quarter. It was a sickening lurch in the wrong direction. "We knew we had to restructure the business," Cowger adds.

By "restructuring the business," Cowger meant, in part, that Wagoner concluded he had to further streamline the management process. The aim was to increase the speed of decision making, a necessary step in tackling the cost structure and many other challenges. So Wagoner completed the reorganization of GM's management that he had begun in 1998 when he created the Automotive Strategy Board. Once and for all, Wagoner concentrated global responsibilities for each function on the ASB. Until that moment, the regions had retained some autonomy, and the authority had never been completely centralized. Now Lutz was fully in charge of global product development, Cowger in charge of global manufacturing, Queen in charge of global engineering, Andersson in charge of global purchasing, and so on. "When we made the change in April 2005, we started to drive the corporate functions on a global basis," Cowger explains. That obviously shifted power from the heads of GM Europe, for example, and other executives in charge of certain geographies, into the hands of the ASB. Not incidentally, Cowger adds, the new structure "looked much more like our competitors from the Far East look."

In other words, it wasn't until 2005 that Wagoner was able to establish a management structure that would allow GM to compete on the same global basis as Toyota did. It had taken seven years since creating the soft matrix in 1998 for Wagoner to be able to push it to the next level and make it a hard matrix. "It took us seven or eight years to get the hard line," Wagoner explains. "Why'd it take so long? 'Cause I didn't think the organization was ready."

This was a critical judgment and explains a great deal about Wagoner's management style. A more cutthroat CEO would have simply mandated that the organization move in a certain direction, damn the torpedoes. But as Alex Taylor would later write in *Fortune*, Wagoner was too much of a "southern gentlemen" to make those sorts of abrupt, discontinuous changes, too much a product of an "insular, self-absorbed culture." In a piece in December 2008, Taylor wrote that "Wagoner's biggest flaw may be that he has been too forgiving." He also quoted a competitor as saying Wagoner was "too fundamentally decent" to shut down divisions and put dealerships out of work. But in this 2005 organizational decision, as with many others, Wagoner wanted to cajole and prod his executives to accept that this new step was necessary.

In large part, they did. John Smith, the former Kansas City boy who became head of product planning, makes a wisecrack about this reorganization, but his remark contains more than a seed of truth. After the company was founded in 1908, he says, "It took us ninety-seven years to get the right structure."

But a management reorganization alone, even when accompanied by another plan announced in June to close more plants, was of course not big enough to address the cost crisis. "I think to a certain extent,

2005 was when it became pretty clear that the approach that we hoped we could use to get the restructuring and to make us competitive, that model wasn't going to work," Wagoner says now. "We weren't going to have enough time to play that out." Despite all the tweaking Wagoner had done, GM's fundamental model was still not working. Costs were still out of whack with what the company could hope to earn.

At the same time, the market was beginning to shift against GM. "It was the first big shift away from full-size utilities and pickups, where we had a disproportionate amount of profitability," Wagoner continues. "So on the one side, the profit model came under pressure, and on the other side, the balance sheet came under huge pressure because of this impact of double-digit increases in health care costs. We began to get this squeeze. It became pretty clear to me that we would not be able to outrun the health care costs and fix it the way we wanted to. We were going to have to come at it more directly and aggressively."

This was a moment of truth for Wagoner, the competitor. After having run the company for five years and earning a measure of respect for how he had played the game, Wagoner now faced the possibility of failure. According to sources inside the company, he began to take some pressure from his normally supportive board of directors.

"It was crystal clear what we needed to do," he said, and that was to fundamentally alter the company's cost structure. "In this case, it relied on reaching an agreement that was acceptable to our union leaders. The anxiety was 'Hey, can we get it done fast enough? And can we come to a consensus on it?'" The obvious first step was attacking health care, and every month that went by without a solution was costing the company hundreds of millions of dollars.

Meanwhile, bad monthly sales and earnings numbers kept rolling in. The company announced in July that it had lost another $318 million; again, the shortfall was in North America. It became apparent Wagoner would not be able to deliver the financial results he had promised to the board. "The 'oh, shit' moments started in August 2005 and September 2005," says one source. "It became clear that we were not going to make the numbers."

Throughout 2005, Kirk Kerkorian started accumulating GM shares. For GM, this was risky territory. Kerkorian, a billionaire investor based in Las Vegas, has a track record of taking big stakes in companies, forcing big shakeups, and walking away with millions of dollars in profit. It wasn't clear what he wanted, but his arrival on the scene added to the pressures on Wagoner.

Then Hurricane Katrina hit Louisiana at the end of August. It was a major shock to the nation, and to the auto sector in particular, because the damage to Gulf Coast refineries caused a spike in gasoline prices. "People said, 'I'm going to park my Tahoe and leave it in the garage. I can't afford the gas,'" says Stephen J. Girsky, an automotive analyst who spent ten months during this time at General Motors as Wagoner's special adviser. "The consumer turned on a dime, and this is a business that you can't turn on a dime."

All in all, everything that could go wrong seemed to be going in precisely that direction. Sales were tumbling. Consumers were wary. Costs were onerous. Kerkorian was scratching at the door. "Other than that, how was the play, Mrs. Lincoln?" Girsky jokes.

In a process that is still shrouded in secrecy, Wagoner and Fritz Henderson opened a discussion with the UAW and its leader, Ron Gettelfinger. A former line worker who earned an accounting degree, Gettelfinger is considered by auto executives to be a shrewd and pragmatic bargainer, much more sophisticated in his understanding of financial issues than his predecessors.

According to media accounts, his bargaining teams and economists at the union's Solidarity House headquarters in downtown Detroit brought in extra help—investment bankers from Lazard as well as lawyers—to advise them in negotiating with GM on health care. That was an unusual step, and the general conclusion was that Gettelfinger used the borrowed help to develop a sophisticated understanding of GM's books. UAW vice president Richard Shoemaker conducted the negotiations with representatives from GM and its struggling parts maker, Delphi Corporation, which was threatening to declare bankruptcy to give itself legal recourse to renegotiate its labor contracts. The meetings were sometimes held in different cities—in Chicago and elsewhere—to avoid the scrutiny of the Detroit-based automotive media.

In public, Wagoner's remarks about the negotiations have been almost banal. "It was obviously a challenging issue for their side," he told me, "so it required a lot of work and discussions, but ultimately came together." There must have been a hard edge to Wagoner's message, though, even if no one outside a very small circle of people (and they're not talking) knows whether he actually spoke with Gettelfinger or communicated through intermediaries. As another GM official explains it privately, 2005 was "the year we stopped playing games with the UAW."

One way or another, Wagoner, was able to appeal to the union to help GM regain competitiveness. The two sides announced a deal in October 2005 that would reduce GM's health care costs for union members $1 billion a year by cutting benefits slightly. This was a breakthrough. There was no trash-talking from either side, and nobody leaked to the media. "Maybe that's why it ended up working," says veteran auto analyst Joseph S. Phillippi. "Everything was done behind the scenes, and no one was embarrassed in public."

But that was just the beginning of addressing six to eight action items that Wagoner had agreed upon with his board. "Once we had the health care deal, the path to us was pretty clear," Wagoner says. "So we moved very aggressively on capacity rationalization and had a very successful early retirement program and made some very aggressive changes in salaried and executive benefits." By capacity rationalization, he means that the company announced twelve plant closings that would eliminate thirty thousand jobs over three years, and salaried workers also saw cutbacks in their pay and perks.

Still, the company would report a near record loss of $10.6 billion for the year. Delphi, which GM had spun off in 1999, went into bankruptcy in the fall of 2005 and has still not emerged. The board wanted more, and health care was still the target. I asked Wagoner in December 2005 whether he blamed internal decisions or external forces for the company's quandary. "It's obviously a combination of both," he said. "I think it would be disingenuous for us to point to things like U.S. health care policy or trade policy and the exchange rates and say they are the whole cause of the problem.

"The flip side, though, is that anybody who says they are not part of the problem just doesn't have their feet placed in reality," he added, in uncharacteristically tough language. "Like it or not, we pay fifteen hundred dollars per car for health care, and our cheap global competitors pay two hundred. That's a disadvantage. We don't have that situation because we're stupid—it's been the U.S. governmental policy for us to pay that bill, and we've been doing it."

Board meetings in March, April, and May 2006 were particularly challenging. (It was in March that Wagoner voluntarily cut his base salary from $2.2 million a year to $1.1 million.) Wagoner was under pressure to get a more sweeping labor deal. Inside sources say the board may have been either seven to four, or six to five, in favor of keeping Wagoner, an uncomfortably narrow margin.

Wagoner was able to tick off another item on the board's to-do list in April by selling a majority stake in General Motors Acceptance Corporation (GMAC) to Cerebrus Capital Management, the private equity group. The financing arm of GM, which provided loans and leases to people who wanted cars (and, it turns out, to subprime home buyers), was profitable, but Wagoner wanted to raise cash by selling control to Cerebrus.

I asked co-lead director George Fisher what was really going on at that time between the board and Wagoner. "Newspapers love to popularize the pressure-from-the-board angle," said Fisher a bit coyly. "If you have the right CEO, he or she is putting himself under so much more pressure than a board can. I think that was the case with Rick. If it becomes evident that change needs to happen at a rapid pace, hopefully it's the CEO who recognizes that, because he's closer to it than the board."

That same spring, Kerkorian's accumulation of shares became a major distraction. In June he proposed that GM strike an alliance with Renault-Nissan, in which its CEO, Carlos Ghosn, would most likely take over Wagoner's job. It would have been a monstrously complex merger, and Kerkorian's goal appeared to be to push GM's shares up in the short term so that he could sell his stake at a profit. But even if Kerkorian's goals were transparent, his proposal added pressure on Wagoner and top management, forcing them to spend crucial time analyzing and responding to Kerkorian's proposals. (Once rebuffed, Kerkorian started selling his shares and went away toward the end of the year.)

The big break on the cost front didn't come until the fall of 2007. It was then that the company and the UAW announced that GM would shift $55 billion in health care obligations in future decades off its own books and into a voluntary employee benefit association, or VEBA, that would be overseen by the UAW. This was a new concept that had never been implemented in the auto industry. GM would put up 70 percent of that $55 billion in the form of cash, stock, and other assets, but after that, health care would be in the hands of the UAW. After decades of steadily escalating costs, GM would be out of the health care business.

The UAW also agreed to a two-tier wage system. The company would be able to hire workers at $15 an hour to replace at least some of the workers making $28 an hour who were accepting buyouts. Such a deal would have been inconceivable even two years earlier. (Gettelfinger would later state that these agreements would have been impossible without Henderson's involvement.)

Lutz describes it this way: "I would say the last big breakthrough of willingness to confront reality was the last labor negotiation, where we finally figured out we can't treat this health care thing like the elephant in the room that nobody talks about. We finally said we've got to do something about health care. I mean, it's going to annihilate the company. We can't afford six or seven billion dollars and someday eight or nine billion off the top every year, just to pay for active and retiree health care. We've got to confront the union and work with it. In the old days, their rhetoric tended to be believed, and we said, 'Gee, that's sort of the core thing that you don't touch.' But we touched health care."

For the moment at least, the board was satisfied. "It took a long time doing it," says Fisher, "but we got all those things basically done, with the exception of Delphi, which is still dangling around. But other than that, we did the GMAC sale, we did Delphi, we got the UAW to work with us on health care in two negotiations. It cost us a lot of money, but in the long term it is going to be wonderful for our structural costs. It was led by Rick. It wasn't led by the board saying, 'You've got to go do something.' The board was totally in agreement with Rick. We had to do something."

Cole, from the Center for Automotive Research, estimates that these steps will allow GM to strip a whopping five thousand dollars from the cost of making each vehicle by 2010. That will fundamentally alter GM's competitive position in the marketplace.

What does it mean for the UAW? It would be an overstatement to argue that Wagoner broke the union; it still has considerable power, enough to close U.S. plants at will. But within the union, dissidents have accused Gettelfinger of "collaboration" with the enemy. Former UAW president Doug Fraser said it was "the most difficult time in the history of our union. Period."

Clearly, there has been a shift in the balance of power. This has come partly because Wagoner had been steadily expanding GM outside the United States. More than 60 percent of the company's workforce is now offshore—and largely outside the influence or control of the UAW. And the number of UAW workers at GM declined from 468,000 in 1979 to 72,000 by mid-2008.

So Wagoner, in a two-year period, carried out the most remarkable transformation in labor relations in GM's history. It represented a fundamental change in the compact between management and labor in the auto industry. It also came at a cost. The toughest question I ever asked Wagoner was, Did you have to destroy the American middle class to save the company? "If you look at the circumstances we're facing today, if we hadn't done that, it would have been very dire for all three of the U.S.-based auto businesses," he responded. "So, unfortunately, the answer is yes.

"But compare the way it was handled with just about any other mature industry. Take steel or the rubber workers or airlines. Basically, the way those companies eventually had to address it was to go into bankruptcy. You talk about something that is tough on people, who worked their whole life, retired with the expectation that they were going to get a certain level of pensions and health care treatment, and all of a sudden, under the system here in the United States, the pensions are reasonably protected but the health care is not. So how would that feel to be seventy years old and have almost no health care coverage? We haven't had to do that."

One saving grace was that the company had overfunded its pension plan by managing it so that it earned a healthier return on its investments than expected. So nobody's pension was going to be stripped away, and the company would be investing heavily in the VEBA to help cover health care costs. "Among the range of alternatives one could have used," Wagoner says, "I think our solution was absolutely as fair as it could be and respected everyone's history with the company, and was done in a way that gives a vision to be quite competitive in the future. But sure, there have been sacrifices by a lot of people."

While all these painful steps were being taken, Wagoner was also investing to create a new General Motors. None of the most significant efforts started in that period, but all of them gained momentum. The first was the drive to close the manufacturing gap with Toyota. A second was continuing to push new product designs, such as the Chevrolet Volt, the extended-range electric car that was unveiled at the January 2007 Detroit Auto Show. "During this tough time," Wagoner notes, "we doubled down and [expended] more resources and tried to advance new products into the marketplace. I think we showed good discipline in fixing the areas of cost that were uncompetitive but keeping an eye out to the fact that we know in this business you can't turn around based just on cost reduction. You need to have a vision for driving your revenue up, too."

Third, the company made big progress with new technologies, such as the lithium-ion battery and its OnStar onboard communications and diagnostic service. And it continued to make strides in becoming a stronger global competitor, particularly in China and other emerging markets. Wagoner didn't start any of these trends, but he set the tone at the top, and he played a key role in putting the right people in place and making sure they had the money to further their goals.

Taken together, these are powerful forces when unleashed by a company of GM's size, particularly if it finally has the right management model and cost structure. Wagoner is taking an enormous gamble, but he could emerge from these difficult years as the unlikely radical who destroyed the old GM while creating a new one.

PART II

The GM Transformation Effort

CHAPTER 6

Mastering the Toyota Way

In the late 1980s, a quiet revolution was starting inside General Motors, though few understood it at the time. Through the joint venture with Toyota at NUMMI in California (and another such collaboration between GM Canada and Suzuki Motors called CAMI Automotive), GM's people were witnessing some substantially different manufacturing methods. What they were seeing led some—but not all—to ask questions about the way their own company made vehicles. GM Europe also embarked upon a journey of learning, hiring executives from several Japanese manufacturers to tour GM plants and offer their insights into lean manufacturing methods. Wagoner, in Europe at the time, encountered the ideas through *The Machine That Changed the World*, the pivotal Massachusetts Institute of Technology book on the Toyota system. "We used that quite a bit in GM Europe to embrace the early stages of the lean concept," Wagoner recalls.

Another source of learning was a new division called Saturn that GM had launched in Spring Hill, Tennessee, in July 1990, for the express purpose of making small cars that could compete against Toyota and Honda. Currents were stirring deep inside GM, even if top management did not fully understand them.

GM's frontline people who witnessed the Japanese lean techniques were flabbergasted to find that the Japanese were not using any production tricks or shortcuts, as top management had suspected. As Jack Smith had discovered, they simply had a better model, thanks in part to the quality gurus, Juran and Deming. The experience at NUMMI was particularly shocking to GM managers because the joint venture relied on workers from the UAW—the same workers who had worked at the failed Fremont GM plant. Fremont had been the scene of bitter disputes between management and the UAW, and many managers liked to believe that card-carrying members of the UAW were the root of what went wrong. Yet here were those same workers producing very different results.

This was partly because Toyota built the production system around the needs of the workers, starting by installing its traditional andon cords, which let workers to halt the line to fix problems rather than allowing a defective vehicle to continue down the line. (Andon means lantern in Japanese.) By giving more power to workers and "inverting the pyramid," or devoting resources to the workers instead of top managers, Toyota was able to largely overturn decades of labor bitterness.

The Toyota system squeezed out waste, too. Rather than having twenty-foot-high stacks of parts clogging up factory space and obstructing managers' view of the factory floor, parts arrived just in time, only hours before they were used, in the kanban system. The workers were organized in teams. In stark contrast to the assembly-line method, where each person repeated the same function endlessly, groups of six to eight workers performed as a unit and were measured on their productivity. They developed allegiances to other members of their team, and they competed against other teams. This created an entirely different set of motivations from the traditional U.S. model. On the mass assembly line, workers had much less incentive to give their best and to fight for the last drop of quality.

At NUMMI, workers were also given standardized instructions. This helped managers identify best practices and make sure they were applied on every vehicle, which is key to achieving higher quality. The fact that workers' jobs were standardized might create the impression that Toyota was not trying to tap their mind power as much as it was their physical power. But in practice, the Toyota system elicited a surge of ideas from workers about how to improve those tasks. They were asked to make many more decisions about how a car would be produced than they were allowed to make in a traditional GM factory. The net effect was undeniably impressive: workers at NUMMI were able to put together a car in twenty hours, while workers at GM plants needed an average of thirty-five.

Toyota had "profound knowledge" about making cars, says Gary Cowger, who paid frequent visits to NUMMI. Although dozens, if not hundreds, of GM people were exposed in the early days to Toyota's methods (and Japanese methods in general), Cowger is generally credited with being the executive who was most effective in pushing them inside GM. Today he oversees 185 plants in 35 countries.

The carefully coiffed Cowger, who sports a trim mustache and wears a GM pin as he sits in his office high in the Ren Cen, seems like an old-school company man, and in many ways, he is. He started out at GM as a student intern in 1965 at the Fairfax plant in Kansas City, Kansas. But even though he was steeped in the traditional GM way of doing things, he was quick to understand the implications of Toyota's methods, partly because he also had spent time with the American experts who inspired them. Cowger was the plant manager in Wentzville, Missouri, when the Pontiac Division invited Deming in for consultations around 1983, during the very early days of GM's attempt to understand the Toyota model. "We had several dinners together and he impressed upon me, 'Unless you understand somebody's profound knowledge, what's behind what you're seeing, it's very difficult to understand what they're doing,'" Cowger says. "What took the most time was to internalize and really get a profound feel of what the Toyota production system was all about. Just walking in and looking at a plant and looking at tooling and the way they process parts didn't give you the whole story. You couldn't see what you don't even know you're looking for. You needed to understand what the profound drivers and processes were behind that system."

Part of the profound knowledge was based on a deceptively simple axiom: Toyota managers relied on workers to make cars, so it built the manufacturing system around their needs. For Toyota, this had led to a completely different relationship between management and labor. In the bad old ways at GM, management dictated what would be built and with what equipment. It didn't really care how the workers made the vehicles; consequently, workers didn't really care how good the cars were.

Cowger and others came back from NUMMI and CAMI converted, ready to revamp the company's production systems. But they had little luck selling their insights to the top brass at GM. "We had a hard time getting traction," recalls Mark Hogan, GM's lead executive at NUMMI from 1986 to 1988. "It wasn't like the folks who went out there didn't try. We needed more [NUMMI graduates] to start changing the company."

Joseph Phillippi, the auto analyst, put it more bluntly: "The expatriates from NUMMI would be in GM meetings and they'd pipe up and say, 'When we were at NUMMI, we did it this way.' Immediately, they would be shot down by the GM establishment, which said, 'This is what we do here. Go sit in the corner and shut up.'"

It was an extraordinary moment. An old system that had proven reliable and profitable for many decades was suddenly revealed to be ossified. Rebels within the empire realized their manufacturing system was no longer competitive, yet top management in Detroit was still resisting their insights.

GM might never have absorbed Toyota's methods if it had not been for Lou Hughes, president of General Motors International Operations in Europe. GM Europe still operated largely independently from North America in the late eighties, so he had the management latitude to build factories the way he saw fit. He could operate just below the radar screen of top management in Detroit. It was Hughes who broke the impasse between GM executives drawn to Japanese methods and those who clung to the old ways. And improbably, it was the collapse of Communist Germany that enabled him do it.

In 1989, the Berlin Wall fell, and almost overnight, East Germany was absorbed by the government of what was then called West Germany. It was a moment of complete economic panic for millions of East Germans, including some ten thousand workers at the Wartburg automotive factory in Eisenach, in the province of Thuringia. Like many other factories, their plant was seized by the Treuhandanstalt, the agency set up to take control of East German assets and sell them or give them to someone, anyone, who could preserve jobs and preserve some semblance of economic order in the East. For the Wartburg workers, this seemed like an end to life as they knew it, which it most definitely was.

Hughes saw an opportunity. If he bought the Eisenach facility, he could develop a new Opel factory on the site. (GM had long owned Opel, based in Rüsselsheim, not far from Frankfurt.) The new factory would serve as a test case for incorporating the best Japanese manufacturing methods, and at the same time would position GM for growth in the new markets of eastern and central Europe.

Hughes tapped a young hotshot named Tom LaSorda, a Canadian who was assistant plant manager at CAMI. (CAMI, confusingly, is simply the joint venture's name, not an acronym.) LaSorda had witnessed the Japanese lean production techniques at CAMI and emerged a true believer.

Although Eisenach obviously had a history, Wagoner and others saw it as a possible greenfield—a place where they could build a factory from scratch. Even more enticing was the presence of such a large skilled workforce. Workers there had made the Wartburg, which didn't meet the quality standards of the West but was still a much higher quality product than the much maligned Trabant, the boxy, smoke-belching, notoriously untrustworthy car that most East Germans had driven for decades.

Because these workers were faced with prolonged joblessness, they were more open to experimentation than workers at other established plants might have been. Plus, even though a worker's council, or union local, existed, the workers decided not to join the very tough national IG Metall union, at least temporarily, which made for a less confrontational labor environment. "We were guinea pigs," says Harald Lieske, a toolmaker at the old Wartburg plant who was one of the first thirty-seven workers hired by GM in the fall of 1990. "GM had no experience with East German employees, who were known for poor quality." Lieske emerged as leader of the local union.

I was driven to Eisenach from Opel headquarters in Rüsselsheim on a rainy morning in April. When we crossed into the former East Germany on the autobahn, my driver pointed out the only evidence that this was once one of the world's most heavily fortified borders—a couple of high watchtowers. All other signs of the brutal Communist system have been eliminated or covered up by post-reunification development. Thuringia is surprisingly green and hilly compared with the flatlands along the Rhine.

Lieske, a kindly looking fifty-five-year-old with a mustache and a completely bald pate, explains what it was like to go through the closing of the old factory and the collapse of an entire economic system. His fear, he says in nearly perfect English, was that "perhaps I would be unemployed for the next twenty years."

LaSorda's team set up an assessment office that began screening job applications from the old Wartburg workers and then started construction of the new plant in 2002. LaSorda began introducing Japanese lean techniques, such as the concept of teams. "We had to change our mindset entirely," recalls Lieske.

At the same time workers were being screened, LaSorda began bringing in managers who had had exposure to Japanese methods. There were first-wave, second-wave and third-wave advisers. Although LaSorda has since moved on to Chrysler, one of the early advisers is still in Eisenach—Arto Savolainen, a Finn who had been working for Saab in Sweden at the time LaSorda was taking over in Germany. The six-feet-tall Savolainen, who hails from Utajarvi, a remote village in central Finland with just eight hundred residents, had made several trips to study Toyota in Japan and was known for his manufacturing acumen. "I have my philosophy based on Toyota," the Finn says in heavily accented but fluent English. We're sitting in the paint shop office, where Savolainen is in charge.

LaSorda "grabbed people" from Toyota's Camry plant in Kentucky, from Nissan, from anywhere he could find them, Savolainen recalls. He needed to completely remake GM management's approach to manufacturing, and do it in a hurry. It was an alluring proposition to Savolainen to move from being an adviser to signing up for the oncoming battle. "I could not say no," he recalls. His value to the team was that he was non-GM and non-German. "As an outsider," he recalls, "I would ask stupid questions."

Even though their products had been shabby during the East German era, the workforce proved able once they were given the right tools and parts. "These people know how to make cars," Savolainen says. "They've been building cars since before I was born." Among other things, they proved to be quite mechanically inclined. They were also good improvisers; they had suffered from mechanical breakdowns on the line in the old era and had learned to make some of their own production equipment rather than waiting for replacement parts to come from afar. That's very unusual at any plant anywhere in the world. Necessity was truly the mother of invention for them.

So the hybrid management team and the recycled East German workforce began inventing GM's future manufacturing methods. It was a stop-and-start process. Equipment was brought in and set up in pilot lines, then set up again to improve the work flow. Workers were asked to develop their own assembly techniques, reflecting the Toyota philosophy. They learned the Toyota method of zero defects. Everything had to be perfect as a vehicle rolled down the line. If it wasn't, they learned how to pull the andon cord. "We would go to the next level and stabilize, then go to another level and stabilize," Savolainen recalls.

The clear goal was to out-Toyota Toyota, and the results were impressive. Eisenach was able to achieve higher productivity levels than anywhere else in the European auto industry—or in North America. It could build 150,000 cars a year with only 2,000 employees. Building one Astra took only twenty-five to twenty-six hours, which the East German workers could not believe. That was roughly half what it took elsewhere in Europe. The plant's requirement for space, including storage and transportation, was also 50 percent below anything that European or U.S. competitors were using. "If you want to beat somebody, you have to take leaps," says Savolainen, who today is forty-eight and lives with his Finnish wife and two sons, ages eighteen and thirteen. (LaSorda eventually left GM to become CEO of the Chrysler unit of DaimlerChrysler and is currently one of three top executives there, now that it is once again simply Chrysler.)

Thus Eisenach was the unlikely birthplace of GM's new manufacturing system. An incredible blend of Japanese techniques and an East

German workforce is what it took to start shattering the arrogance of managers back in Detroit who thought that the traditional GM way was the only way.

What GM learned in Eisenach started to percolate around the world, starting in Argentina and Brazil. The first plant to imitate it was in the city of Rosario, Argentina. And in 1991, even before Eisenach was finished, Wagoner transferred to Brazil and began pushing lean techniques there. It was a good place for it because Brazil had fewer existing plants than the United States and hence less resistance. "I remember very clearly at the first budget review having a pretty direct conversation with the head of manufacturing and saying, 'Hey, we are going to drive this lean stuff,' " Wagoner recalls. "We began to get huge improvements in productivity and responsiveness. I got a chance to see that firsthand."

One of the Brazilian plants, code-named Blue Macaw and located all the way south in the state of Rio Grande do Sul, became the first plant to completely alter GM's relationships with suppliers: rather than accepting delivery of hundreds of parts in a dashboard/steering wheel subassembly, for example, it asked suppliers to deliver the completed subassembly, which could be quickly integrated into the body of the car. It proved to be a far more cost-effective way to assemble cars.

Blue Macaw also was the first factory GM built in the shape of a T, because that allowed trucks to deliver parts precisely to where they were needed on the line. A regular factory might have one set of docks for all parts to arrive; workers would then have to move the parts to where they were needed in the factory. But the T shape, with docks all along its sides, allowed for specific parts to be delivered by truck to within thirty or forty yards of where they were being used on the line, so they didn't have to be stacked up or moved through the factory. Cowger says the company at this time was asking itself, "How can we take the lean model and drive it even leaner?" GM wasn't content to merely copy Toyota's methods; it wanted to improve on them.

This was when the company really got serious about the lean concept. This was the tipping point. "For many years, we didn't have one person in charge of manufacturing," Wagoner recalls. "We had seven or eight operating units with seven or eight heads of manufacturing, where some ideas were the same, but a lot of stuff was done very differently between Car and Truck, between Saturn and Lansing"—different parts, different equipment, different processes.

Cowger was the man who pulled it all together. He left his job at Cadillac in 1992 to head up a new thing called the Manufacturing Center, which was the beginning of Smith's movement to "run common." "At that time," Cowger recalls, "we were trying to get the U.S. onto one system. We had seventeen different engineering groups" before the Manufacturing Center got started.

Cowger codified all that GM had learned about lean manufacturing from its various channels and called it the Global Manufacturing System, or GMS. Other plants using GMS were built from the ground up in China, Poland, and Thailand. "We were taking our learnings and moving them," Cowger says. The goal was for every plant to "be driven by the same organizational structure." GMS, which was not officially announced until 1996, has five principles: people involvement, standardization, built-in quality, short lead time, and continuous improvement. All are borrowed directly from Toyota. *People involvement* means that workers are asked for their opinions about how to do their jobs, for example. *Standardization* means that every job is done in a prescribed manner, rather than according to local standards. *Built-in quality* suggests that every step of the process is geared toward building quality; it is not an afterthought. *Short lead time* means that model changes happen quickly. *Continuous improvement*, meaning just what it sounds like, is the heart of the Toyota method.

After GM recognized the incredible value of replicating Toyota's manufacturing system and began improving upon it, it was relatively easy to start building new U.S. plants that relied on lean manufacturing. Two of these so-called greenfield plants were Lansing Grand River and Delta Township, on the outskirts of Lansing.

Lansing Grand River was the first, and I toured it in 2003. GM had indicated that it was considering shutting down its Lansing facilities, some of which were nearly a century old. But the community responded with a "Keep GM" campaign, and UAW Local 652 agreed to give GM the flexibility to build a new-style plant. The company knocked down eighteen buildings and put up a new factory, at a total cost of $585 million. It opened in January 2002 and started making the Cadillac CTS.

Lansing Grand River was shaped like a T, just like Blue Macaw. I was excited and intrigued to see the andon cord, which I had never seen before in an American auto plant. The just-in-time delivery of parts to each workstation was another clear Toyota method. And areas had been created near the line where teams could have their meetings and breaks. While totally embracing the Japanese methods, GM learned to add massive amounts of computerization and wireless communications to improve upon the original model.

In the traditional Toyota system, for example, when a worker on the line started running out of parts, he would hand a card to a materials person, who would go get the right components and return to the line. But at LGR, I saw that information was communicated wirelessly to small vehicles called tuggers. Drivers of the tuggers would see the information flashed onto their computer screens. They would get the necessary parts and simply arrive at the line with the parts at precisely the right time. "Wireless is starting to reinvent the factory floor," Cowger told me at the time.

To eliminate errors, GM also devised a system of scanners that checked bar codes on parts to make sure they were the right parts to install. And the company improved on the traditional andon cord system by creating large electronic displays overhead, much like those in sports stadiums. When a worker pulls the cord, the team leader can look at the display board and know immediately where the problem is. "We think in some ways we have improved on what we originally saw at Toyota," said Mark Hogan, the former NUMMI executive. It was the Toyota system on steroids.

Yet despite the success of Lansing Grand River and Delta Township, those facilities were exceptions to the rule. The key question was whether GM could bring the GMS system into dozens of its existing, or brownfield, plants. It was one thing to build a new factory to fit the new methodology. To reform an old one—where traditional practices had prevailed for decades—would be a different challenge altogether.

CHAPTER 7

Going to Kansas City

Making GMS Work

Fairfax Assembly, the GM plant in Kansas City, Kansas, is a 3.2-million-square-foot compound that occupies a huge piece of land left by an oxbow in the Missouri River. The facility was originally a military base, located in the center of the country so that it would be outside the reach of German and Japanese raiders during World War II. In 1940, Jimmy Doolittle raided Tokyo in a B-25 bomber flown from Fairfax. At the end of the war, GM took over and built a plant that started making Buicks, Oldsmobiles, and Pontiacs. During the Korean War, it made F84F Thunderstreak fighters on one production line and cars on the other. The roof collapsed in 1979, so a new plant was built next to the old one. In all, the two incarnations of the plant have produced ten million cars since World War II.

It's the kind of place that has a long and proud history, and also the kind of place that can have trouble letting that history go when it's time to change. The story of how plant manager Michael L. Dulaney is pushing lean manufacturing at Fairfax is a short version of the story of GM's turnaround hopes; the factory is now running five days a week, in two shifts, pumping out Chevy Malibus and Saturn Auras, which have been in hot demand. That demand intensified in the second quarter of 2008 as Americans began an even more pronounced shift away from larger vehicles. If GM can carry through its program of change in the United States, the Fairfax plant is the look of its future.

Dulaney, fifty-two, is a big, beefy guy, bespectacled and graying at the temples. He's been at the Fairfax plant since May 2007, but he's been with the company for twenty-nine years. He's an African American from an inner-city section of Columbus, Ohio, an area that was once called Flytown, but that now has been revitalized and renamed Victorian Village. His father was an hourly worker in the casting industry, and his mother was a teacher's assistant in the public schools, and they had a family of six. "I grew up in a middle-class area, but an area that didn't have college graduates," Dulaney recalls, sitting in his spacious but utilitarian ground-floor office looking out over the plant's parking lot. "I didn't have role models to lead me. There were not a lot of people in my neighborhood with suits and ties on." Dulaney became the first of his family to graduate from college, working his way through nearby Ohio State University. After he graduated, he joined GM.

He got his first taste of the Toyota system when he was an assistant plant manager at Flint Assembly in 1997. "My first exposure was going out to the NUMMI operations and benchmarking them," he recalls, referring to the process of comparing operations at different plants. "We'd go out for four days," he says. "I had an experience of actually working the production line."

He was shocked at what he found. "I walked away from there being fearful that General Motors couldn't compete against Toyota, because the employees were so knowledgeable and so disciplined and so embracing of continuous improvement."

Dulaney was particularly impressed that the NUMMI workers had the confidence to recommend ways to eliminate their own jobs to improve overall efficiency. "They felt that 'If I eliminate my job, it creates a better opportunity for me somewhere else.' I'm hearing these employees talk about these things and they're sincere, yet I'm at Flint Assembly where, definitely at that time, we weren't working real closely together." That is a major understatement. Labor relations in Flint were among the worst at GM; the following year, the Flint plant would be the focal point of a bitter strike that shut down the company's U.S. operations.

The experience at NUMMI turned Dulaney into a kind of miss "I made up my mind that I was going to make a difference," he was going to help prove that an American facility could be as proc as a Toyota facility." Back in Flint, he started introducing GMS prir like small teams and became plant manager in the process. Recog: that Dulaney was someone who could improve labor-management tions and push GMS at the same time, GM moved him in rapid from Flint to the Oshawa truck plant in Canada, Pontiac Assemb Pontiac, Michigan, and then to Wentzville Assembly in Wentzville, souri, where vans are made. From there he went to Fairfax.

Over the past decade or so, Fairfax has been known as a plant wl management and labor knew how to work together better thar plants like those in Flint. But labor relations haven't always been cordial as they are today. John Melton, chairman of the local UA says of the 1970s and 1980s, "I'd file a grievance just as soon as look ya." The tone regarding quality at the plant, he says, was "If it has fo wheels on it, send it out the door." Other old-timers tell stories abo how workers who had problems on the line had to take a hammer an beat on an iron post to attract the attention of a supervisor. There wer certainly no andon call systems, and workers could not stop the line i they had problems. There were seventy-seven job classifications back then, which made for extreme complexity in assigning and reassigning workers. A welder could not become a glass installer, for example. (There are just two job classifications today, team member and team leader.)

One part of what Dulaney is pushing is cultural change because the GMS system, like the Toyota system, requires a deep restructuring of the traditional management-labor relationship. One principle is "support the operator"; rather than building the company around their own needs and goals, managers are expected to support workers and help them do their jobs, not the other way around.

As Dulaney explains it, "I want the management team to understand the leadership behaviors that they need to change to be able to work in a GMS culture. The behaviors involve giving a lot less direction. At the old GM, eighty percent of the time, a leader would be giving direction and

telling an operator what to do, when to do it, and how to do it. Twenty percent of the time they may support the operator on how to solve a problem."

That model has to be stood on its head. "Today," Dulaney adds, "what we're looking for in leaders is, we want you to spend eighty percent of your time supporting the operator, coaching and counseling and teaching, helping, resourcing. Twenty percent of your time should be on giving hard directions: 'Okay, change over and do this. Move to that line. Move to this line.' That's a big shift. For a lot of years, older leaders have been recognized for being very good know-it-alls. They are knowers versus learners. Now we're looking for learners and teachers and motivators and coaches." Rather than telling workers how to do something, now a manager might ask them to come up with solutions that make the most sense to them. Then the manager would work with engineers and others to accommodate the worker. This is pure Toyota; it's very unlike the old GM.

Dulaney is a talker and a communicator, which might imply that he's a softie. But he also has a hard edge to him. He's trying to drive the plant's GMS compliance rate—the measure of how well the plant is conforming to the GMS principles established by Cowger—from the current 68 percent to 95 percent. Cowger sends "GMS calibrators" around to every plant to measure how it stacks up. Until recently, Fairfax had a much higher rating, but then the company decided to raise the bar and institute a tougher grading system. This ratcheting up of pressure is the very heart of the kaizen (constant improvement) philosophy.

To achieve a 95 percent rating, Dulaney has to tackle two issues that are quite sensitive for the local UAW leadership; one is how team leaders are chosen, and the second is how large the teams are. There are national agreements between GM and the UAW, but in this case the issues are local. On the first issue, the UAW has wanted to make sure that team leaders are chosen on the basis of seniority, which would keep the teams solidly in the grip of older UAW members. But Dulaney says team leaders should be selected on the basis of their skills and proven leadership ability, which would open up the jobs to some younger people. "A team leader shouldn't go into the job based on his or her seniority," he argues. "In the traditional union environment, if you have the most whiskers,

if you have the most gray hair, if you have the highest seniority, if you apply for the team leader job, it's your job. The person may not know how to read or write. The person may never have communicated in front of a group of people. The person may not have any teaching or motivating skills." He's making some progress on this issue; the second morning I was at the plant, the UAW local agreed to start a pilot program that would test the concept of choosing team leaders on the basis of skill. "A training team is going to put together a team leadership selection process," Dulaney says. "We'll try it out on existing team leaders, then tweak it, but basically move forward."

Second, he has to reduce the size of the teams that build the cars. (Each team performs a specific function, such as installing dashboards; altogether, dozens of teams may be involved in building a single vehicle.) The GMS ideal is four to six people per team, a substantial difference from the historical number at Fairfax of around ten. The reductions Dulaney is working for mean that everybody on the team has to work harder to get the same amount of work done; the union is resistant. As any good negotiator does, Dulaney has set a goal that probably cannot be attained; but movement from an average of ten per team to, say, seven would represent big progress. "I'm moving fast," he says.

To accomplish his goals, Dulaney is playing close to the edge. The local contract calls for an 11 percent absentee pool, which means that 11 percent more workers are on hand than are needed, in order to cover workers who may be out on a given day. He's pulling his team leaders from that pool and building smaller teams around them. That has the net effect of lowering the average size of a team. "I'm not really violating anything in our current agreement," Dulaney explains. But, he says, "We have to work on getting that [absentee] language modified or else I'll be in violation." It's obviously in Dulaney's interest to do this because he can build more cars and his GMS scores will improve; it's equally obvious that the UAW will be skeptical about it because it suggests that everybody will need to work just a little bit harder.

Dulaney is pushing an ambitious agenda. Just as he's pushing these new concepts, Fairfax is accelerating its line to accommodate demand, for the Malibu in particular, making a big jump from forty-seven vehicles an hour to fifty-nine. To help, the plant is increasing its number of employees from 2,600 to 2,900. But this entails a total reshuffling of the deck; new recruits will have to be trained; current workers will have to learn new jobs; all will have to work harder.

Another layer of complexity is that the plant is getting ready to launch a new product, a Buick based on an architecture code-named Epsilon II, which means that many people at the plant are gearing up new tools and preparing to launch production. Many teams have traveled to Rüsselsheim, Germany, which is GM's homeroom for midsize cars and where design and engineering for the new Buick has been overseen. After successful launches of the Aura and the Malibu, the pressure is on for a perfect launch of the new Buick; the first cars that roll off the production line have to be flawless.

Dulaney is asking people to work harder and handle a new product launch without sacrificing quality. He's squeezing blood out of a stone, and that is causing increased tension with the UAW. Walt Wedow, who represents the second and third shifts for the union, tells me that Dulaney "is moving too fast." The number of grievances filed against him has increased. It's obvious that there is tension between management and labor. What's difficult to discern is whether it's normal and acceptable tension or something more.

With so many employees, Dulaney cannot possibly oversee how everyone in the plant does his or her job. It's up to him to create a climate in which people are motivated to do their best. He has to find good deputies and help them create a positive culture that surrounds both union and nonunion people, from the minute the first components enter the plant until finished vehicles are shipped to dealers. A tour of the plant, from where the parts come in to where the cars go out, reveals some of the inherent difficulties and also a great deal of progress.

Two people on the front line of the plant's bid to improve quality are surprisingly young. Called dimensional managers, they are in charge of examining the stamped metal parts that enter the factory from the factory's stamping plant. These are the parts that will be welded together to create the body of the car, and they need to be perfect. Randy Cartwright, a thirty-three-year-old from the Missouri side of the river, has been with

GM for ten years. David Pacheco Jr., thirty-two, is a friend of Randy's, even though he's from the Kansas side. Both are salaried engineers and arrived at the plant as student interns.

I meet them in the plant's Coordinate Measuring Machine Room, which is filled with large, imposing machines that measure the body panels that arrive. They loom like dinosaurs in a natural history museum, yet they are very precise; they measure as many as five hundred points on each part and can detect variations down to a millimeter. Cartwright concentrates on parts for existing models; Pacheco is the dimensional launch coordinator, which means that he is focused on the Buick that the plant is going to launch. GM has just spent heavily to refurbish the measurement machines and make sure that they are as sensitive as possible. One machine has a glass probe that actually touches the parts and can find variations of less than a hundredth of a millimeter.

Cartwright and Pacheco, armed with computers and clipboards, are looking for any imperfections that might later affect how the pieces of metal fit together. The problem could be in design or from a mistake at the stamping plant; either way, the name of the game is making sure that the tolerances, or gaps, between doors and door frames, for example, are perfect. As data comes from the machines, they are on the lookout for any dings, imperfections, or variations—anything that compromises the perfect fit. "When we talk, we're talking millimeters," says Pacheco.

Pacheco, though younger, has been here slightly longer than Cartwright because he worked as an intern for three summers and one Christmas break. His father works at the plant as a team leader in the body shop, which means he's a member of the union. The younger Pacheco has a thin goatee and spiked hair. Cartwright, clean-cut and boyish, is single and races a Giant Anthem mountain bike in his spare time.

Pacheco, with a wife and two kids, is more family-conscious than Cartwright. He says friends think he's pretty lucky. "I had a job before I left college. That was a huge relief. I didn't have to worry that last semester. Working those three summers really helped me and helped secure my future."

The two men can each make over $100,000 a year, particularly if they accept all the overtime work that is constantly requested of them.

They are often asked to work odd hours during evenings or on weekends, but they haven't allowed their jobs to completely take over their lives. Both men own Pontiac Trans Ams from the 1990s that they have souped up. Each Trans Am has 400 horsepower "at the rear wheels," as they say in typically precise engineer-speak.

I ask them why so few young Americans go into engineering at a time when so many young Indians and Chinese are pursuing those degrees. "I went to the University of Missouri," says Cartwright. "Dave went to the University of Kansas. Big rivalry. At engineering school, I'd say only fifty percent of the people were Americans. The rest were Indians and Indonesians and others." So why did you go down the engineering path? "My dad has a master in mathematics," Cartwright replies. "I'm one of those weird people who enjoy math. I enjoy crunching through the data and the charts. I get a lot of satisfaction fixing problems. I take a lot of pride in these cars."

Pacheco's reasons are somewhat different: "I always liked cars and always thought I wanted to do something that was mechanical," he explains. "My mom also printed out an article from the *Kansas City Star* that showed starting salaries. I saw that engineering was at the top. That sorta guided my decision."

Both men see a connection between what they do each day and the survival of the Fairfax plant. "I think it's on a lot of people's minds here," says Cartwright. "They've shut down a few plants. You've got the hub in Detroit. But look at what they're shutting down—Linden, New Jersey, and Atlanta, Georgia. Here, I feel we gotta continue to improve, or maybe in ten years, this place will be gone."

Pacheco is concentrating on the launch of the new Buick and hopes to be around long enough to launch many more vehicles. "If we fail on one of these, we're probably going to be in trouble," he warns. But he notes that Fairfax has had back-to-back winners with the Saturn Aura and Chevy Malibu. "If we continue to do that, we have a chance to stay in business in Kansas City. Every day is important."

After the metal body parts arrive from the stamping plant, they are welded together in the body shop, a big room full of fierce-looking but incredibly precise robots. At this point, the shells of the cars, with doors on but no motors, transmissions, interiors, or wheels, go to the paint shop. That's where they come under the care of Patti Bitler, forty-two, who has been with GM for twenty years. She started out working on the line and was promoted to become a seal cell electrician in the paint shop, meaning it is her job to make sure that the robots seal the bodies of vehicles against the elements of nature. "Nothing inside the cabin is applied by human hands," she says, so she needs to make sure all the sealants are "applied dead center." Bitler supervises 120 robots and re-programs them if she detects any imperfections. "I make the robots work," says Bitler, who is wearing overalls and safety glasses. She is all business, very intense.

We talk as we watch robots made by Japan's Fanuc apply a noise blocker—she calls it LASD, for liquid applied sound deadener—to the interior floors of the cars. It's a kind of asphalt, laid on precisely three millimeters thick. I impulsively touch it with a finger, and it's quite wet, so I get some on my finger and have a sudden fear that they'll have to use some seriously intense, industrial-strength chemical to get it off. "Don't worry," she reassures me. "It's water soluble."

She explains that the LASD prevents some sound from penetrating the cabin of the car, which means drivers and passengers hear less road noise. Her robots also apply a waterproofing sealant to the interior of the car. After her work is done, the bodies enter clean-room-like envi-ronments to get spray painted by robots; I can peer in a window, but can't actually go inside.

Even though she's standing amid robots, seemingly disconnected from the world outside, Bitler sees a real connection. "To me, the biggest problem for GM is perception," she offers. "People perceive that their Lexus is a better quality car than a Cadillac. That's not necessarily true, but that's their perception. In order for me to change that perception, I have to make sure that every car that leaves my area is one hundred per-cent compliant. 'Just try it. You'll buy it.' That hasn't been true for a very long time."

Earlier in her career, she didn't feel the company was sincere in pushing for quality. Top management just wanted the numbers to look good; they didn't really care about the quality of the cars. But she feels that has changed. "It's coming from the top down," she explains. "They kept preaching quality. But what I had never seen in the past was that management was standing up for what they were saying. They're finally starting to do that. That motivates me because they're backing me up. When I say I've got a problem and ask, 'Can you address it?' they say 'sure.' That's a huge turnaround in attitude."

This is the heart of why Toyota's system—now the GMS system—is so powerful; people who are doing the real work feel that they have a sense of ownership and control. Bitler says she wants to continue at GM for many more years and not take a buyout offer. "I'm confident I will, in fact, have a job here in seven years," she says over the robotic din. "I'm really proud of this process. Management is giving us so much control. Rather than coming in and saying, 'You will do it this way,' they're saying, 'What do you think we should do?'"

Bitler recently met with her seventeen-year-old son Doug's teacher. When he asked her where she worked, she told him she programmed robots at the Fairfax plant. "Then we started discussing quality, because he owns a Toyota," she recounts. "It was an interesting conversation. You don't want to put people off. You don't want to offend them. So I said, 'Go in and drive the Malibu. Just test-drive it even if you're not in-terested in buying it. See how it feels, how it handles. I think you'll be impressed."

After passing through the paint shop, the shells of cars enter General Assembly, where they will be fitted with interiors, wheels, and the chassis, which include engines and transmissions. The first team that greets them on the day shift is headed by Linda Flowers, fifty-six, an African Ameri-can woman who is a native of Kansas City, Missouri. She says she works "on the wall," the place where the bodies enter the assembly area. Her team of six takes the doors off, both to make it easier for operators to get in and out of the vehicle and also to avoid damage or mutilation. (The doors are reattached near the end of the assembly process.) Additionally, Flowers's team attaches a manifest to the car, a sheet of paper that tells all the operators on the line just what options to install. "We're go-betweeners," she explains. "We're problem solvers."

Flowers feels pressure to support all her team members in a timely fashion. "It's my job to know all their jobs and then some, and to understand the different personalities," she explains. "I make sure that they have everything they need to do their jobs." When a worker pulls the andon cord and lights up the computerized board high overhead, "that lets me know which operator I need to go see." Flowers relies on her decades of experience to quickly size up any problem. If the worker has to pull the andon cord a second time, that shuts down the line, and that has a cascading effect that interrupts everybody's work.

I sit down with Flowers at a table in a team meeting area just off the line during a break. We're joined by Cheryl Christwell, fifty-three, another team leader who is also African American. We talk about how they do their jobs, but their personal stories are powerful and deeply intertwined.

Both started at GM in 1979 (Flowers at Leeds; Christwell at Fairfax) and have participated in huge changes in how GM makes cars. At the same time, they have been single mothers who overcame sexism and racism in the plant to achieve modest versions of the American dream. "I would have never thought in my wildest dreams that I would still be here today," says Flowers, who speaks slowly and thoughtfully. "But I paid the rent and got the kids through college."

Her husband died at a young age, and she was left alone with two daughters. At the time, she was working for Greyhound in Arizona, and the company wanted to transfer her to New Mexico. But she heard about GM hiring back home and got a job there.

Christwell's parents were originally from Kansas City, Kansas, but since her father was a chef on Kansas City Southern Railroad, she was born in the big railroad center of Ogden, Utah. She was working at a hospital there for about $2 an hour when she heard that GM Fairfax was hiring at $7 an hour. She started immediately. "I went straight down to the floor after the interview," says Christwell, who is wearing big hoop earrings and a black blouse. She's more outspoken than Flowers. "I like to run my mouth," she jokes.

"The plant has changed one hundred percent since I walked in," Christwell adds. "Back then, you didn't have a choice: You did the job or you was gone. We did a lot of crying. We took a lot of *stuff*. Men said,

'I'm not going to work with you.' Or they'd walk up and say, 'Women shouldn't work in a plant.'"

The plant was making a station wagon at the time, and there was a particularly big window that had to be installed. "The men would help each other," she remembers. "But I had to carry that glass by myself and set that glass in that door."

Everything was set up for men. The jobs required more physical labor because there were fewer supporting machines, and the ergonomics were primitive; even the work gloves that the plant offered were designed for men's hands. "We had to hold ourselves together," Christwell says. "We would get together in the bathroom at lunch and just cry. 'We gotta make it. We gotta make it.'"

When jobs would be posted, Christwell would say, "I want that job," but she would be told, "No, you're not a man."

"I was kinda upset. I really was. But a friend of mine said, 'Cheryl, learn all the jobs in the group.' That's what I did."

There was more overt sexual harassment. When a woman bent over, to reach into a trunk, for example, men would comment on her shape. "It was rough," Christwell says.

Race was also a factor. Soon after Christwell was hired, she was told by a coworker, "We don't need any more black people in here." "Nowadays, it would be a whole different story," Christwell says. "But back then, you couldn't say anything about what people said. The world has changed."

Flowers is not as talkative as Christwell, but with a few words puts a hard edge on what it was like: "Each day, I thought I was walking into hell. I used to say, 'Lord, give me strength.'"

The fact that both were single mothers made it more difficult. Christwell has been married twice but has mostly raised her three children on her own. Flowers had two daughters at home. Because Flowers and Christwell sometimes had to work the second shift, they were not home for the crucial dinner and bedtime hours. So they would leave the plant during their breaks to rush home to spend a little family time, mete out discipline, or respond to a sudden health problem.

Despite the difficulties, neither woman seems bitter today. They laugh as they tell their stories, and it's obvious they feel a sense of personal accomplishment. One of Flowers's daughters graduated from college; the other studied for a year before deciding to get married. Christwell has a thirty-year-old daughter and two sons, age, nineteen and seventeen. Her daughter, who loves her job as a dental assistant, is more aggressive than her mother was. "She gets whatever she wants," Christwell says. The older son is studying computers in college; the other is still in high school. "I bought them their first car," she says. "After that, I told them, 'You have to have a job. You have to pay the insurance. You have to pay the gas. I just buy the car. Everything else is on you.' That teaches them responsibility." The kids "know they have to buy General Motors or something that is American. Nothing else is allowed in my driveway." She was able to buy a four-bedroom home in an older neighborhood.

Both women are proud of what they've achieved at Fairfax. "Believe it or not, people get along," says Christwell. "They like each other. The management people and the union people, we get along. Yes, we have personalities. We have fun. We talk. We laugh."

Many more women now work at the plant, which as changed the dynamic of how jobs are organized and who gets promoted. "If the women walked out, the plant wouldn't run," Christwell says. "We have say-so today."

Ultimately, in her view, that makes for a better factory. "We have been building good cars a long time," she continues. "There has to be a reason. And it must be us. I tell anybody who wants to hear. We have the best plant."

After the cars are finished, they are put through a few rudimentary tests in the assembly area. But the real scrutiny is meted out by people like C. J. Griffin, a fifty-year-old woman with shoulder-length brown hair and a wicked sense of humor. What does C. J. stand for? "Carol Jane," she says. "People will tell you it's Calamity Jane, but don't believe 'em."

She started on the line at the Leeds plant in 1978. The following year, she was divorced, which left her to raise her two daughters alone. "Thank God for GM because it helped me get out of a very bad situation," she recalls.

The good times didn't last forever. Griffin was laid off in 1986, before

Leeds was closed. Back then, there was no Jobs Bank program, a program that guarantees laid-off workers 90 percent of their regular compensation, so she was largely on her own in Kansas City, Missouri. "I was working two jobs in 1986 and 1987," Griffin says. "One was in Wal-Mart and the other was at a Mexican restaurant called Santa Fe. It did not feel good. I was always tired. What bothered me the most was not having health insurance for my children. I did not like having to take them to the clinic. I'm not putting anyone down who does that, but I didn't like it. I also didn't like not having more time with them because I was working so many hours."

Eventually, in 1989, she won a transfer to GM's Tarrytown plant in the New York metropolitan area, where she and her daughters spent five years. That plant, located on the Hudson River just north of the Tappan Zee Bridge, was also closed—"not because of me, trust me," she jokes.

She was able to win a transfer back to the Fairfax plant, which meant disrupting her daughters' educations, but keeping a high-paying job with benefits was obviously important. (Both daughters were able to go to college; one now has three children, making Griffin a grandmother.)

After working on the line for twenty-nine years (counting some of the time she was laid off), Griffin was trained last year in quality inspection techniques, which the company calls "audit." Now she is "in the pool" of quality auditors, who inspect finished vehicles. If an auditor is absent or on vacation, she covers for him or her. She floats from one area of the plant to another, including the body shop, paint shop, and materials, relying on her wide base of knowledge to spot potential problems.

We're standing in a quality inspection area underneath a Saturn that has been raised up on a lift, similar to one that might be found in an automotive shop. Not every car that comes off the line is subjected to a quality audit; cars for inspection are chosen randomly. Of those, though, "we inspect every inch," she says, wearing plastic safety glasses and earplugs and carrying a flashlight. "The best thing they did was train me in audit, because once you're trained in audit, your eyes catch everything. In audit, we inspect every inch of the car, every nut, every bolt, every clip that's feasible. We don't take it apart, obviously."

Griffin checks for air conditioner leaks, fluid problems, anything that is a "customer dissatisfier." Are the brake lines okay? The exhaust lines? All the welds on the muffler and gas tank? She carries a gauge in her pocket to measure the tolerances between body parts, which should be two millimeters in most cases. Manufacturing techniques have improved so much that she says she has never found a "significant" mistake.

"The technology and the tools, those are the most important things we have now," Griffin adds. "Thirty years ago, we were doing the best we could with what we had."

A major reason quality has improved is that "management and the union get along better now," she says. "Back in the seventies at Leeds, management and the union fought constantly." And everyone has gotten the message about global competition. "The Americans are trying harder," she says. "The jobs are leaving the country."

The result of a series of inspections like the one that Griffin does can be glimpsed at quality meetings attended by team leaders, auditors, and management. At one such meeting I observe, the differences between management and labor are completely invisible. It was all about the cars. Dulaney is there to demonstrate that he is willing to sweat the details.

In one case, the auditors have discovered that the gaps on either side of a Malibu's trunk are off. On one side, the gap is 5.5 millimeters, and on the other it's 3.5. The car will have to be fixed. That sort of attention to detail used to be inconceivable at GM plants (at any American plants, really), where small imperfections were routinely allowed to leave the factory. The old rule of "if it has four wheels on it, send it out the door" has been repealed.

One particularly interesting quality catch the day I'm there is on a Saturn Aura. An auditor has found three tiny scratches on the right A-pillar, the metal structure that connects the roof to the car's body and separates the front window from the windshield. The scratches were near the side mirror. I can't see them at first glance; I have to be directed where to look. But, yes, there are tiny scratches in the paint.

Once a problem of this nature is found, hourly "mutilation coordinators" track it back to where it originated. In this case, they discover, a

line worker had been in charge of putting three studs with nuts into the mirror to secure it to the A-pillar. GMS instructs each worker to do each job in precisely the same way, and in this case the standard operating procedure was for the worker to approach the door, take three sets of studs and nuts from a pouch he was wearing, and use his torque gun to put them in.

But this operator thought he had a more efficient method: He approached the job with the studs and nuts in his hand, not in a pouch. As he grasped the mirror to put it into place, the hardware in his hand scratched the paint. That happened to two hundred cars. The worker was identified, and his practices were corrected; the problem was knocked out. "That was a good kill," says Dulaney.

Walt Wedow, the UAW representative, was laid off from Leeds in 1987 and spent years working part-time jobs while receiving severance pay. His new wife at the time, also laid off, got a full-time job, but it didn't pay much. With two children in tow, they moved to Lordstown, Ohio, to work at the GM plant there, before returning to Fairfax, following the work. Now he's receiving twenty-eight dollars an hour from GM, even though he is working full-time for the UAW. He has a thirty-five-year-old stepdaughter and a thirty-two-year-old stepson, in addition to two daughters, ages twenty and seventeen.

Wedow seems to have figured his life out after some earlier reversals. Although he grew up in Missouri, he now lives across the river in Kansas, a few miles south of Overland Park. He has a three-bedroom home and recently bought a Saturn Aura for his wife. When he retires, he anticipates a pension of $3,150 a month, and Social Security should also kick in when he's sixty-two. He was hospitalized in December 2007 with an irregular heartbeat for two and a half days. The bill was ten thousand dollars, but "I didn't pay a penny," he says. He has health care coverage for the rest of his life, and he's not worried that GM is transferring control of his health care plan to the UAW through the VEBA. "I have probably as much or more confidence in the UAW managing it as I do General Motors," he says.

Yet Wedow knows that union workers of the next generation aren't

going to have it quite as good as he does. Under the dual-wage system that the UAW negotiated with GM, the company can hire younger workers at a fraction of what Wedow, as a tier 1 employee, now makes.

Has he betrayed the next generation? No, he says. He thinks they ultimately will get raises and be able to afford decent lives. "The tier 2 people have a chance to move up to my tier because of the way the contract is written," he explains. "There are going to be a designated number of tier 2 people in this plant. Let's say three hundred people. Once those people get hired, then if there's an opening in the first tier, management will go to the highest-seniority person in the second tier and say, 'We have an opening in the first tier. Would you like to move up?' That guy or gal will say, 'Hell, yes.' If they did not have that opportunity, then it would be unacceptable. But as long as they have the promise that 'I'm making lower wages now, but there is that opportunity for me in the future to make a better wage,' then I'm okay with that."

Was it necessary for the union to make all those concessions to GM? According to the contract, GM can turn to outside companies to perform certain jobs if the costs of doing it internally are higher. "I think so," Wedow says, "because we were losing the work to outsourcing." The fact that the UAW agreed to take the health care burden off General Motors and to start the two-tier wage system helps protect Wedow. "That's probably the only way somebody like me who is first tier is going to stay at first tier," he acknowledges.

Even though Wedow himself seems largely immune from downward economic pressures, he can see how his children's families may be affected. His stepson works at the plant as a tier 1 employee, but his daughter's fiancée is working two jobs, one loading and unloading trucks at a United Parcel Service facility, part-time during the week. On the weekend, he's a security guard. One pays $8.50 and the second pays $10.50. He just took a test to work at Fairfax as a temporary employee, which would pay $15 an hour, a significant raise, but with considerably less pay and benefits than Wedow receives. "It's rare anymore that anyone will do what I have done, and that's spend my whole career with one company," Wedow says.

What would happen if the UAW stuck to its guns and did not allow GM to reduce its cost structure? "I believe General Motors would end up being no different from Toyota or Honda or Nissan, just maintaining a presence in the United States with four or five plants but for the most part manufacturing their cars overseas and shipping them over here," Wedow answers. "The American public obviously doesn't care where the cars come from. They just care about the price and the quality. So there has to be an incentive for General Motors to maintain its current presence. I believe General Motors does need that kind of relief. I haven't looked at their books, but the UAW has looked at them extensively, and the mutual funds and the investment bankers have looked. I don't think General Motors is fooling the whole world when it says, 'Hey, we're losing money.' Some of my coworkers would disagree. There are a few. They would tell ya, 'Hey, they're making billions in China. They just hid all the money and took all the profits they made in America and invested it in China.'" Wedow clearly is not buying that argument.

What do you have to do to make sure this plant will still be here for your stepson and perhaps your son-in-law? After the tasks of building a much-higher-quality car and reducing the plant's cost structure, the major task, Wedow thinks, is "to convince the American public. If you read trade journals and the J.D. Power reports, you see that GM's quality is just getting better and better. The trouble is convincing the American public of that after they sat through the last twenty-five years of *Consumer Reports* and most of the media saying, 'If you want to buy a good car, you have to buy a Japanese car, a Toyota or Honda or whatever.' It's hard to turn back twenty-five years of ingrained mentality."

I cannot resist asking Wedow a question that must be on the minds of millions of Americans as they contemplate an economy that seems to have come off the rails: Who do you blame for the tough situation? Who failed you? He thinks about it for a moment, keeping his eyes locked on mine, and says, "I would never put all the blame on *anybody*. There are some of the trade agreements that the United States has made that were unwise, and are hurting us. I think there are some decisions that GM made that were unwise, and the UAW made some decisions that were unwise. And I have to look at myself and say that I made some decisions that were unwise.

"I mean, it's a tough argument. Me and my wife have a lot of discussions about her shopping at Wal-Mart. I pretty much convinced her not to do a lot of that. I said to her, 'You have to understand what Wal-Mart does to our society in general.' One, they treat their workers like crap. They're forced to work through lunch and breaks with no pay, and the company discourages any unionization. They'll fire people for even talking about unionization. Second of all, we'd like to blame the Chinese for shipping things over here with lead in the paint. But Wal-Mart is telling the Chinese manufacturer that it doesn't own, 'You will build us this for X amount of dollars or we'll find somebody else to do it.' And the only way they're going to meet that price is to cut corners and do things they shouldn't do. I just don't believe in doing business with people like that."

At the end of the day, even a union official who in the old days might have wished General Motors ill believes that GM matters. He doesn't agree with everything that Rick Wagoner has done, but he wants Americans to buy more GM cars. And it's interesting to note that he thinks the quality of the jobs GM has created—and its overall economic profile—is more robust than what the company's Japanese competitors are offering. He sees a big difference between manufacturing jobs and service sector jobs—between a job at the Fairfax plant and a job at the Wal-Mart.

A few months after I visited, the union did go on strike, at least partly support of American Axle, a parts supplier to GM that was also striking at the time. But the changes that Dulaney was pushing were the primary issue.

The strike lasted sixteen days. Both management and labor made compromises to end it. So it's clear that there's only one direction for the plant to go, and everybody knows it. Says Local UAW chairman Melton, "GM cannot survive without the UAW, and the UAW cannot survive without GM. Not everybody believes that all the time. But the old style is gone."

Because of what is happening at plants like Fairfax, GM's manufacturing ability in North America has improved dramatically. Rankings and data from *Consumer Reports* and J.D. Power support GM's view that it has almost eliminated the manufacturing gap with the Japanese transplant factories. "There are some manufacturing managers still around today who still joke about the days in the early or midnineties when I was running North America and when they had to come in once a quarter and tell me how they were doing on their implementation of lean manufacturing," Wagoner recalls. "But now just look at the raw Harbour data on the number of hours it takes to assemble a vehicle. We were about twice what the transplants were maybe as late as 1990. Within ten or twelve years, we were within about five percent of them." The company benchmarks itself against Japanese plants in the United States, the so-called transplants, rather than their factories back in Japan, which are more efficient than any in the United States.

"While it took a while to get it going," Wagoner continues, "our manufacturing leadership took this to heart and did a terrific job. I also give a lot of credit to the UAW leadership. Obviously, it's not easy for them." Throughout this period, Wagoner's style in engaging with the UAW has been absolutely essential. Rather than treating the union as an enemy, he engaged with the UAW leadership and persuaded them to take unprecedented action.

Today, Wagoner does not believe that manufacturing efficiency or quality are a significant barrier to competing against Toyota or any other carmaker. "Ten years ago," he says, "I used to spend a ton of time on this, but today I check in with Cowger every once in a while—'Is it going all right?'—and he shows us some charts. It doesn't require a lot of attention from a guy like me anymore."

One of the reasons it doesn't require a lot of attention from a guy like Wagoner is that the push for GMS has been deeply institutionalized. Wagoner and Cowger have elevated an entire generation of managers who have been exposed to the Toyota system and are committed to beating it. One is Mary Barra, who started working in a GM plant after high school and is now in charge of global manufacturing engineering.

Barra says she began to understand the need for dramatically different manufacturing methods during the 1998 strike. At that time, she was assigned to internal communications, tasked with helping persuade GM employees that the company faced some fundamental challenges. "I did that for two years, but my heart was in manufacturing," she recalls. She spent time in industrial engineering and was responsible for spreading the GMS gospel. But before she could do that, she had to learn a great deal. "I didn't have a NUMMI or an Eisenach assignment," she explains. "We had Kaz Nakata, who we had hired from Toyota as a consultant. He had been working in GM Europe. I spent time with him and came to see the plant with him through his eyes. I also spent time with many of our people who had lean experience to understand it in depth. It's like continually peeling the onion back to understand the deep issues."

One of her responsibilities was developing the calibration system for measuring how well plants were adopting GMS. "We developed a set of questions that were very objective," she explains. "You ask questions on the fundamentals of quality and people involvement. 'Did people understand the mission? Did people understand their roles? Were small teams involved in problem solving, recognizing that the best place to solve a product or process problem is with the people who do it day in and day out?' And in continuous improvement workshops, 'How do I make continuous improvement and achieve waste reduction?' We'd ask a series of questions and it was either yes or no. You either have it or you don't."

Lean manufacturing is "built on human nature," she says. "It's engaging people's hearts and minds. No one wants to come to work and spend eight-plus hours a day and do something fairly repetitive without being valued for how they can improve it."

Today her group helps decide what equipment and processes a plant needs to make vehicles. The goal is to have the same equipment and the same processes at every GM plant in the world. "We deliver machinery to a plant," she explains, "and it has to be integrated with material flow and the people. It's the integration of man, machine, and material. We can put equipment in a plant, but if it's not integrated with how we design the jobs for employees, we haven't done our whole job."

So the minute the company assigns a chief engineer to work on a new product launch, Barra's group assigns a manufacturing chief engineer to make certain that at the end of the process, the company has the tools and wherewithal to actually manufacture the car. The two engineers "work hand in hand, shoulder to shoulder," Barra explains. "Even before we start doing physical builds, when we're doing virtual builds, we're then involving representatives from the plant. We want to get their viewpoint."

That's a pretty radical departure from twenty years ago, when management simply told workers, "Here's what you're going to build and here's the equipment." Now, once the company decides where it is going to make a new vehicle, "long lead" workers from the plant join the launch team. "The earlier we look at the fundamentals from an operator's perspective, the better," Barra says. She doesn't want problems on the factory floor to force engineers to redesign a part, which is time-consuming and expensive.

Barra's group wants to listen to workers to avoid problems in assembling parts. "Maybe the way I have to fasten something is not ergonomically correct, and if I change the orientation, I don't cause an ergonomic stressor. We want to get all that input in early. We can eliminate issues that we might fight later in the process." All of this has been adapted from the Toyota method, and all of it is now deeply inculcated throughout GM's North American plants, including Canada and Mexico. The calibration experts who measure each plant's compliance with GMS assign green, yellow, or red status (just like a traffic light) to each of the plant's practices. Cowger says 80 percent of these findings were green in 2007, and he expected to reach 85 percent by the end of 2008.

Even if GM has fully embraced lean manufacturing, the burning question remains, why did it take so long? Why were there so many years of denial? As Ross Perot once famously remarked when Roger Smith told him it took five years to develop a product, "Heck, we won World War II in four years."

Wagoner won't criticize his predecessors. "So the guys before us, were they bad? Did they miss this? The answer is no," Wagoner argues. "When we built the company, we were the benchmark in productivity and quality in the forties, fifties, and sixties. But a new model arose. It's hard to change when you're successful. There are a lot of reasons not to change. There's a lot of resistance. And it's not just management. It's labor and the dealers. You've got to be ready for change, and you've got to have your people ready for change, and then you have to take advantage of opportunities that are provided to you to change. It seemed slow while it was going on. But now I look back after what is a period that is closer to twenty years than I want to admit, and say a huge amount of progress has been made. For a company this big to make that kind of conversion, in retrospect, that was a very important initiative."

It is, in fact, very rare in the annals of business history for a large-scale manufacturer to be able to completely remake the very heart of its production system, particularly when that implies such a deep change in relations between management and labor. Whenever a clearly superior new system or a new model emerges to challenge an incumbent, dating back to the time of the steam engine and the Industrial Revolution, the far more common outcome is that the incumbent gets blown away. The U.S. clothing, consumer electronics, shoe, and tire industries are obvious examples of industries that couldn't adapt and essentially disappeared from American soil or American ownership. What made the process of adapting particularly difficult at GM was that the company was still the world's largest auto manufacturer and for many of those twenty years was profitable. It was difficult for management or labor to accept the need to radically reinvent its manufacturing system. But however long it took and however uneven a process it may have been, GM's nearly complete absorption of the Japanese lean manufacturing system is one of the largest and most profound industrial transformations in history.

CHAPTER 8

Design Rides Again

It was 2001 and Rick Wagoner had a problem. Less than a year into his term as chief executive officer, Tom Davis, who was in charge of global product development, told him on a flight in Europe that he wanted to retire. Wagoner was stunned. Davis wasn't even fifty-five, and he wasn't under pressure to step aside. But he told Wagoner that he had made a personal choice. "He said he didn't need to leave right away but would appreciate my moving as expeditiously as I could," Wagoner recalls.

This was a serious concern. The head of global product development is a big player, the guy who is ultimately responsible for deciding what cars to put on the road. Wagoner needed to find someone good, and fast. There were two ways to go. He could look internally, or he could turn to an established expert to tell him who the hot young guy might be. Wagoner chose the latter. The expert was Bob Lutz.

Wagoner had met Lutz at a function in Detroit where Lutz was being honored as business statesman of the year. The two men chatted. "It got me thinking," Wagoner says. "Hmmm, maybe I should talk to him sometime about who he thinks are the best product people in the business."

Lutz was a giant in the auto industry, someone with an outsize lifestyle, perhaps, but universally respected for his car savvy. Born in Zurich,

Switzerland, in 1932, Lutz grew up to become a jet pilot in the U.S. Marine Corps from 1954 to 1965, the last few years on reserve. After serving in the Marines, he attended the University of California at Berkeley—a real neck-wrencher for an ex-military guy in those days.

After graduating with a degree in marketing, Lutz started at GM in 1963 and made his mark in Europe. He pushed for the creation of the Opel GT, which was like a small version of the Corvette Stingray. It was considered a breakthrough car. He also spent time at BMW and helped that company devise its system for naming and marketing its cars—the 3 Series, 5 Series, and 7 Series.

In 1984, he moved to Ford Motor, where he spent twelve years, working mostly on trucks. He then moved to Chrysler in Detroit, from 1986 to 1998, where he was vice chairman. At Chrysler, he surprised the auto world by pushing the Dodge Viper into production. With more than 400 horsepower—more than the Corvette of the time—and a stunningly aggressive design, it was a halo car, one that was intended not to sell hundreds of thousands of units but rather to attract attention to the Chrysler line.

But Lutz had never been able to make it to the top of a car company as CEO. He eventually took the job of chairman and chief executive of Exide Technologies. It was a battery company, but at least he would be the top boss. That's where he was in the summer of 2001, when Wagoner came calling.

Lutz had an office in Ann Arbor, about an hour west of Detroit, and one Friday that summer, Wagoner went to have breakfast with him. "His assistant had gotten enough breakfast buns for the Russian Army," Wagoner recalls. "He and I were seated in this not-huge office. I said, 'I just wanted to talk to you about who you think the best product guys are in the industry today.' I was really wide open. There were people in GM, but did he know people on the outside who he thought would be strong candidates? We got to talking about people and what characteristics are important to lead product development.

"Bob was so into this. He couldn't sit in his seat more than one second. He stood up and he's walking around, talking passionately about products, how it's more like the movie business, there's a lot of fashion, you need technical expertise. At one point, he was trying to eat a grape-fruit. I wasn't sure if he was gonna drown me, him, or both of us. But his passion really showed through.

"Then we started working through who the people were in the busi-ness and what he thought of them. Who's the fifty- or fifty-five-year-old Bob Lutz in the industry today? We went through the list, and in con-clusion, it didn't really seem like there was anybody like that. I looked at him and said, 'There's no chance that you'd be interested in this job, would there be?'

"And he looked at me and said, 'Don't assume that.'"

It was a counterintuitive, almost contrarian idea. Wagoner was forty-eight; Lutz was sixty-nine. The age gap was sensitive; very few CEOs will fill key positions with someone who has decades more experience, plus a reputation for flying his personal Czech fighter jet and heli-copters. The other delicate issue was that Wagoner had been criticized over the years for not being a "car guy." Lutz, the quintessential car guy, might outshine Wagoner in certain automotive circles. How would the two men get along, much less work together? Nonetheless, the conver-sation ended amiably, if inconclusively. Wagoner told Lutz that if he had any ideas, "holler."

That evening Wagoner received a visitor at his home, a former GM communications person who now worked for Lutz. "He had something for me," Wagoner says. "I opened it up. It was a fairly long letter, written beautifully in Bob's handwriting, with a lot of thoughts and ideas. But bottom line—he was interested."

Perhaps this really was the right fit. "I had this sense," Wagoner said, "that we were making a lot of progress across the range of important functions in the company: quality, manufacturing, productivity, things of that sort. But it wasn't a hundred percent clear to me that we were putting it together in the most dynamic way. As I talked to Bob, this passion, the role of fashion, the importance of design, it clicked. He was going to bring the spark that we needed in the area where we needed it. He had a tremendous amount of credibility, and I thought he would be a terrific addition to the company. He was a guy who could 'work inside,' too," meaning he could be effective inside GM's sprawling hierarchy.

Wagoner took the idea to members of his board, and they were enthusiastic. Lutz started September 1, 2001. Within days, the terrorist attacks hit New York and Washington, sending a ripple of panic through the auto industry, and through the country. People needed jobs as much as ever, maybe more so. But with everyone stunned and hunkering down, was anyone going to buy a car, GM or otherwise? For its part, GM focused its energy on its "Keep America Rolling" campaign of rebates, aimed at staving off a collapse in car sales.

As the country returned to normal, Lutz started to settle in. "I think one of the things that Bob said when he came in was, 'Hey, we need really great designs. If you do a high-quality vehicle [with] very good value that's sort of passé in design, people aren't going to give you a look. You've got to get a reason for people to want to be in your car.' As Bob says, this is a fashion business. It needs outstanding design, which is leaning forward rather than leaning backward."

Lutz became an agent provocateur within the company, acting on behalf of Design in the inevitable (and legendary) turf battles with Engineering, Manufacturing, and Finance. Ed Welburn runs the studios and is solidly in control of the design process. Lutz, as head of new product development, travels a great deal and takes some of the pressure off Wagoner by giving speeches and attending auto shows. He also floats above Welburn and acts as Design's advocate.

Even though Lutz came from the outside, he had worked at GM before and understood its history. GM's cars once captured the American imagination, with robust rear-wheel drive, bold designs, rocketlike shapes, and lots of chrome. But by the time the baby boomers came of age and started buying cars, it was hard to find a single GM car that appealed on any level. GM had completely lost its design leadership. "Bob really kind of reminded us of something, sometimes not too subtly, of our history and the historical success of GM," says Wagoner.

As a result, GM was able to regain its design mojo faster than it was able to reinvent its manufacturing systems. "When you have a clear vision there and strong leadership, you can move more quickly," Wagoner says. "I think it's fair to say that what took us fifteen years to do in manufacturing, we were able to do in five years in design."

Lutz-isms are nearly inescapable inside GM. In the main reception area of Tower 300 at the Ren Cen, the wall behind the reception desk is plastered with pictures of General Motors people and a quote from each of them, most appealing to a vague sense of feeling good about GM. Somewhere in the midst of this mom-and-apple-pie display is Bob Lutz's quote: "We can all love one another, but what good is that if the amorous lemmings are all running off the same cliff together?"

Lutz is famous inside GM for being able to say things that no one else can say, not even Wagoner, because he is at such a late stage in his career—the "extra innings," as he puts it. "One colossal advantage of being in extra innings is you can tell it like it is, say what you think, and largely eschew political caution," Lutz told *BusinessWeek* in 2008. "I often ask, rhetorically, if they don't like it, what are they going to do? Force me into early retirement?"

Most Friday mornings at seven, Lutz joins Wagoner at the Design Center in Warren, along with Fritz Henderson, Troy Clarke (president of North America), Mark LaNeve (head of marketing and sales), and John Smith, to look at cars being designed, sometimes in Welburn's virtual reality studio, which contains three life-size screens. Viewers can don 3-D glasses to get a particularly good look at a vehicle being displayed on one of the screens.

The brass also will duck into particular studios to look at models on which decisions must be made. Sometimes the cars are positioned in the Design Center's silver-domed auditorium or nearby brick-walled patio. These management sessions are called "reviews" and are usually conversational and unscripted. This is very different from the old days, when top management would never be seen anywhere near the studios.

Wagoner says he is listening and learning "ninety-nine percent of the time," but Lutz is busy persuading people through a combination of humor and keen insight. "He's hilarious," says Bob Boniface, a hot youngish designer, "After any Lutz review, you'll always have a one-liner from him to tell your buddies about at lunch. He just cuts through all the b.s. People make these well-meaning presentations with all these charts and graphs, and he'll just cut through it all and say, '*That* doesn't mean anything, and *that* doesn't mean anything. *This* is what we're going to do.' Everyone in the room says, 'You know what? He's right.' "

One line that Lutz uses, if designers come up with something he thinks is ridiculous, is the "kosher pork chop." "When people describe a high-performance car, but it's got to have the world's best fuel economy or they describe a radical sports car, but it's going to be environmentally sound," Lutz explains, "I say, 'You know, you're inventing the kosher pork chop again. I mean, you got to make up your mind—is it kosher or is it a pork chop? You can't have both.' "

There's a stark difference in personality between Wagoner and Lutz—Wagoner doesn't like to be provocative, but Lutz loves to be. One Lutz episode left an impression on Wagoner and everyone else. The company was gearing up to introduce the 2005 Buick LaCrosse sedan. Joe Spielman was a manufacturing guy running metal fabrication, the process by which sheets of metal get stamped into parts that are welded together to form the body of the car. Lutz wanted a sharp angle where the front fender and the headlamps come together. (Imagine that you're folding a piece of paper in preparation for making a paper airplane. The sharp point, resembling a bird's beak, is what Lutz had envisioned.) A rounded or "crimped" edge is easier to manufacture, but the angle obviously is not as sharp. "If you're a stamping guy, if you can round these corners off, the quality of execution is better," says Wagoner. But it's not as visually appealing.

"Bob kept saying, 'I want this sharp bird's beak here,' " Wagoner says. Lutz kept rejecting Joe's trial stamps because they weren't what he wanted. This was heresy—a design guy holding up production of a car and telling the stamping people what to do. Lutz took several executives, including Spielman, out to the company's proving grounds and showed him how Japanese, Korean, and European manufacturers were executing the sharp angles.

"Finally," Wagoner says, "Joe went into the [design] studio, because Bob kept rejecting him, saying 'no, no, no.' "

The metal man was clearly exhausted after the long battle with Lutz.

As Wagoner recalls it, "Joe said, 'Just tell me what you want, and I'll build it for you.' Bob said, 'I want this.' And Joe said, 'Okay, we'll build it for you.'"

"That was good. That was symbolic," says Wagoner. "If that's the design we need to distinguish ourselves in the marketplace, then we're going to give it to you rather than saying, 'You make my job easier by rounding these bird beaks off.' We needed to really get behind and let our designers execute."

At lunchtime, Bob Lutz is seated at a conference table in his office in Design, looking out over the huge pool of water designed by Finnish architect Eero Saarinen when he created GM's steel-and-glass Technical Center in the late 1940s. Lutz is dressed in a dark blue shirt, a bright yellow tie, and a tan suit, although the jacket is hung up. He's wearing a GM pin on his shirt. It's a fruit lunch with strawberries and grapes and exactly one chocolate chip cookie.

Lutz is seventy-six but looks at least ten years younger, despite his white hair. He's been out on his 160-acre farm near Ann Arbor this morning with a camera crew from CNBC television. They were shooting Lutz and his toys—fifteen cars and ten motorbikes. Lutz had fallen off one motorcycle. He wasn't going that fast—only about ten miles an hour—but that's dangerous enough for a morning in May. "I have high-risk hobbies," he explains in his gravelly voice. On his wall are pictures of his two jets, one German and one Czech, and two helicopters, one of which is flown by his third wife, Denise, who is much younger (her actual age is a closely guarded secret). The aircraft are not kept on his farm.

We discuss whether GM has got its design working again. "I worked for GM in the sixties, and it was a good culture because it was customer focused and it was design driven," Lutz explains. "We're trying to bring a lot of that back, and I think with some success. So the answer to your question is yes. In a way, I am the person that connects, because I'm the only one who was around in the sixties in a position of semiresponsibility."

Lutz is a product guy in a way that Wagoner does not pretend to be.

"The reaction I want from people when they see a Chevrolet Malibu is—pardon the vernacular—'Holy shit! I can get that for twenty-one thousand?' And when you have that reaction, you know you've got a winner—as opposed to people looking at it and saying, 'So that's the new Chevy. Yeah, it's not bad. I still kinda like the Honda Accord better, but if I wasn't going to buy a Honda Accord, yeah, I might consider this one.' Number two doesn't get you anywhere anymore because people don't have to settle for second choices.

"Look at the products we're bringing out. Look at the Cadillac CTS, look at the Enclave, the Acadia, Saturn Outlook. Look at the full-size trucks—even though that segment is contracting, we're getting a higher and higher market share of an unfortunately ever-smaller segment. And look at the Chevrolet Malibu. I mean, dealers are still screaming for more cars—the average transaction price is up from sixteen thousand dollars on the old one, which was clearly loss-making, to almost twenty-two thousand now. So we're up between five thousand and six thousand."

Lutz is also excited that the Malibu, in particular, is beginning to get "conquest" from Toyota and Honda. (*Conquest* is an industry term for taking sales away from another company.) "The conquest rate is way up, and both Honda and Toyota on the Accord and the Camry have like seventy and eighty days in inventory and are offering incentives," Lutz says as he pops a strawberry in his mouth. These conquest sales have a markedly different effect from doing repeat business with an existing customer. It's also very unusual for Honda and Toyota to have significant inventories of their top-selling models; this is the first time in their history they have had to rely on incentives.

One sensitive issue for Lutz is that he challenged some of GM's financial mavens and insisted that the company invest in "content"—the features and creature comforts that customers want. For too long, GM was notoriously tightfisted on investing in its interiors, which was ill-advised for the simple reason that the interior is where the customer sits. Lutz railed against the molten black plastic interiors. He didn't like the materials that were being used and didn't like the shapes. He felt that the interiors were not designed to match the exteriors of the cars, which was often true. He also didn't like the tactile sensations that the typical GM interior offered. In cars that had ashtrays, he wanted them to gently rise, not pop open. The glove compartments did not open as smoothly or as quietly as he felt they should.

Nor did he like the controls. He knew that drivers want to be able to operate their cars intuitively, without having to read the owner's manual. And they should also be able to operate the radio and air conditioner and other devices without taking their eyes off the road for any longer than is absolutely necessary.

Lutz insisted that the interiors and controls be improved, which of course cost money. "I will willingly admit that the new generation of vehicles under my oversight cost more money," he says. "But what we were doing with our overly tight cost targets was we were losing sight of the fact that it doesn't matter how well you manage your costs. If the customer doesn't buy the car, nothing happens. And that's what we were doing. We were meeting our cost targets, but we were winding up with a car that nobody wanted. So then we had this great margin on paper, but when the car came out, we had to put four thousand dollars worth of incentives on it, so there goes the margin. And I said to the finance people at the time, 'Let me put five hundred to a thousand more in to take 'em from good to great and from acceptable to truly beautiful, and I think we can get the incentives down from four thousand to two thousand dollars.' So that to me sounds like we're ahead a thousand bucks a car."

The next challenge was to convince the public. "We got [*Motor Trend* magazine's] Car of the Year with the Saturn Aura, a year later we got Car of the Year with the Chevy Malibu. We got Truck of the Year with the Tahoe. The Buick Enclave has won a number of awards; the new Cadillac CTS was *Motor Trend* Car of the Year. And we just heard that Toyota has commissioned a consulting firm that specializes in benchmarking to dig into the Malibu and figure out how we were able to do that. The Japanese competition may also have gotten a little complacent. Toyota may have figured, 'Well, we'll just do another new car and we'll just astound the public yet again, and we don't have to expect any big retaliation from GM because we doubt that they really know how to do it.'"

───────────

One of the first signs that GM still knew how to design cars was the makeover of the Cadillac, which began before Lutz came aboard. John Smith and design chief Wayne Cherry started the look in the late 1990s with the Escalade SUV and the first-generation CTS sedan. This came at a time when "we had begun to let Cadillac be defined by the luxury standards generally out of Germany," Wagoner explains. "We said, 'Okay, to be successful in the luxury business, the design form should be like the German luxury cars.' But then we said, 'That's a fool's errand. Why would we want to mimic somebody else when the best you can be is the best mimicker of somebody else? If we want to be a great brand and a leader in the luxury business, we have to do it our way.' We very specifically do not want our Cadillac CTS to look like a BMW 5 Series. We want people to look at the CTS design and say, 'Whoa, that's a little different.'"

Cherry and Smith gave them different. The hip-hop crowd adopted the Escalade en masse. And the new creased-look CTS with its very distinctive angles was a clear hit. The new look, which GM called "Art and Science," was a stunning design breakthrough.

That strategy had worked. But as in all such cases, when a car company has a hit on its hands, the pressing question is, What do you do next? The task of figuring that out in 2004 fell to John Manoogian II, director of exterior design, Cadillac Studio. With graying, thinning hair, Manoogian is in his late fifties. He resists the notion that people of age are not creative. "If you look at music and cinema and literature, most people are pretty much written off by the time they're forty or forty-five," he explains, sitting in the A111 conference room in Design, under those portraits of Cadillacs through the decades. "I refuse to take that lying down. I'm going to keep doing it as long as they'll let me."

Manoogian's grandparents were born in Armenia, which at the time was part of Turkey and the scene of a bitter, bloody conflict between the Turks and Armenians. Armenians fled en masse, and the Detroit area attracted a large number of refugees because jobs were available. "They all came here because they were uneducated," Manoogian explains. "Five dollars a day with Henry Ford. That was a big deal."

Grandfather Manoogian worked at Dodge Main on the east side of Detroit, and his son worked at Ford Motor for fifty years. "I was born into a car family. That's what I know," he explains. "It's kind of funny—three generations of Manoogians all worked for different companies." (The fourth generation, Manoogian's son, works on websites and lives in California.)

Having been at GM for thirty-two years, Manoogian has seen the best and worst of what the company can offer. "It was pretty dark during some of that era in the eighties," he recalls. "As a young designer, I'd think, I spent all those years in college for this?

"Most people just wrote us off. I did a summer program at Columbia University in 1997, and one of the professors there spent the first two hours of his lecture one morning talking about how terrible General Motors was, how foolish we were, what buffoons we at General Motors were, and what buffoons the entire auto industry in Detroit was. I took that personally. I didn't say anything, of course. But I said to myself, these people have really written us off. They're acting as if we don't exist anymore. I said to myself, if I do nothing else in the next however many years I work for General Motors, I need to make sure that everything I do and everyone around me in the organization is going to prove that gentleman wrong."

Manoogian's chance to do that was the redesign of the CTS, a critical vehicle in the Cadillac lineup when it first came out because it was the first car to reflect the new, edgy design. The Escalade was out, but it was an SUV. The CTS was the flagship of the Cadillac car design; it set the direction for the Seville (now the STS) and the Deville (now the DTS), not to mention the XLR sports car and SRX crossover.

But to keep the CTS fresh, it was time for a redesign. Manoogian had a team of five people ranging in age from twenty-nine to fifty-five, and from a variety of ethnicities and professional backgrounds. As head of the design team, Manoogian saw his job as that of a maestro: "It's my job to conduct the orchestra—not so much to play the clarinet and the french horn, but to direct so that they can be the most creative and make them play in harmony."

The team worked for a year. The natural temptation when doing a redesign is to stick pretty closely to the design that has already proven itself a winner in the marketplace. But Welburn had "thrown down the gauntlet," Manoogian recalls. "He said, 'You guys have to reinvent

Cadillac's next step. You need to design the whole philosophy. Show us your stuff. Show us what you got.'"

The new CTS was scheduled to be unveiled at the Detroit Auto Show in January 2007. That meant that final and formal approval of the design had to occur in the first week of January 2005. That meant that by October 2004, it was time to wrap up the creative process so that the car could be engineered and manufacturing could be geared up. Time was running out. "At that point, we pretty much had the car dialed in," Manoogian says. "We had everyone in the organization looking at the car and saying, 'John, the car looks good. You guys are getting there. Just finish it up.'"

On October 7, the designers took a full-size clay model of the new CTS, along with an older first-generation CTS, outside to look at them in natural light. (Designers don't trust artificial lighting.) The Design Center's patio was taken that day so they used a small outdoor enclosed area called the Ponderosa. "We had the two cars sitting there. And one of the things I always liked to say to kid my team is, 'If my mother or John Q. Public on the street saw this car, would they know, number one, it's new, and number two, would they recognize it as a Cadillac?' I kept looking at the car, and I said to myself, 'The car really looks good.' We had done a good job. Everyone was happy with it. I could have kept my mouth shut, and we could have gone home, and everyone would have been happy with the car.

"But I had this nagging sense, this voice in the back of my head saying, 'John, we're not quite there yet. We can turn this crank a couple more times.' My attitude was, 'We've already got this design done. It's finished. It's in the bank. The only thing you've got to lose by wanting to make any changes is the wrath of the engineering organization.'" Engineers tend not to have a sense of humor when designers want to make whimsical last-minute changes, which force the engineers to change the way the car is manufactured. That drives up the cost of the car and also raises the risk that it will be late. With design sign-off scheduled for the first week in January, the last couple of months "should have been the refinement phase of the program, not the reinvention phase," Manoogian says.

He knew that if he missed his deadline, it could have a ripple effect that would reach through engineering all the way to production. "It can mean a delay of weeks or months" in getting a car into showrooms, he says. "And every day you're not selling the new car, you're losing money."

All this was going through Manoogian's head as he stood on the Ponderosa with his new boss, Mike Simcoe, head of GM North America exterior design. Simcoe had been transferred to Michigan from Australia the prior week, and "this was his first opportunity to come outside and see the car. He said, 'John, the car looks great. You guys are doing a good job.'

"I said, 'Mike, I gotta tell ya. I just think we need to do this thing a couple more times. I'm not sure we've gone far enough.'

"He said, 'If you guys really believe that, if you really think you need to give it a few more cranks of the creative wheel, have at it.'

"So we went back, and with paper and tape and pins and odd materials, we literally mocked up a whole car with paper, on that clay model, in probably a day and a half," Manoogian says.

On October 20, after two weeks of feverish work, the team was ready to show top management what they had done. Manoogian explains, "We called Ed Welburn down, with Mike Simcoe, and said, 'This is what we want to do.'"

Welburn and Simcoe walked around the model, looking carefully from different views, imagining the car that would take shape. Finally they said, "If you guys believe in it, have at it."

That almost certainly would never have happened in the design world that prevailed during the 1970s and 1980s, and certainly not at the eleventh hour. Designers would have been told to stay in their sandboxes and let the real decision makers—the engineers and finance guys—make the tough calls. "I was going outside the process," Manoogian explains. "I was running the risk of delaying the program."

What Manoogian's team did during this frenzy was radical in car terms. The original CTS had a creased front grille shaped like a V. The V shape ended at the bumper, so it was somewhat muted. But Manoogian's team wanted to continue the V below the bumper, closer to the ground. "We did that as part of the eleventh-hour thing, where the grille kind of comes down and looks like it's one big shape," he says. "Prior to that, everything was just on top, like the old CTS. The big change was that lower aperture suddenly tying in to the upper one, as one common harmonious texture. That was a big change from a strategic and philosophical point of view. The clinic results from that were not stellar. It was a very controversial front end that we were asking for. It was an aesthetic issue. It made some people very uncomfortable."

Manoogian was breaking another rule by ignoring the findings of clinics, or customer research. But the net result was a much bolder look. If you stand in front of the new CTS, it does appear that the V effect continues below the bumper and plunges toward the ground.

A second big change was that the design team came up with a decorative chrome vent that they wanted to insert on either side of the car, between the front doors and front wheels, just above the belt line. The vents were striking visually, but they would require that the metal be stamped in an extraordinarily difficult process. It's one thing to stamp a piece of metal into a certain shape; it's quite another to also stamp a precisely shaped hole in it.

The engineers said the side vent was impossible. "That was just a constant battle, back and forth, to get that to work. We went around and around for a month," Manoogian recalls. "They could have hit me over the head and said, 'We're not going to do it.' But the engineering organization finally said, 'You know, John, that's a very unique feature. No one has ever done that before.' And it became a challenge for them as well. They carried the ball to the finish line." The vents went in.

The willingness to take big risks is arguably the signal difference between great design and mediocre design. "A lot of the people who were here prior to Mr. Lutz coming on board are still here—we didn't just get creative overnight," Manoogian explains. "It's not that we were stupid or dumb. Nobody ever came to work and said, 'Let's design a dumb car.' That didn't happen. But he provided the catalyst that allowed the design organization to really show our stuff."

Perhaps the ultimate ratification for Manoogian came the day the new CTS sedan was unveiled at the January 2007 Detroit Auto Show. "There were a lot of people who were enthused about [the CTS], all day long," he recounts. "I could see because I happened to be standing next to the car. Many competitors were there as well. I won't say which company it was, but a major competitor from Europe, the CEO and his entourage, came by the CTS stand. They stopped and they were looking at the car, admiring it. They were speaking in their native tongue. They didn't realize I was with someone who spoke their language.

"The CEO was convinced that the fender on the CTS could not have been made out of metal—it had to be plastic—because nobody could stamp a fender like that. I thought, 'Boy, that's kind of cool.' And half an hour later, two people came by with tracing paper and they traced that part of the car. Yes, someone was actually using General Motors as a benchmark. I don't have to be dragged around by my ear and be shown every European and Asian car that has an example of something we haven't done. Now they're using us as one of the benchmarks. How cool is that?"

After finishing the CTS sedan, Manoogian continued having fun by designing a sleek and sexy CTS coupe, and other derivative models that have not yet been unveiled. "The cars I'm working on right now would never have happened without Mr. Wagoner and Mr. Lutz and the rest of the organization saying, 'Okay, let's do those cars.' They were never part of the corporate plan."

The CTS coupe is another illustration of how GM's design processes have changed. What's unusual about this car is that it was not planned—it just kind of happened. "I encouraged them to develop those ideas for the coupe and [said] let's not take a set of documents into a boardroom and present our case for this vehicle," explains Welburn. "Let's develop the design, a full-size clay model, and show that to Bob Lutz and Rick Wagoner, which is what we did. Frankly, I think if we would have gone into a boardroom and said, 'We want to do a coupe for Cadillac,' we would have been thrown out of the room."

Lutz, even more than Welburn, stands as a kind of insulator who will take the heat if designers try something and it doesn't work. "The CTS coupe just stuns people," Lutz explains. "And the production car will be indistinguishable from the concept car. That just floored everybody. Even designers of other automobile companies just stood around with slack jaws and said, 'Holy mackerel.'"

Manoogian had continued to break rules. "There are a lot of things in [the CTS] that violate the hallowed GM principles," Lutz says. "Like, the rearward visibility is going to be awful, because of that extremely high deck. People are going to say, 'Gee, I wish I could see out the back a little better.' Well, you know, you pays your money and you takes your choice. The high-style customer is never functionally oriented anyway. If she were functionally driven, she'd never buy a coupe in the first place. So that's what I call putting design first and then you work out the business equation afterward."

CHAPTER 9

Battling for the New Camaro's Soul

Bob Boniface and Sang Yup Lee grew up on opposite sides of the world in dramatically different family environments. But the two have some things in common. Both were rebels at a young age. And both got to try their hand at resurrecting one of the most iconic of American cars: the Chevrolet Camaro.

Boniface grew up in Youngstown, Ohio, where his father was a psychiatrist. All other seven siblings went to medical school, but not Boniface; he wanted to design cars. Lee, just four years younger than Boniface, was born in Seoul, South Korea, to a father who owned and ran a small business and a mother who served as a school principal. They were wealthy by Korean standards and expected the younger Lee to mimic their values of hard work and sacrifice. But Lee had other ideas: he wanted to be a fine arts sculptor, a profession his parents found positively bohemian.

When the new Camaro appears in showrooms in the spring of 2009, it will have been the intense competition between these two men and their teams that pushed it into the limelight. How Boniface and Lee arrived at General Motors and competed against each other to define the face of the new Camaro, starting in 2004, is a case study of how

Ed Welburn uses "bake-offs"—not for cakes and pies at the state fair, but for automotive designs.

There were four generations of Camaros, the first one created in 1966 for the 1967 model year. It was still an era of relative innocence. President John F. Kennedy had been assassinated, but Bobby Kennedy and Martin Luther King Jr. were still alive. The Vietnam War was in progress but hadn't yet erupted in the Tet Offensive. Race riots had not yet consumed American cities, and the Watergate scandal had not yet engulfed President Richard Nixon. When the first Camaro came out, it was still the America of post–World War II optimism and hope.

GM introduced the Camaro to compete against Ford's Mustang. It was touted as having the same rear-drive, front-engine configuration as the Mustang, and it captured the American imagination while it was in production. The Ramones sang "Go Lil' Camaro Go"; Pearl Jam praised it in "Wishlist"; and Bruce Springsteen referred to it in "Racing in the Streets." Madonna's music video "What It Feels Like for a Girl" showed her hot-wiring a Camaro. And John Cusack starred in the 1985 film *Better Off Dead,* which featured a black 1967 model.

The Camaro appealed to the fantasies of many young people, including Rick Wagoner and Ed Welburn, whose first cars were Camaros. But as they rose up the ladder at GM, they reluctantly concluded that the Camaro had grown long in the tooth. There was a limited market for pony cars those days. Gas was expensive, and there were production problems in Canada. In 2002, GM decided to end the Camaro's long, action-packed life.

But in 2004, the Camaro was starting to come back from the dead.

When Boniface was a kid, he collected race car models. "I built a lot of models," he recalls. "That's a common thread with designers. They all built a lot of models when they were kids. I collected all sorts of die casts. I always used to modify the unassembled model kits. I'd put a motor from one into another one. I'd take the wheels from one and put them on another one. Designers are tinkerers. We never accept the status quo. That's boring. In your mind's eye, you're always playing those games."

Two weeks before his sixteenth birthday, he graduated from models to his first real car, a metallic brown 1975 Camaro. He got the car in a time-honored way: "I inherited it from my older brother," says Boniface, now forty-two and not happy about being over the age of forty. "He went to Dartmouth. Then when he went to med school, he was done with it. After there were a bunch of rust holes in it, he decided to give it to his little brother."

It was love at first sight. "I blacked out all the chrome. It had a 350 two-barrel engine, and I put an aftermarket intake manifold and carburetor on it to wake the car right up, and headers. It was *fast*. It had fog lights, which is what you did back in the eighties. I loved that car. I drove that car for eight years. I drove it all through high school and all through college, and I drove it to my first job in Boston."

That first job—doing accounting work for a mutual fund—taught Boniface what he didn't want to do in life. Its only advantage was that it allowed him to sketch more cars in his spare time. Soon he was applying to car design studios. His father couldn't understand. "My dad collected cars," Boniface says. "You would think he would understand why I wanted to do what it is I do. But it took him years to figure it out."

"What is it you do again?" his dad would ask.

"I design cars, Dad."

"Yeah, but what do you do?"

"Well, I draw pictures of cars, and they go into models, and then they go into production."

"Yeah, but what do you *do*?"

Boniface jokes, "He gets it now, after about eighteen years."

After he left Chrysler to join GM in 2004, he and a couple of designer pals were contemplating what products GM had in its portfolio. "As an outsider, I assumed that GM would have had a Camaro in the works, but it didn't. I was surprised to see that."

He started talking to fellow designers, and they felt the same way. "It was really just a couple of us sitting around saying, 'GM without a Camaro just doesn't feel right.'" Boniface, with long dark sideburns, is wearing what seems to be the uniform of designers: black striped shirt, blazer, slacks, no tie. He's sitting in the Design North studio at the Tech Center in Warren.

The designers asked themselves, What would be the purpose of a new Camaro? "We asked, 'What does it want to be? Does it want to be like a Pontiac Vibe, a car that meets people's everyday needs? Does it want to be a muscle car? Does it want to be a pony car? Does it want to be a Chevelle replacement? In the end, we went back to its roots, which was an affordable, handsome, performance pony car."

For the hard-core enthusiasts who distinguish between *muscle car* and *pony car*, a muscle car is larger and more rigged to accelerate in a hurry, like a drag-racing car; pony cars are smaller and lighter, with more emphasis on handling in curves than performance down the straightaway. Suffice it to say that both varieties are hot cars—cars that are meant to be *driven*.

Shortly after Boniface had arrived at GM, he traveled to the Geneva Auto Show with other top design executives. On the way back they stopped to visit GM's advanced design studio in Britain. Among the traveling execs was Welburn. In the bar of the hotel in Coventry, Welburn said, "How's the new job going?"

"It's going great," Boniface replied. "We're working on the Sequel fuel cell vehicle."

"Any ideas crop up you want to work on?"

"I want to do a Camaro," Boniface said. Each man knew the other was a Camaro fan.

"Don't start with me," Welburn said. "Camaro has issues with the Canadian Auto Workers, and we closed that plant down. Planning tells us there's no market for coupes."

Boniface recalls of the conversation, "I'm just getting more and more down at the mouth. I was going to leave it at that. But he looked at me and said, 'Well, I'm not telling you *not* to work on it. Just don't let anyone see it. Just keep it under wraps.'" As Boniface read the conversation, Welburn really wanted a Camaro but was skittish about running into opposition before he had something to show; he wanted something tangible.

So Boniface and other designers, collectively known as the Design North team, very quietly started work on a Camaro design. They did it after-hours, collaborating with a couple of sculptors to build a one-third scale model. But they had other demands on their time, and after some months, they ended up sticking the Camaro model on a shelf in a back room.

In the fall of 2004, Boniface received a call from Mike Abelson, then the executive director of architectural engineering for GM, asking whether Boniface had ever been able to find a way to use the Zeta architecture, which was GM's code name for a particular car platform. (A platform consists of a chassis and other core building blocks of a car.) The company was considering killing Zeta, and Abelson wanted to keep it alive.

Boniface told him yes, he had; he and his associates had used it to design a Camaro.

"How come I didn't hear about it?" Abelson asked.

"Because we didn't tell anybody about it," Boniface replied. "We just built the scale model, and it's sitting in the back room."

Abelson came over immediately to see what they had come up with. "I remember taking the model off the shelf with one of the sculptors," Boniface recalls. "It was really heavy, and I hurt my back. We sat it on a table."

Seen from above, Boniface's model was wasp-waisted—meaning it protruded in front and back and had a narrower midsection. There was "a swelling around the front, then it was tucked in at the waist, and then flared back out at the rear. The original '67 through '69 Camaro had that, and we thought the new one should have that as well," Boniface recalls. The model had a very aggressive stance, the kind of attitude a kid playing with models might give his most badass creation.

Abelson liked it. To Boniface's delight, he agreed to "put some resources behind it to see whether what we had thrown together really held water." Boniface stuck to the original inspiration of the Camaro, its aerodynamics and the iconic shape he describes as "a fist in the wind."

"It became an internal concept at that point, just something under study," Boniface explains. "Lutz got wind of it and we had an audience with him. Ed knew about it all the time, obviously. And the next thing you know, it just started snowballing."

Boniface and the Design North team worked on the Camaro more or less full-time in the spring of 2005. Says Welburn, "They established the whole proportion of the vehicle, the whole stamp of the vehicle, the architecture, and it really looked like a sixty-eight Camaro." Welburn had driven a 1969 Camaro SS, so he was a purist in his personal taste. "That was good to a point," he says. "But I wanted the vehicle to have even more of an edge to it, be even more expressive."

It was the last day of June in 2005, and the Design Center put on a show of models under development for the board of directors. Wagoner attended and made a comment that reverberated throughout the studios. Boniface recalls him saying, "You want to do that? That looks like it should be on the road today," rather than in the three or four years it takes for a car to go from design to production. "You guys aren't pushing it hard enough."

Both Lutz and Wagoner—in another example of their friendly rivalry—claim insight for this view. "But I can tell you, it was really me," says Wagoner. "We went in to see the design and our designers were proud of it, and they had almost exactly reproduced the 1969 Camaro. I said, 'But there's one problem, guys. I don't think we want to sell a 1969 Camaro with current year's technology. We need to do a modern interpretation of what the car stood for.'

Wagoner told the designers to "think about what the people who were doing the 1969 Camaro were thinking about, and use today's shapes, forms, technology, and execute a Camaro today. That's one way to use our heritage to our advantage."

So Welburn, as he had done before (and obviously reading the politics above him), decided to bring in a rival team. In late July 2005, he tapped rear-wheel-drive studio design director Tom Peters, also the owner of a 1969 Camaro, to launch a Camaro squad of his own. Many members of this team, including Lee, had been involved in designing the new Corvette Z06, an incredibly powerful and sleek machine. They worked out of Studio X, an unmarked, isolated room buried deep in the basement of the Design Center. Boniface, of course, was told that he now had competition. Also on the Studio X team were Steve Kim, a California-born Korean American, and Vladimir Kapatonov, a young designer who had grown up in Russia. Peters was a classic GM middle-aged white guy, making his team a veritable United Nations. But Lee was the design director, and it was his design vision that competed against that of Boniface. They had just weeks to come up with an alternative—a brutally short deadline in automotive terms.

Boniface and Lee had very different histories. When Boniface was mixing and matching parts from car model kits as a youth, Lee was trying his hand as a performance artist before deciding he wanted to become a fine arts sculptor. "I was always fascinated by beautiful shapes," Lee recalls.

His parents urged him to find a professional career path. Anything but sculpture. The young man persisted, pursuing a degree in sculpture at a Korean university. "It wasn't a happy family," he says.

One day, however, he visited Itaewon, a neon-lit tourist district of Seoul, once favored by American troops stationed nearby. Lee saw a white Porsche 911 in the reflection of neon. "It was beautiful—it looked totally sculptural," he says. "Man, that's the job I wanted to take," he said to himself.

So the Lees—unlike Boniface's parents—were relieved that their son decided to apply his skills to what they regarded as something practical: transportation design, particularly cars. He applied to the Art Center College of Design in Pasadena, California, one of the most prominent schools for automotive designers, and was accepted. He spent six months in Italy as an intern at Pininfarina—where dream cars like the Alfa Romeo Spider and the Ferrari 612 Scaglietti have been designed—and then a year at Porsche in Germany before graduating from the Art Center and joining GM in 1999. Lee, today thirty-eight, has mussed-up hair that builds into a fashionable spike. Sitting in A111, he wears a long-sleeve olive-green shirt beneath a blue blazer with faded blue jeans.

The starting point of Studio X's design efforts was a copy of what the Boniface team had done. "It was a beautiful car," Lee recalls, "well-proportioned, very solid. But it was too faithful" to the '69 model. Lee's goal was to capture the attitude of the earlier car without being captive to it. "It had to be a modern design statement," he said. "I loved the '69 Camaro, but I grew up in a totally different environment. I had a very different perspective about what this Camaro should be over the next ten or twenty years. Because of that, I pushed myself to achieve a more modern design."

Lee was not a young man whose father had a hot rod in the garage, and he didn't drive a fast car as a youth. Nor is Seoul known for its car culture—the roads are crowded, and gasoline has long been quite expensive because of tax policies. "I didn't grow up with this muscle car, but I understand what this muscle car is," Lee says. "I understand the essence and the history. Tom, my director, always used the word *juice*. 'If you understand the word *juice*,' he said, 'then apply it to the car.'"

The Boniface team, in his view, had taken a traditional rectangular approach to the front grill of the car, for example. They made the headlamps circular, "which was very '69," Lee says. Lee went for a much more angular approach, with the headlamps shaped like sunglasses. Whereas the Boniface design was two-dimensional, Lee tried to make his three-dimensional, with more shadows and a more aggressive look. He wanted to suggest a V shape, which is what gives a sense of boldness and movement to a car, much like what his fellow designers had done with the front end of the Cadillac CTS.

One inspiration for Lee was the Transformers cartoon series. Transformers toys and cartoons had been a big hit with children and teens for many years. All the characters were machines that transformed themselves from cars to human-shaped robots and back. Lee was only four years younger than Boniface but he was plugged into a younger way of thinking—critical for an entry-level car marketed to younger buyers.

Armed with that set of cultural insights, Lee took many of the 1969 details that Boniface had replicated and reinterpreted them in what he saw as a more modern idiom. "This is GM's future," says Lee. "If you take a look at the car and walk around it, it sort of smells like 1969 all over the place. But there is no direct relationship between this car and the 1969 Camaro. It's just the smells."

The Camaro was a high-security project, but everyone in the Design Center knew about the bake-off. (Also, between bouts of work, the two squads spied on each other, conducting "recon missions" to see what the other was doing.) The competition was going to be over in a hurry, just a matter of weeks. Top management brought the teams together for periodic reviews of full-size clay models. Ed Welburn noticed the advances in Boniface's design as the bake-off heated up. "It got much better once he knew there was competition," Welburn says.

The teams continued their frenzied competition until it was time for a decision. Welburn and Lutz went to Warren in the second week of August 2005 for a final showdown between two painted full-size clay models. They were displayed on the Design Center patio in natural light. Simcoe, Peters, Boniface, Lee, and a handful of others were there. It wasn't a large group.

Lee recalls, "Bob and Ed took a look at the cars and then they went off for half an hour to talk."

They didn't reveal what they were thinking while they were in the studio. "It was hard to say which way they were leaning," Boniface says.

During the half hour they were gone, Lutz deferred to Welburn to make the call. "He said, 'I'll leave it up to you, Ed,' and he left," recalls Welburn. "Frankly, it was one of the most difficult decisions I had to make, because both designs were strong." It essentially was a choice between remaining true to the old Camaro or allowing a newer identity to emerge.

Alone, Welburn returned to the patio and started walking around both cars. He pointed to features on each car that he wanted to be part of the final design, but still didn't reveal which team had prevailed. "We were waiting with bated breath," says Boniface.

Finally Welburn said the Peters team, with Lee, would execute the final design. "At the end of the day, I think everybody felt good about the decision we made," Welburn says. "I know for the team whose design was not picked, it had to have been difficult initially."

Indeed it was. "I think of the Camaro as being the highlight of my career," says Boniface. "The low point was the day I found out the other team was going to execute the final project. You can agree with the decision and still feel bad about it. You pour your heart and soul into it and then boom!"

Did you take it personally? "It was very difficult not to take some of this personally," Boniface acknowledges. "But Ed made the right decision. He had to stay out of the emotional part. He had to say, 'Look, this is what the car needs to be,'" and that's what he did."

It was difficult for Welburn too, because after all he had been the one who encouraged Boniface to start designing a new Camaro. "Yeah, it tore me up," says Welburn, "to tell somebody who had done a great job on the vehicle that we weren't going to go with it. They did a terrific job. But the other one was, frankly, better. I'm not so sure we would have gotten to that point with this if it wasn't for that initial foundation of what Boniface did." Boniface was rewarded with a promotion to start work on a new prototype hybrid car.

For Lee, it was obviously a sweet triumph. "It was a great moment, probably the biggest moment of my career so far," he says. And he believes that Wagoner's statement that the car had to look more modern helped carry the day. "Rick was getting hammered all over the world, but he walked into the studio," says Lee. "He shook my hand and he was looking at the car."

Soon after Lee won the bake-off, the producers of a new movie based on the Transformers approached GM and said they wanted the hero of the movie, Bumblebee, to be based on the Camaro. The plot was a war between two breeds of robots fighting for the future of mankind and the planet Earth. The leader of the good robots was Bumblebee, a Camaro that changed into multiple shapes. The movie came out in 2007 to rave reviews from the under-twenty-five age bracket. "For Generation Y, this car is the Bumblebee to them," Lee says. "They don't really care what the '69 Camaro looked like." He adds, "My mom back in Korea still thinks I'm a Bumblebee designer. That's how powerful that movie was."

After winning the bake-off, Lee spent a year and a half in GM's Holden subsidiary in Melbourne. Australia has a heritage of affordable yet robust rear-wheel-drive cars and a car culture very similar to that of the United States. That's where Lee's Camaro design was translated into parts that could actually be melded with Holden's Zeta architecture and then be manufactured. The Holden subsidiary is the design center that Welburn has designated to engineer mid-range rear-wheel-drive cars.

As lead designer, Lee had to continue fighting the tough-minded pragmatists in Engineering to retain his original design inspiration, but not so hard that it prevented the car from staying on schedule. He made some concessions: his show car had 22-inch wheels in the front and 21-inch wheels in the back, but the production car's tires had to be smaller. There were other slight changes in dimensions, an inch or two here or there, to make sure the frame would work with the Holden power train.

With that stage complete, the next step was gearing up to actually manufacture the car in Oshawa, Ontario. Lee transferred back to Detroit, closer to the factory that had been doing pilot builds of the Camaro. All the pieces of sheet metal have been stamped, and Lee has seen them assembled. "I get emotional when I see that," he says.

The car was scheduled to go on sale in the spring of 2009, starting around $20,000 as an entry-level sports car. Base cars had a V-6 engine with 300 horsepower, same as in the Cadillac CTS. A base V-8 version had 420 horsepower. And the new Camaro Z28 will have 550-plus horsepower. Those are seriously powerful vehicles, but GM's latest engine designs give then reasonable fuel efficiency, not like the gas-guzzlers of old.

Before letting Lee depart from the A111 conference room in Design, where we've been talking, I had to ask some of the big questions: Can GM use its historical designs to appeal to the American soul in a way that Toyota cannot? Can GM outdesign Toyota?

"I feel very, very strongly about this. GM has a strong, rich, deep history. This," he says, gesturing at his surroundings, "is the world's first car design studio. All the methods of car design started here in the thirties and forties and fifties. This is the place that has all the history. I can take any of the GM cars back in the forties, fifties, or sixties and totally refresh them. They can be the most modern cars.

"I can do that not only here in North America but also in emerging markets, like China and Brazil. The Japanese are lacking that. Toyota is going global too. But their strategy is if they try to sell their cars in Europe, they want to be as European as possible. If they want to sell in North America, Toyota is really good at NASCAR these days. So they want to be American if possible. That is Toyota's global strategy. But at GM, it has the rich history of design. Our design can be strong globally.

GM can totally lead the trend. That's the difference between Toyota and GM. We can be the design trend leader. They are the trend follower. GM has a strong soul." Lee's missionary enthusiasm aside, GM does have several decades of design history in the United States that Toyota lacks.

So isn't it ironic that the Camaro, an American icon, was redesigned by a Korean, engineered in Australia, and manufactured in Canada? No, no, he says. "That is this country's strength. That's what makes this country so powerful."

CHAPTER 10

The Chevy Volt

In late 2005, Bob Lutz was losing patience. Part of his job was to figure out the way forward for GM—to help dream up the next big thing. And having come from a battery company, he was intrigued by finding new ways to power vehicles.

But the GM hierarchy was extremely skittish about batteries, hybrids, or electric cars, especially after the misadventure with the EV-1. The EV-1—GM's first foray into eco-friendly engines—was an all-electric plug-in car introduced in California in the early 1990s. The company leased 1,100 of them to customers, but the program was stymied by the fact that the EV-1 had such limited driving range and the cars cost far more to build than the company could ever hope to sell them for in the market. GM did not believe they could become a commercial success and took all of them back from customers at the end of the leases, inspiring a critical documentary, *Who Killed the Electric Car?* In terms of both commerce and public relations, it had been a disaster. GM leadership felt they had lost a huge amount of credibility. So when Lutz pressed for some form of electric car, as he had on at least two occasions since his arrival, he was shot down. The data didn't support his thinking, he was told.

Meanwhile, Toyota was getting huge PR mileage out of its Prius hybrid, even as the automaker was gearing up to make inroads into the least energy-efficient segments of the market, large SUVs and pickups. Adding insult to injury was that Lutz heard in late 2005 about a Silicon Valley company called Tesla Motors that was developing a high-performance electric car, which would sell for $100,000. Such a car would not be commercially viable from GM's perspective, but the idea that a start-up company in California could be doing something so technologically sophisticated—when the mighty GM couldn't—ate at Lutz.

Soon thereafter, Lutz says, he "just lost it." In a fit of pique, he demanded that GM snap out of its paralysis on the issue. He turned to veterans like Jon Lauckner of Engineering and John Smith of Product Planning, both of whom reported to him, and also to Larry Burns, the head of R&D, and urged them to find a solution. With the help of an informal skunkworks that included veterans of the EV-1, they developed an internal white paper, a vision statement aimed at launching something they called the iCar. (The name was borrowed from the iPod, in hopes that the new vehicle would transform the auto business just as Apple's MP3 player had transformed the music business.) The paper was presented to Wagoner's Automotive Strategy Board in March 2006, and the board approved it.

It was the equivalent of an Apollo moon shot: the company was going to both invent a propulsion system and design an entirely new vehicle at the same time. "We don't normally let people do that," notes Wagoner. Such a plan is generally seen as too complex (there are literally too many moving parts), and the potential for failure too high. But despite those misgivings, Wagoner and his team had now set a goal of unveiling a new design—not a fanciful concept car, but a real car that could go into production—at the January 2007 Detroit Auto Show, only nine or ten months away. By the standards of the automotive industry, that would require blazing speed.

In April 2006, the call went out to Tony Posawatz to start making it happen. Posawatz, who likes to joke that his name rhymes with *kilowatts*, is a first-generation American with deep loyalty to GM. His parents met on the boat coming to the United States from Germany and Austria in 1955, when both were about twenty years old. Because of World War II, "the countries and the infrastructure and the economic opportunities were torn apart," Posawatz explains. "And this was the land of opportunity." The young man and woman were soon married.

The elder Posawatz got a job at the Tech Center in Warren as a skilled tradesman working for an hourly rate. He also worked at Fisher Body for many years. Young Tony was the first generation of his family to go to college; he got his degree in mechanical engineering at General Motors Institute, and the company then paid for him to get an M.B.A. from Dartmouth. His diploma is proudly displayed on the wall of his office at the Vehicle Engineering Center (VEC) today. "We are a GM family," Posawatz says.

Throughout the 1980s and 1990s, the burly, mustachioed Posawatz grew increasingly tired of being accosted at cocktail parties or barbecues with complaints about GM products. He had a deep desire to change that. "One of the reasons I originally came to General Motors was because it stood for something," he says. "It stood for the best. It stood for automotive leadership, both from the technology perspective but also satisfying customer needs. I would say that's one of the reasons I'm still here today and one of the reasons I'm probably one of the more competitive people you'll ever meet."

Posawatz, who was considered the iCar's employee number one, meaning the first one, was tapped to become project leader for a combination of reasons. He had been involved in the EV-1 project and was known for his interest in alternate propulsion systems. (His two sons are amused that he has earned a reputation for being "the electric car geek.") Partly because of his M.B.A., he was more than a gearhead—he also had business savvy. And he had been involved in product launch efforts for twelve of his twenty-four years at the company, on such projects as the Escalade SUV and the Avalanche pickup truck. There was also a personality factor: Posawatz was someone who could operate in a loosely defined, somewhat chaotic environment. He could be creative. He could hustle different departments for resources. He could get things done unofficially.

Still, he almost didn't take the iCar job because he thought it would be a "science fair project," a term GM people use to describe something that may be interesting but has no chance of moving into commercial production. "I got the tap on the shoulder from Messrs. Lutz, Burns, and Lauckner, asking me, 'Would you like to do this program?' I said, 'No, I'm not interested in doing a concept car. I do real cars.' Then I got the second call. 'No, no, no. You don't understand. This is more than a concept car.' "

Even though top management desperately wanted the project to succeed, it created a skunkworks environment with minimal resources. It would have been a mistake to commit to a huge budget before the team had a clear direction. So the team met in an abandoned auditorium in Design North. "It was geared toward being a very undercover team," Posawatz recalls. "That is why I was told I was selected. We didn't want to form committees and groups and staff this thing. They just said, 'Tony, you know how to do these things.' "

In effect, the promising but risky idea had to operate with as much independence as possible. Lauckner, Smith, and Burns would be champions for the project, but they knew that ideas on how to execute the car had to bubble up from below and earn some credibility before they could be shared with the larger organization. "Our leaders recognized that if they made iCar too formal and had too many committees, it would drown in its own weight, if you will," Posawatz says.

He was given about a dozen people from various parts of the company to get started part-time. Only Posawatz was assigned to the project full-time. "Everyone else had other jobs," he says. "It was purposely set up as a team with a lot of different types of diversity. I'm not talking about just the general diversity, but diversity of thought, from age to different types of individuals, different backgrounds."

The charge to the team was very clear and exciting. "The leadership message we got was 'Try to find a way to displace petroleum.' They didn't say 'Be the greenest or be the most environmentally friendly.' Those are all nebulous terms. But when you tell engineers, 'Try to find a way to displace petroleum,' oh, boy, engineers can solve those problems."

Lutz asked the team to do a pure electric vehicle, but they pushed back; they weren't going to be stampeded into any particular course of action. "I gotta tell you, we had some knock-em-out, drag-em-out sessions," Posawatz recalls. "We had the debates with the various advocates for the different types of technologies. Because they wanted their technology to be the best."

The problem, as the team launched into engineering simulations and feasibility studies, was that GM's engineers were intensely divided over whether future cars should be powered by diesel, E85 (a fuel made of 85 percent ethanol and 15 percent gasoline), pure electric batteries, hybrids of various sorts involving both electric and gasoline engines, or fuel cells that might operate on hydrogen or methane. It was an emotional, high-stakes war among the tribes. "We had to work through the issues. Which is the right bet? Does this go against any of the bets we've placed? Is this productive?"

The starting point was a review of what was right and wrong about the EV-1. "We went through a point-counterpoint process," Posawatz explains. "The EV-1 was a two-seater. There's a limited market for two-seaters in the world. So we said, 'We can't do that again, whatever we do.' And the EV-1 was a unique vehicle in terms of components. It shared very little with any other product. And that's expensive, to do every part new.

"Plus, the EV-1 had a limited range. The term that we knock around is that EV-1 customers did not like living with 'range anxiety.' The EV-1 came with a 220-volt inductive charging system," which required rewiring many customers' garages. "That's not going to work either. The EV-1 had no cargo space, and it had lead-acid batteries." Ideas were created, tested, fought for, and shot down. The debate raged on.

In May 2006, the project was given official clearance to grow and receive more resources. A vehicle line development team was formed, and Bob Boniface was named director of design. Even if his design for the new Camaro had lost the bake-off, management could see that he was a player.

One of his key designers was Jelani Aliyu, who was born in a northern Nigerian town called Sokoto, an hour's drive from Nigeria's northern border with Niger. The town sits in a semidesert region, one of the hottest places in Africa, where there are very few modern vehicles. Yet Aliyu always really loved cars. "My dad and two older brothers were also into cars," he recalls. "We always talked about them. I've always liked drawing. I thought I'd put the two together and be a car designer.

"I imagined I had my own car company. When Mercedes would come out with a new car, I would do my own, and I would compete against Mercedes-Benz. I did my own sports cars. And I built models of them out of tin. I'd get a tin [can] and cut it out and make the exterior. Then I'd make the interior out of paper or cardboard. The doors would open. The hood would come up and down.

"A lot of the cars that moved my imagination were in magazines—Ferraris and Lamborghinis. Most especially, the one that really pushed me into saying, 'I've really got to become a designer,' was a 1982 Corvette. A family friend was studying in the U.S. and I asked him to send me a magazine. He sent a *Road & Track* magazine and on the cover was this red Corvette. But there was nothing like that in Nigeria. There was no design and no manufacturing of automobiles. I knew I had to travel overseas to do that. I really wanted to go to Italy because of Italian cars. I wrote to a couple of schools in Italy, but I discovered that I had to learn Italian to study in Italy. I didn't want to do that." He spoke English, the official language of Nigeria. Ethnically, he is a Hausa-Fulani, meaning he is from the dominant tribe of the Nigerian north.

Aliyu contacted a cousin of his who had a book listing all American colleges. "I hadn't heard of any of them," he recalls. "I went to the art school section and I picked out the ones with the names that sounded good, like the College for Creative Studies in Detroit. I wrote to that and I wrote to the Art Center College in Pasadena. I got both brochures and I looked at them and I decided to go with CCS because the brochure was more captivating, and also because of its proximity to the Big Three.

"So I put together my portfolio. I was all 2-D, but I sent it to CCS. A lot of it was paintings of cars, but most of it was side views and technical drawings of vehicles—side view, top, front, rear. I got admitted. And I got a scholarship from the Nigerian government."

He would be gone for a long time, finishing a four-year program. Did your parents and friends think you were crazy? "Yes, yes, a lot of people, even within the family, thought I was no good because I couldn't get a job back home. A lot of people did say I was crazy. That was a hurdle. But I didn't care. I knew what I wanted to do, and I went for it."

Aliyu graduated from the program and was hired by General Motors in 1996 at age twenty-nine. He was a lead interior designer on the Buick Rendezvous, a crossover vehicle, and spent a year and a half at Opel in Rüsselsheim, taking his Nigerian wife and two small children with him to Germany.

But the big moment came in May 2006. "Not long after the 2006 auto show, Bob Lutz said he wanted the most technologically advanced vehicle for 2007. He didn't want a science project. He wanted something that could go into production." Aliyu was going to try to define the look of such a vehicle.

As the project team grew, it became a rallying point for people who had been involved in the EV-1. The chief engineer, Andrew Farah, had been a junior engineer on the earlier project, and John Bereisa had been the propulsion chief. Their expertise flowed into the iCar. "We could do this project because we did the EV-1," says Posawatz.

One raging debate was how far the new car should be able to go on a single battery charge. "Why forty miles?" he asks rhetorically. "What's so magical about forty miles? We rassled with that and worked it over, left, right, and sideways." The winning argument was that 78 percent of Americans drove less than forty miles a day. The forty-mile car, Posawatz says, also ended up being ideal because of the amount of "tunnel intrusion" the appropriately sized battery would create.

To translate: The "tunnel" is the central cavity in the car where the battery is located. It is T-shaped, going down the middle of the car and then splitting under the back seats. The team did not want the tunnel to intrude too deeply into the passenger seating area. "The tunnel of that size allowed for a comfortable four-passenger seating environment," Posawatz explains, about the equivalent of a standard rear-wheel-drive vehicle. "It also allowed for a nice cargo area. When you looked to go beyond forty miles, you could put more battery in there, but now it gets more costly. There's more mass. And when you looked at the amount of available energy, sixteen kilowatt-hours of energy, and you said, 'Okay, the bigger the battery, the longer it takes to charge. How much time is an ideal charge time?' "

The EV-1 had taken about seven hours to recharge on a high-amperage

220-volt circuit. "That's great if you're a seven-hour sleeper and you use off-peak electricity," Posawatz says. But the batteries under consideration for the iCar were going to be more efficient. The idea was to "cut the time in half, and it's a three-hour charge." The other alternative was using an ordinary 115-volt household outlet, which would require seven hours.

To avoid giving drivers range anxiety, the team decided to add a 1.4-liter, 4-cylinder gasoline engine. It could never actually power the vehicle; it was there to recharge the battery, and thus extend the range of the vehicle past three hundred miles. Drivers running short on power could simply stop at a gas station and fill up, obviating the fear of running out of juice on a long and lonely road, always a risk with the EV-1. (This is also the fundamental difference from the Toyota Prius—the Prius has a battery and a gasoline engine that alternate in powering the car. When the car accelerates from a standing stop, the gasoline engine takes over; but when the car goes downhill, the battery charges. It is not possible to operate the car over any distance in pure battery mode.)

As the battery experts on the team were aware, rapid advances were being made in lithium ion batteries, which were becoming the batteries of choice for cell phones, laptop computers, and the iPod. They sketched out a battery of about 375 pounds, far lighter than the EV-1's 1,200-pounder. Despite its smaller size, they reckoned that the battery should have reserve power so that it would typically operate at a fraction of its full discharge potential, making sure it would endure for 150,000 miles or ten years.

Posawatz's breakthrough was getting the warring tribes to rally around a unifying concept, which became known as E-Flex. (This name would replace the iCar moniker.) The idea was to make a frame that would be flexible enough to accommodate the various energy strategies GM engineers were pursuing. "If you're a fuel cell advocate, the way we configured the E-Flex, the flex part of it is that the engine generator set can be replaced by a fuel cell stack. The gas tank in the back could be replaced by hydrogen. And we could allow that technology to go forward. If you're an E85 advocate within the company, we can burn E85 fuel in the engine generator set. So, ultimately, when people finally understood the value of it, and its connecting qualities, it became something that the whole organization rallied around. Ultimately, we ended up coming together. It reached the point that everyone felt, 'This is my idea.' Everyone had a kick at the can."

On the design side, Ed Welburn's three advanced studios—at Design North in Warren, in Hollywood, and in Coventry, England—submitted hundreds of sketches. Eight "themes" were chosen. Aliyu's was one of them.

His design, perhaps unsurprisingly, was inspired in many ways by growing up in Africa. "I get my best ideas when I'm watching the Discovery Channel," says Aliyu, who is forty-one but looks twenty-nine. He wears his hair closely cropped, and like other designers, wears a jacket over a dark long-sleeved shirt—no tie.

"I was home alone one night, and I started with doodles probably not bigger than two inches. I came up with something I really liked. I'm always fascinated by nature because humanity, I believe, as a species is really on the verge of a major philosophical evolution. That evolution will dramatically and forever change the very pattern of the human experience. This will be brought about by exponential advances in the sciences, arts, and technology. A result of this new way of thinking will be our relationship with the environment. Nature will no longer be seen as a force to conquer. Rather it will be seen as a medium from which to learn.

"That really spurred me to come up with the concept for the Volt, something that is highly practical and highly beautiful, a perfect balance of beauty, efficiency, and practicality. I pulled from nature to come up with a dynamic stance for the Volt."

One of the things that Aliyu did was to adjust the overhang of the body over the rear wheels. BMW and other leading designers have recently gone for car bodies in which very little of the body overhangs the rear wheels. But Aliyu wanted to go one step further, to have "negative overhang," meaning the rear wheels extended beyond the body. "So the wheels are the last thing you see in the back," Aliyu says.

Aliyu achieved a dramatic, sleek look by placing the wheels right out on the corners. And then he added a daylight opening (or "window," for civilians) that reached down to the car's belt line, much lower than most windows reach. The net effect suggests an animal getting ready to pounce.

The eight themes for the Volt were taken into the next stage of development, which was scale models about a third the size of full clay models. Aliyu then made a presentation to Bob Lutz and other top brass. "Bob decided that he felt mine was the one that should be the show car," Aliyu recalls.

Aliyu remained lead designer as the project progressed. He helped create a full-size clay model of the vehicle, for example. The style obviously had to evolve to make the car manufacturable and it was also changed because wind-tunnel testing revealed that it was not as efficient as possible. But it retains much of Aliyu's early inspiration.

"I grew up in Africa. Just minutes and you're out there in the middle of nowhere, in the middle of nature," he explains. "I see nature as a source for answers to the problems of transportation, not just transportation, but life in general. We can see a lot of answers in nature because it has been there for millennia. It provides solutions in a most beautiful and efficient manner."

There wasn't a specific animal or plant that drove his design. "It was more the philosophy of nature," Aliyu says. "Simplicity, efficiency, harmony, and continuous adaptation to new environments. The Volt does that. It suits the challenges of the future. It doesn't just produce the same old answers to an evolving problem."

By November 2006, two months before the Detroit Auto Show, the E-Flex team had made enough progress that Wagoner and the ASB decided to start production engineering work on the car, now called the Chevrolet Volt. That was an unusual step; typically, the company doesn't start the very expensive engineering work on a model until after it has gauged the market's response to an unveiling. Wagoner made a key speech in Los Angeles at about this same time, promising that GM would take the lead on a new generation of fuel-efficient vehicles. Few in the outside world believed that GM was serious. But internally, the mood was upbeat. "The company," says Posawatz, "was in a position to say, 'Hey, we're going to go do this. We're going to try to be leaders again.'"

The team realized it needed to push battery development harder and faster. So GM tapped Denise Gray to be in charge of all of GM's battery development efforts, including the one for the Volt. (She's technically the director of energy storage systems, but her nickname is Battery Lady.) At age forty-five, Gray wears her hair in a bob and sports a blue pinstripe pantsuit. She's a small African American woman from Detroit who has a big smile and lots of energy; her enthusiasm is infectious. She's also an avid sports fan who beats her husband and two teenage sons to the sports page every morning she's home. She's trained as an electrical engineer.

GM was putting enormous responsibility on the shoulders of Gray, who grew up in Detroit about six miles south of the Tech Center. Her family came from humble origins in the American South. Beginning in the 1950s, "they came up here to Detroit because the jobs were plentiful at the parts plants and the assembly plants. In all, my grandmother had fourteen kids. Probably about seven of them came here to Michigan." The majority of them, including Gray's mother, ended up in UAW jobs working on the line.

Not surprisingly, Gray grew up in a car environment. "It seemed like everybody on my block were all GM, Chrysler, or Ford people. My family were all GM people, and they all had GM cars," she recalls.

She and her future husband went to Cass Tech High School, one of Detroit's premier public schools, and she spent some time at GM during her senior year. From there, she went to GMI, where she developed an interest in becoming an electrical engineer, not a mechanical one. "It was a big win for me to go to college. I was the first in my family on my mom's side to go to college—and then to end up working at the Technical Center, at what was then called the Chevrolet Engineering Center." She began full-time in 1986.

Over the years, she was involved in systems integration and software engineering, which were solid building blocks for her current battery role. "In an era where emissions and regulatory requirements were heavy upon us, controls were what enabled us to make engines like our V-8s more fuel efficient. I worked on a lot of the software for E85 for ethanol blends. The last twelve years before I came to this appointment, I was working on propulsion systems, diagnostics, fuel-efficiency algorithms, and controlling mechanically driven parts or controlling hydraulically driven parts. So really I came [to GM] in the time where more computers, more electronic devices, microprocessors, were really beginning to be a part of the overall engineering activity." In effect, her experience spanned the move from mechanical and hydraulic controls to electronic controls, which were central to the Volt project.

The Volt was unveiled at the Detroit Auto Show in January 2007. Auto shows are the auto industry's equivalent to debutante balls, where each manufacturer showcases its latest vehicles and tries to gain momentum in the media. The car companies show both concept cars and production cars, and it's sometimes hard to tell them apart. But even if the competition and some in the press were skeptical about the Volt that the company showed in January 2007, GM had, in fact, decided to go into production. The Volt wasn't a science project.

There certainly was no doubt in Aliyu's family. It was a moment of huge personal triumph for him. His brother and family friends came from Nigeria. The boy from Sokoto had fulfilled his dream.

Meanwhile, Gray was just beginning some of the most critical work, and it wasn't easy. Current GM hybrid and fuel cell vehicles primarily used nickel-metal hydride batteries, so she had no hands-on experience with any of the lithium-ion batteries that were under consideration for the Volt's main propulsion system. Her team was struggling to hit its targets. "It was important that we learned as much as we could as early as we could," she explains, sitting in her glass-walled office in the VEC looking out over a sea of cubicles. "It may not be perfect in the beginning, but if we can get some product and we can get it tested, we can begin our learning—that's the most important thing."

One key partner was Compact Power Incorporated, a subsidiary of South Korea's LG Chem (part of the old Lucky-Goldstar group). It specialized in a very particular kind of lithium-ion battery, one that relies more on manganese than others of its kind. Compact boasted the ability to both make the battery cells and then assemble them into the packs that the auto industry could use. (Another kind of lithium-ion battery under GM's consideration was made by Continental Automotive Systems of Germany, using battery cells designed by A123Systems, located near Boston.) Lutz and other top execs "all emphasized that at the very beginning—learn, learn, learn," Gray says. "Get product, start learning it, start touching it so we can learn. With new technologies, that is the key. The more learning you get, the quicker you can see the problems or the issues. You can confirm your assumptions—or not."

When I met with Gray, she was holding in her hands an oblong, multilayered thing that looked like a big Kit Kat candy bar. "These are plates, and the plates are positive-separator-negative, positive-separator-negative," she explains. "So it's really back to electronics 101, where you get a positive and you get a negative and you can get current to flow through and can get some electricity. But in order to get the voltage that you need, you need several of those. Then we take those cells, the cell stack, and we put several of them together, and we call that a module. We have several modules that will give you an overall battery pack. Then they come in different shapes and forms."

One other variation is cylindrical, where the positive-separator-negative plates are wound together. She affectionately refers to that one as a "jelly roll."

Whatever the physical structure, another key question is what the plates should be made of. Compact Power was championing the manganese variation of the lithium-ion battery. But Continental/A123 was working on a formulation of lithium ion relying on nanophosphate, which was developed at the Massachusetts Institute of Technology.

The battery manufacturers all have their own secret recipes for their batteries, Gray explains. "We call it 'recipe' because if you ever walked into a battery plant—last year I think I was Platinum on my credit cards because I was flying so much to go see these plants—you go into what they call the mixing room. They've got all these huge Kitchen Aid mixing bowls. The material comes in like flour or sugar. They come in and they've got certain concentrations, they measure 'em.

"It's a little bit of that and a dab of this, and everybody has their secret recipes," she continues. "It's like how my mother's and my grand-mother's cakes taste totally different because they all have their own recipe." Each configuration of plates—every variation in thickness and constitution—gives a different characteristic to the power the battery produces. The "recipes" for making and aligning plates are carefully guarded trade secrets. "You want to team up with companies who've done it before because it takes time to really wring out the recipe and then the process control."

Another technical challenge was this: a little bit like Goldilocks, the Volt battery wants to be at the "just right" temperature and therefore needs a thermal system to keep it happy. "I was in a meeting the other day," says Gray, "and a thermal guy said, 'You know, we've designed this thermal system for this car, and it's a four-passenger vehicle, but we actually have a fifth passenger, and it's called the battery.' Because it's just like people—they don't want to be too hot or too cold. My thermal guys have to make sure they comprehend in the overall design."

When the battery is not in the right temperature range, it cannot be used. Bitter cold conditions are a particular problem. "If it's minus thirty, you may not get the battery to work because the electrons don't move very fast at those low temperatures."

There also had to be an intelligent system that fine-tunes battery conditions and communicates them to the driver. The company has patented software—what Gray calls "logic"—that it thinks will get the job done. "We've got monitors on these cells, and that information goes into the computers as a part of my battery system. Then I can say, 'Okay, it's good to use it now,' or 'No, we're not going to use it now,' based on voltage and current and temperature of the electrochemistry of the cells themselves." But some important technical questions were not yet fully resolved, and the clock was ticking.

Taking a new car from concept into production is like a relay race; no matter how skilled the individual, no one can handle all aspects of getting it done. So in March, two months after the Volt was introduced, a German by the name of Frank Weber arrived from GM Europe to take over the project from Posawatz and push it through to completion.

(His wife and three young children followed in August.) Weber's title became vehicle line engineer and chief engineer, meaning he was responsible for bringing the vehicle to market and meeting its cost "boundaries," as well as for resolving all technical questions.

The VLE position is one of the toughest jobs at GM, and Weber's measure of success is simple: either the Volt is launched in November 2010, or it's not. Tony Posawatz was called in because he was good at getting projects started; Weber is in the business of finishing them.

Weber, forty-two, is tall and slender, and has horn-rimmed spectacles and graying curly hair. In a tie and white shirt, he's dressed a bit more formally than many other people at the Tech Center. He speaks very fast, and I have trouble telling whether he's so smart that I can't understand every word or if he's adapting the English language to a Germanic model. Referring to Weber, Bob Lutz says, "We've got some of our absolute best people in the world in charge of the Volt program." (Weber's selection has been featured prominently in the German auto press. "The German media are fun as usual," Lutz wisecracks, making up the headline: "GM makes progress on electric vehicle, thanks to German technological aid.")

One reason GM has put a European in charge of the Volt launch may be that Europeans in general are ahead of the Americans in attempting to adapt to a world in which energy costs are high and there are constraints of space, money, and resources. "The one key to our sensitivity is energy cost. Fuel is nine dollars per gallon in Europe," Weber says. "This is what is driving the pattern. But there is definitely another piece, which is European history in dealing with limited space. That's driving our search for efficiency. Because of the war also, I think there is something in Europe that makes everything a little leaner. You go with less."

Whatever the historic backdrop, Weber's sheer enthusiasm is impressive. He talks with his hands with an energy befitting a Ferrari designer. With a background in both advanced engineering and in program management, he is a risk-taker with a strong technological bent. He's young and ambitious enough that he's willing to put his career on the line: If the Volt is launched successfully, Frank Weber will have stood on the

If there is a single car that represents the high-water mark of GM design, it's the 1959 Cadillac Eldorado, with its huge fins suggesting the shape of a rocket ship.

The 1960 Corvette; in the background is GM's Technical Center, designed by the Finnish architect Eero Saarinen.

Rick Wagoner (center), with Gary Cowger (left) and Jack Smith (right), at the 2003 North American International Auto Show in Detroit.

The XLR, one of the most distinctive of the Cadillacs to embody GM's "Art and Science" design theme.

Bob Lutz introduces a concept Corvette at the Detroit Opera House, January 4, 2004. Wagoner recruited Lutz, a well-known "car guy," to rev up GM's design capabilities.

Ed Welburn unveils the Saturn Curve concept vehicle in January 2004. Welburn, the first African American designer to work at GM, ultimately became head of design.

Above: Designer Bob Boniface, who helped revive the Camaro, checks out the lines of a clay model.

Right: Sang Yup Lee competed against Boniface's team to give the new Camaro design a more modern interpretation.

Left: Wagoner with the winning Camaro design on the patio at the Design Center.

After years of poor interiors in its less expensive cars, GM created a winning interior design for the Malibu that resembled an airplane cockpit.

The 1969 Camaro Rally Sport Coupe captured the youthful enthusiasm of the era. Many top GM executives still own this model.

GM has emerged as the largest automaker in China, the company's second largest market after the United States.

The Chevrolet Aveo, designed and manufactured in South Korea by GM's Daewoo Automotive unit, is one of GM's new entries in the small fuel-efficient car category.

Designer John Manoogian won several auto awards for scrapping an in-progress redesign of the Cadillac CTS at the last minute and championing a dramatic new look.

Manoogian also pushed through a new model, the CTS Coupe.

Jelani Aliyu (center), born in a remote town in northern Nigeria, came up with the design for the exterior of the new Chevrolet Volt.

The Volt, due out in late 2010, is an extended-range electric vehicle that may help transform GM's product lineup—and its image.

shoulders of many other people, but it will be counted as his success. If it doesn't happen, he may never again have an opportunity for a day in the sun like this one.

He's late to our meeting because he just came from a meeting where decision makers locked down the exterior design of the Volt; though it's lunchtime and everyone else is eating, Weber's assistant will bring him lunch later. "Actually," he says, "I'm happy if I get anything to eat at all."

His cell phone rings and rings again. It's obvious he's under intense pressure. How many hours a day do you work? "With all the electronics and having to respond constantly, it is something that I cannot even answer. How do you know that you are not working?" he asks, laughing.

For Denise Gray, Halloween night 2007 was an exciting evening, not because of the trick-or-treaters but because that was when she received shipment of the first lithium-ion battery for the Volt from Compact Power. "People here were saying, 'Is it on its way?' All day long, all kind of communications were happening. Then the truck comes into our gate. 'It's here!' The excitement was mounting and everybody got their cameras ready. It was like the delivery of a first baby."

Getting shipment of a lithium-ion battery that worked, she adds, was a "big check mark." For the first time, she could say, "Hey, this thing is plausible. It is real."

So far, lithium-ion batteries have been used mostly in consumer electronics products, which obviously are much smaller than cars and operate in a much narrower range of temperatures. They also have a life expectancy of perhaps three years, not the ten that GM is seeking. So gearing up full-fledged manufacturing for the automotive industry is filled with challenges.

For one, contaminants that might be introduced in the manufacturing process could short out the battery. That's what forced Sony to recall ten million of the lithium-ion batteries inside various brands of laptop computers. Some had burst into flames. The other challenge is that people expect their cars to last longer, a lot longer, than their consumer electronics. It's a big deal, she says, to "move from a small-scale kind of battery size to a larger battery size and make sure that the manufacturing of the battery is flawless and make sure that it is going to last the life of the vehicle."

So where will the batteries be made? This is not only a technological question—this is where the economic opportunities are for entire countries. "I've spent a lot of frequent flyer miles," she says. "And guess what? Most of the companies are in Asia. They're in Korea, they're in Japan, there's a few trying to do some things in China. There are very few battery cell companies here in the States." Toyota's lithium-ion development efforts are located in Japan.

Could it be that the United States could play a big role in manufacturing these batteries, repairing some of the economic damage that's been done by the contraction of the auto industry? "There will be an opportunity for an investment in this area and so there's an opportunity for the United States to invest in having a footprint when it comes to the battery technology as well," she says. According to an estimate from Alliance Bernstein, the investment firm, the lithium-ion industry could have $150 billion a year in sales by 2030. It could be a major industry in its own right.

"Yeah, I think a market is being created. It's kind of like the chicken and the egg. Now that we're heading toward batteries being an enabler for fuel economy, there's a market, and folks are saying, 'Hey, maybe I can invest now.'" GM believes that if it succeeds in launching the Volt, at least some part of the process of building the lithium-ion cells and designing and engineering the packs will occur in the United States.

So Gray is at the heart of a battle not just between car companies but also between national economies. And of course it's personal, too, because her career is on the line. She's not afraid of making mistakes, but she doesn't want to make the same mistake twice. "I'm a Cool Hand Luke kind of person—you want to make sure you never see that lesson again."

She knows that her family is watching. "I've got a thirteen-year-old, Nathan, and a seventeen-year-old, Taylor, and my thirteen-year-old already says his first vehicle's going to be some kind of electric vehicle, because the kids today are a lot more conscious of what's happening. They understand, because we're still in a war in Iraq, they still see the prices of gas up, especially those who are becoming drivers. But they also hear about just overall emissions and how it's important that we're earth-conscious.

"So my kids are saying, 'Oh, Mom, this is awesome.'"

The pressure on Weber kept intensifying. Reporting to him are people from Engineering, Manufacturing, Finance, Purchasing, Battery, Power Train, Quality, and Human Resources, among others. "A VLE is the person who has full commercial and technical responsibility, and the priority during the product development phase is to find something that is commercially successful and within the technical boundary conditions," he explains. "I have a fairly unique role, being the VLE and chief engineer at the same time. This was a model that was chosen for this program because so many decisions can fundamentally impact the technical nature of this program. What was wanted was somebody who was commercially overlooking the program at the same time that person was technically overlooking the program in one role."

What's also unusual is that Weber reports to a leadership board, which includes Wagoner, Lutz, and all the top product people inside the company. Other product development teams don't have those boards, which is one reason they have traditionally taken more time to resolve conflicts and force decisions. "It was clear from the beginning," says Weber, "that you could not delegate this program to a team and say, 'Now go off and develop this program.' On the leadership board, we sit down and talk about the fundamentals of the program. How is this thing operating? What are the policies? Is the engine starting properly, or why isn't the engine starting? What are the aggressive boundary conditions and how far do we go and how do we achieve commitment?" He had spent two hours the previous week with the board, and Wagoner was there. The board was to meet again the following week for two hours, again with Wagoner in attendance. "This is a very, very close dialogue we're having with the senior leaders of the organization."

Weber's key challenge is making the GM matrix work. Each of the vertical functions, like engineering or design, report up to their top managers in what are called silos. They also have very real but less formal responsibility to Weber, so the challenge for him is to use his personality, expertise, and sheer energy to persuade the technical experts to work together smoothly. "Everybody is connected to very strong silos," Weber says. "But the reason why the VLE is in place is because at the end, it is only the integration aspect that brings the vehicle program together. Building consensus is the mechanism to bridge the functions."

In the old days, and maybe still on other vehicle launch teams, a technical argument—over whether manufacturing people can bend the metal in a way that the designers are demanding, say, or whether the power train people can squeeze out extra horsepower without costing more money—would be elevated upward through each vertical silo, and the people high up in the company would try to sort out the issues. But that takes too long and is grossly inefficient. "This is why we have all the functions sitting on that leadership board," Weber says. "Whenever I have an issue, we go there, we make the argument, and within days or weeks, I don't even need another meeting, we make those decisions. Either I make the decisions myself because I am empowered or I go to the leadership board if we need strategic direction."

Weber is a motivator; rather than being a careful bureaucrat, he's taking risks, and his personal example encourages others to "go fast" too. "There is complete transparency on all the issues. If somebody comes in with an issue, we try to resolve it immediately," says Weber.

"It is a transformational aspect of what this program means culturally to GM where each individual knows that it is not my boss telling me what to do," he continues. "It is dialogue and I am the expert. It is very interesting what this is creating on the people side. Even though you cannot run every program like the Volt, it is interesting for all levels of the organization to see how a change in priority can help do something that is truly needed."

Don't you sound a bit like a cheerleader? He glares at me through his glasses. "The timetable that has been established for this program is so aggressive that it needs this kind of attitude," he replies. "Otherwise, it would kill you."

The technical complexity of what his team is trying to master could indeed slay a less energetic person. Much as Posawatz passed a baton to Weber, so too, in a way, has Gray. She needs to pick the right battery and get it manufactured; Weber has to make the battery work as part of a car. "The battery in itself is a challenge, and then the battery inside the vehicle is a challenge," Weber explains.

"If you look at the whole system in an electric vehicle, you have a very sophisticated overall thermal system; you have the cabin, you have the battery, you have the power electronics, you have the engine to generate electricity, you have a very, very complex system. Most of it is all new technology, chilling, heating, high-voltage electric devices that create cabin heat. All this is challenging for the industry. You cannot say, here is a technology, so I will go to supplier one, two, or three, and I'll pick the best one. In many cases, we have just one supplier, the only one worldwide. For example, when we talk about the high-voltage heating system, there is only one key supplier worldwide that can deliver that." Perhaps coincidentally, it is a German company.

One of his key challenges is helping customers understand how their vehicle is really functioning. The Toyota Prius has a screen on the dashboard that helps the driver understand when she is using the gasoline engine and when she is using the battery-driven engine. The car has two propulsion systems, and the car is in either one mode or the other.

The Volt will be different because an electric motor is the only propulsion system. The gasoline engine will be used to recharge the battery but will never actually power the wheels directly. That's why it's called an extended-range electric vehicle. "This is definitely not a hybrid vehicle," Weber explains. "We are creating a propulsion category in itself."

Weber also says the Volt will not force customers to accept trade-offs between what is environmentally friendly and what is fun to drive. He says the Volt will accelerate from zero to sixty miles per hour in less than eight seconds, which is not bone-crunching but still quite robust. And the top speed will be capped at a hundred miles per hour. "People are going to say, 'Okay, I don't need gasoline [to drive forty miles].' There are no tailpipe emissions. It makes no noise. The whole driving of this vehicle will be like from a different planet. It will be a big surprise.'"

The fact that a driver can extend the car's range from forty miles on battery to three hundred miles if the gasoline engine is tapped is the key differentiator from purely electric vehicles. "The old problem of range anxiety, of plugging it in, will be a major issue for those vehicles," says Weber. "All pure electric vehicles will have constraints that we don't want for the Volt. We are pretty sure there is nobody out there who will have an extended-range vehicle which will give you the normal comfort of range. This will be a unique proposition."

While Weber pushes the project across the finish line, Posawatz's success at moving the project into commercialization has been a hit with his two sons. "I'm cool now—it's hard to believe," he jokes. "My kids never thought of me as too cool." On Take Your Kids to Work Day, he brought in his younger son, a ten-year-old, and gave him a ride in the EV-1. "He thought that was better than any day at school. It is a nice feeling. In all honesty, we're doing something beyond creating a great car. Most of us view this as a much more noble mission. It's our turn to change the world."

"The Volt is on!" Rick Wagoner announced at a press conference before the annual shareholders meeting in Wilmington, Delaware, in May 2008. The board of directors had just authorized funds to gear up production.

Not surprisingly, Wagoner approaches the Volt more from a business and economic angle than from a technological or design point of view. "The first cars out are going to be pretty expensive," Wagoner explains, sitting in his office in the Ren Cen. "That is the key issue we need to be confronting. We really have to be able to drive down the costs.

"What we also need to remind ourselves is that we've worked on the internal combustion engine for a hundred years. It's an amazing machine. It has quality and durability, and the power generated is unbelievable. It has the ability to perform in an unbelievable range of circumstances, from your grandmother driving it twenty miles an hour in one-hundred-degree heat in Arizona to your cousin starting it up in the morning in Alaska at zero degrees and wanting to drive it immediately at eighty-five miles an hour on the highway. These are tough conditions. We can do that with internal combustion because we've been working it for one hundred years.

"Now we're going to substitute in these alternate propulsion systems that don't have the benefit of being gradually improved over a hundred years," says Wagoner. "The team has got to come in and meet this high standard. The way we're going to do it is with belts and suspenders [extra safety systems and safeguards] in a lot of areas. That means high cost. Then we have to drive the costs down. California guys ask, 'How come Tesla can do this car?' That's terrific what they're doing. But it's a completely different matter to do a vehicle that you're going to sell a thousand units of at a hundred thousand dollars each versus something you're going to do five hundred thousand units of for twenty thousand each."

Most commentators say the Volt will cost consumers about $40,000 when it first comes out, almost guaranteeing that GM will not sell enough to make money on the first generation. And if in fact Wagoner's goal is to drive the price tag closer to $20,000, that is going to require a massive investment to create the right economies of scale.

But sheer scale is what makes the Volt project potentially so powerful, and the fact that GM decided to make it a Chevrolet is an obvious sign that it hopes to sell large quantities because Chevy has traditionally been GM's lowest-cost, highest-volume brand. "We are not going to change this environmental-energy equation until we get into the middle of the market and get huge volumes," adds Wagoner. "The one thing you know about U.S. consumers is that you'll only increase volume if you give them very good value. There aren't that many people who will pay a premium for the technology. They want the value with it."

Will you be there alone with the extended-range electric vehicle? "No one else is talking about being there with us, but I suspect a lot of people are hustling," says Wagoner. "This is a new idea. It's a big idea. But we're not the only smart guys in this business. This is going to be a race. Just because you get the first handoff doesn't mean you win forever. We're going to have to hustle on this technology for a while. But we do have a chance to be out very early and set the tone in a lot of ways."

Lutz says the Volt will be an "absolute game changer." That's not to say he isn't concerned that the cars will be priced so high that it discourages customers from buying them, or that GM will have to subsidize purchases, meaning it will lose money on each sale. "But as the technology becomes more normal and more lithium-ion batteries come in, it will be like the first generation of computers or the first generation of everything," says Lutz. "There isn't a well-developed supply base for the stuff that you need in an electric vehicle, and we're having to pay exorbitant prices for a lot of the stuff. But some of it we'll integrate in-house. We already have seen areas where we can save a lot by switching to making something instead of buying it. So the second and third generations will be cheaper."

A company with GM's global scale should be able to quickly find many markets for the Volt. "There is huge worldwide demand," Lutz argues. "I think it has the potential to be almost the Model T redux, because the Volt is in demand all over the world. That's why we've designed it to where it would comply with all known crash and exterior and interior protrusion regulations around the world. It'll be available in right-hand drive and left-hand drive, and it'll go to China and Latin America, Europe, everywhere. Clearly the technology is such that once we've got it into mass production as a Chevrolet, there's no reason why we can't do larger versions, smaller versions, more luxurious versions, truck versions, and so forth. It may just be our ace in the hole. It may be the only thing out there that will permit us to meet the U.S. fuel economy regulations— because we're going to get a label of over one hundred miles per gallon for it." That figure is widely debated. Some analysts consider 50 miles per gallon to be more realistic; it will depend a great deal on how the U.S. Environmental Protection Agency conducts its mileage test. If it operates the Volt only on the battery, that means it would use no gasoline and could meet Lutz's goal of 100 miles per gallon. But if the EPA pushes the Volt to its full three-hundred-mile range, using the gas engine to charge the battery, the miles per gallon would be fewer.

Lutz believes that in the early stages of the Volt's development, the media overstated the challenges of the lithium-ion battery—with help from Toyota. "Toyota started [the negative media coverage] because they have such an enormous equity in what they call the Toyota Synergy Drive system, which is based on nickel-metal hydride batteries, which are okay. But they are last generation. They are very mature, they're very reliable. We use 'em, too, in our full-size hybrids. But the energy storage is only half of what you get with lithium-ion."

Neutral observers agree with Lutz that Toyota was not eager to make the move to lithium-ion because of its huge investment in three factories in Japan that made nickel batteries. It also was concerned that a successful lithium-ion battery would render the Prius obsolete. "There is only one company that has a stranded cost in nickel and that's Toyota," says Alex Molinaroli, chief executive officer of Johnson Power Controls, a unit of Johnson Controls, which makes lithium-ion batteries for BMW and Mercedes-Benz in Europe. "They [Toyota] would be least motivated to move to a new technology."

Lately, however, Toyota has gotten on the bandwagon and has announced that it, too, will unveil a plug-in hybrid in 2010 using lithium-ion batteries. Thus a high-stakes technology race is fully engaged.

Even though Lutz was the prime instigator for the Volt, there's no question that Wagoner is personally involved and will be exposed to allegations that he personally failed if the Volt project runs into a brick wall. Aside from attending the Volt board meetings, he and Fritz Henderson have visited the Hybrid Battery Development Center at Milford, where experimentation with vehicles is under way. "We talk to the people doing the work, and they tell us what we can do differently," he explains. "We're strategizing on our feet. And we get a chance to put in our two cents, too."

As 2008 progressed, it became increasingly clear that enormous attention would be focused on the Volt. "It's gotten to be bigger than life for us," Wagoner told the PBS talk show host interviewer Charlie Rose in August 2008. "It is really important. It's important because it's a rallying cry within the company to show, even in some tough financial times, our commitment to really drive the industry to the future, drive ourselves, but drive the industry."

The Volt is not the only bet that GM is making on alternate propulsion technologies. By early 2009, the company had eight hybrid models available for sale, and it was pushing ahead on fuel cells, biofuels, and other technologies such as hydrogen, which was used in the Chevy Equinox. In the final analysis, no one can really know which propulsion system will prevail. Ultimately, there may be several different kinds of engines and vehicles on the road at the same time.

If the Volt fails (and many auto writers are still skeptical), it will be a signal to everyone inside GM and to everyone who watches the company that its woes were as deep as its harshest critics suggested. It either could not make the right bets or could not break free from its bureaucratic shackles to innovate. If, however, the company starts production in November 2010—or comes close—it will be a wake-up call to those same people and to the whole market; GM can once again stake a claim to design and technological leadership in the auto industry.

CHAPTER 11

OnStar

"Pretty Good for an Ex–Locomotive Salesman"

After the great innovations of the 1950s and '60s, culminating in the invention of the catalytic converter in 1974, GM's ability to innovate ebbed dramatically. For the next two decades, its internal research and development operations kept getting cut back as the company was thrown on the defensive. The prevailing culture discouraged breakthrough ideas because they involved financial risk. The company did acquire two tech companies, Electronic Data Systems and Hughes Electronics, in the 1980s. But the cultures clashed, and GM was unable to unlock its acquisitions' technological treasure chests.

So it is remarkable that General Motors was able to snap back with one of its greatest technological achievements in modern times: the OnStar communications and vehicle diagnostics system, which links millions of GM vehicles to a comprehensive set of services based on wireless communications and satellite technology.

The success depended in large measure on a small-town Midwestern boy from one of the lowest-tech industries around. Chet Huber was born in 1954 in Hammond, Indiana, right up against the perfectly straight border that divides Indiana and Illinois. As a teenager, he worked for the Certified Grocery Store in Worth, Illinois, on the southwestern outskirts of Chicago.

At age eighteen, he left the grocery store to go to General Motors Institute in Flint. He got a degree in mechanical engineering, and then GM sent him off to Harvard Business School to get his M.B.A.. Afterward, Huber joined GM's locomotive business, which was headquartered in Illinois and run quite separately from the auto business. "I loved the locomotive business," says Huber, who sports a mustache and whose bluish eyes are piercingly clear. "It's the perfect business for a mechanical engineer. It's a 450,000-pound moving science project, right?" Huber, a natural storyteller with an Indiana twang, worked his way up the ladder to take charge of global sales and marketing.

Then, one day in 1994, after twenty-two years in the locomotive business, his life took an abrupt turn; "I'd say somebody had a sense of humor," he jokes. Unbeknownst to Huber, that somebody was GM vice chairman Harry Pearce, who oversaw the locomotive business. He had plans for the young man, then forty, and told Huber's boss.

"What happened is out of the clear blue in the summer of 1994," Huber recalls, "my boss, who was running the locomotive business, took me to lunch and passed me a brochure from something called the National Defense University. He never took me to lunch, so I didn't know what was going on. I thought only bad kids get sent to military school."

In fact, it was not a disciplinary school at all—it was a special educational program for military leaders, plus rising stars at the Central Intelligence Agency and the State Department. The university, which was trying to expend into the civilian sector, was at Fort McNair, Virginia, near Washington, DC. Huber's boss told him he didn't have to accept, but then added, "You've been accepted." Huber could hardly refuse. He was being groomed.

"I flew home every weekend," Huber recalls, "so I was the classic definition of what military guys call a geographic bachelor. I was in Virginia for the week, and I'd do homework on the phone every night with the kids." That lasted for ten months.

When it was over in 1995, Huber thought he'd go home and start selling locomotives again. But Pearce called him and told him about Project Beacon, a three-way joint venture among GM, Hughes Electronics, and EDS. GM was trying to tap their communications, software, and electronics know-how to create a new service for cars, something it hoped none of its rivals could imitate. But representatives from the three companies pursued different agendas. Plus, they weren't quite sure what their purpose was. All in all, it was an example of precisely how *not* to manage a joint venture.

Pearce diplomatically told Huber that he wanted to try a different corporate governance model for Project Beacon. Huber puts it more colorfully: "I was like the human equivalent of Switzerland to these guys, right? I wasn't from Hughes, I wasn't from EDS, I wasn't from the car business, I couldn't possibly know anything about anything." Huber may have been a neutral player, but his lack of experience in any of the core technologies put him at a huge disadvantage. He was being asked to move from selling locomotives to railroads, an old-fashioned business in many ways, to starting up a consumer services business based on new, untested technology. This was an abrupt shift if ever there was one.

From an office along I-75 in Troy, about forty-five minutes north of downtown Detroit, Huber began trying to put his arms around the project. The guiding vision was that exciting things were happening in cellular communications, which meant that cars were now able to communicate. But nobody seemed to know what the cars should communicate *about,* or *to whom.* Global Positioning System (GPS) technology, which started in the U.S. military's spy satellite program, was also becoming more widely available commercially. Huber took over an existing staff and reported to a board of directors consisting of two representatives from Hughes, two from EDS, and two from GM. "They said, 'Okay, come up with a plan.'"

Once again, Huber was commuting, this time to Detroit. "It would have been crazy to uproot the family and move 'em," Huber explains. "The kids were in school. They loved where they were. We were in Western Springs, a really nice suburb of Chicago."

In Troy, Huber and his team papered the walls of their office with Post-it notes, trying to figure out what they wanted Project Beacon to offer. There was a dizzying array of possibilities; the latest technology made it possible to deliver traffic alerts, music, and games to a vehicle in new ways. Customized news, sports, stocks, and weather were also within the realm of possibility, as were video entertainment, mobile shopping, and a range of more futuristic possibilities, such as linking a car with a home security system. But no one knew what customers would actually pay for, and there were few guideposts to help Huber's team figure out what was realistic. "We didn't understand the bounds of the technology that well," Huber recalls. "We didn't have a strong brand position to help guide the range of possibilities, and we had no experience with customers or alliance partners."

Ultimately, the team concluded that safety, security, and peace of mind were the key features to concentrate on. If cars were now smart, how could they get help for the driver and occupants in the event of a crash? The team also wanted to link their system to the car's airbag modules, door locking and unlocking systems, diagnostic systems, and other increasingly computerized functions.

Huber didn't know it at the time, but he was on the front lines of the telematics revolution, the marriage of wireless communications and computing with the automobile. It was virgin territory; no one knew how much communications and computing power to put into a car. There were issues of driver distraction; it was possible to cram so many functions into a dashboard that it would resemble an airplane cockpit (which is why OnStar created a simple three-button system that is built into the rearview mirror in most vehicles). But the burning question remained, What will customers pay for?

The crucial moment came around Thanksgiving 1995. Wagoner had called a North American management meeting. Huber had met Wagoner only once before, in passing, and had had scant exposure to the top brass, other than watching them on the company's internal television system when they made announcements. "So we go upstairs to this conference room and Rick's got his entire executive staff," Huber recalls. "I'm thinkin', 'Wow, I've never been at a meeting with this many big shots.'"

Wagoner sat at one end of the table and Huber at the other, giving his pitch for how Project Beacon should evolve. The vision that Huber outlined was far from the concrete, detailed business plan that top management typically demanded. He didn't have market research to back him up. He didn't really know how all the technologies would work together. Huber was able to tell the meeting that his team had identified a set of customer needs and thought the technologies could be used to satisfy those needs. But by the tough-minded standards of the top brass, this was a very soft proposal.

Huber then proceeded to tweak their sensibilities again by telling them that if GM wanted to launch the business, it would have to be with a very different kind of model. "I said if we have to live inside the typical vehicle development program, we shouldn't even start doin' this because we'll be selling 8-track tapes when everybody else is selling CDs."

In other words, the business had to operate on principles more like those of the electronics business, which changes every season and quickly goes through multiple generations of products. It couldn't operate on a four- or five-year basis, like most new vehicle development programs do. "We shouldn't even start unless we manage this differently," Huber said. "We won't get business results, we'll look silly, and everybody will get frustrated."

Wagoner, then forty-two, a year older than Huber, looked around the table and started asking his direct reports for their opinions. One of the goals Wagoner had been stressing to this set of executives was the need to standardize GM's engineering functions so that the company could improve its quality. This was part of Jack Smith's vision of "running common." Now Wagoner was asking them to zag in another direction.

As he went around the table seeking reactions to Huber, Wagoner arrived at Arv Mueller, who was running GM engineering at that time.

"So, Arv, can you do this?" Wagoner asked.

Mueller looked at him and said, "Yeah, if you make me."

Mueller was in charge of trying to make GM's vehicle development process more consistent. This would introduce a significant wild card. "Every part of our DNA would say, 'No, we can't do this,'" Mueller said. "Now, if you tell me to make an exception and to manage this outside the process, I can do it. I can't do everything this way, because then we're going to go back and say we've lost control."

Wagoner was facing other pressures, too. Wall Street was angry with GM for diversifying into unrelated fields, as it had with the EDS and Hughes acquisitions, and wanted Wagoner to stick to autos. And he knew that the success rate of start-up companies located deep inside huge existing incumbent companies was not high. To be exact, it was infinitesimal.

But Wagoner bought Huber's argument. "We're a big company," Huber recalls him saying. "One of the things a big company gets to do is we get opportunities to try different things because of our scale and our resources. They don't all have to work, but we ought to pick the ones that have a good chance to work."

Wagoner knew that OnStar would challenge the company's core processes, and he also knew that he didn't want Hughes and EDS as joint venture partners because they would greatly complicate any decision making. According to Huber, "Rick announces to the room, 'I unilaterally terminate the partnership.' And he looks at the lawyer in the room and he goes, 'Okay, make that happen.' And then to me, he said, 'Okay, now you're the newest division of General Motors.'"

Huber was in shock. "I left the room and, God, I didn't even know what to tell my wife that night. She knew that I had this meeting and asked, 'What happened?'

"I said, 'I don't know. I'm certainly not selling locomotives. But this is just really interesting.'"

Wagoner set OnStar up as a separate subsidiary, with a separate board of directors that would report to the company's marketing division rather than engineering or manufacturing. But in reality, Wagoner ran interference for it. He set up monthly one-on-one sessions in his own office with Huber to force the pace of decision making and protect the adolescent company from the rest of the GM bureaucracy. The meetings were unscripted. "I was able to control the agenda, which was actually pretty amazing," Huber says.

Only much later did Wagoner tell Huber that he was experimenting with how GM reacted to a new idea. "I just wanted to figure out what you were running into," the CEO said. "I just want to kind of get a sense for, when we run a play like this, what it's going to feel like to be on the other side."

I asked Wagoner how he knew that OnStar was viable. "It was a good

vision," he says simply. "We were convinced that if it did work, it woul[
be a pretty interesting business for us. And the good news as we starte[
it was that we didn't think it would cost that much. That sort of wa[
true. The up-front investment wasn't high."

Although the numbers have never been disclosed, Wagoner acknowledges that it required more investment than he foresaw. But the first
OnStar services were installed in the fall of 1996 on the 1997 Cadillac
Seville and Deville—and OnStar started developing into a formidable
platform, one that was unique in the auto industry.

True, the customer take-up rate in the early days was disappointingly
low, mostly because OnStar was sold for $895 and had to be installed at
a dealer. But as time passed, it became clear that OnStar was arguably
the most practical way to integrate advanced technologies into an auto,
because of the simplicity of the driver interface.

Today, OnStar is solidly profitable, and no other automaker offers a
service that is directly competitive. Wagoner deadpans, "It's pretty good
for an ex–locomotive salesman."

The relative simplicity of how the driver engages with OnStar was important. The three-button OnStar approach was not as distracting as
other systems that demanded drivers look at display screens on the
dashboard or fiddle with knobs. It allowed drivers to "keep their eyes
on the road and hands on the wheel," a mantra of the industry. Plus,
drivers could use the car's cell phone system to speak to OnStar special-
ists located in two call centers, one in Michigan and the other in North
Carolina. The human touch, it turns out, really mattered.

What also proved powerful about OnStar was that it was a platform
that allowed the company to keep adding new layers of service. The capabilities had exploded but there was only so much space on the dashboard for various controls and buttons. No one wanted the front seat of
a car to resemble a fighter-jet cockpit. Different manufacturers tried
different strategies. BMW, for example, tried to cram more than two
hundred functions into its iDrive knob, which was positioned between
the front seats and linked to a display screen. It was radically simple in
concept but confusing in practice, because drivers had to memorize

how to find air conditioning and navigation controls. BMW drivers rebelled, forcing major changes in the system. Other manufacturers toyed with allowing drivers to read e-mail and get stock updates, but these created the problem of driver distraction. The central issue was that drivers should keep their eyes on the road and their hands on the wheel while taking advantage of new computing and communications capabilities. The OnStar advantage was that it had such a simple interface that huge complexity could be "hidden" from the driver.

One such added-on project was called Virtual Advisor, and Huber hired a man named Mike Peterson to head it up. Peterson arrived from A.T. Kearney, the consulting company, in 1996, when he was thirty-eight. He had come to GM because he was tired of being on the outside of a company looking in. "You have no closure, no accomplishment," the boyish-looking but intense Peterson said.

The goal of Virtual Advisor was to allow drivers to get their weather, stocks, sports scores, traffic conditions, and even horoscopes by pressing a single button and talking to the system through a microphone located just above their heads. Peterson wanted to deliver the Internet to the automobile and do it all by voice.

He had to rely on his persuasive skills because no one on his twelve-person team actually reported to him. He had to "borrow" people from other OnStar departments, such as finance, marketing, and engineering. This was more like the culture of Silicon Valley than the hushed, buttoned-down corridors of the Ren Cen.

The key challenge was voice recognition technology. To address it, Peterson found Silicon Valley companies such as General Magic, Nuance Communications, and SpeechWorks International that had know-how in voice portals, speech recognition, and speech-to-text, respectively. Getting voice recognition technology to work in a car is particularly tricky because of all the background noise. Peterson and team needed to "purify" voice commands from inside the car by stripping out background noise and to "tune" the software to improve its ability to recognize a driver's words. (Virtual Advisor understands not only "yes" but also "uh-huh," "yeah," and "yup.")

In December 1999, Peterson and Huber teamed up to persuade Wagoner to cough up $15 million for a formal alliance with General Mag

whose technology was the most important among the three outside companies. During this period, Peterson was a full-blown workaholic, acting more as an entrepreneur than an executive. In view of the three-hour time difference between Detroit and the West Coast, Peterson would routinely work until the Californians went home, at nine P.M. Detroit time, and even longer. "It's not uncommon to find Mike running around the GM parking lot testing OnStar on different cars at eight or nine P.M. California time," said Jeff Adamson, vice president of applications services at General Magic. That was eleven P.M. or midnight in Detroit. Peterson's monster hours persuaded others to take the project more seriously.

In the next months, it all clicked. An alpha version of the Virtual Advisor was up and running by June 2000; the first customers received access to it that December. The way it works is that a driver goes to the OnStar website from a personal computer and creates a profile of what information she wants read to her while in the car. That data is transmitted to the car's computer, which then obtains the information wirelessly. (Sports results, for example, come from an ESPN online service.) A voice then reads the information aloud to the driver.

Peterson, who stayed at OnStar until 2007, got it all done by ignoring many of the rules in the GM playbook. "My bosses would ask me, 'How many rules did you break today?' " Peterson says. "But I prefer to think of it as working on the edge." The fact that GM has allowed a free-wheeling subsidiary to remain alive deep inside the empire is surprising. But it has an ally at the very top.

OnStar solved one of its major problems by deciding to have its latest systems installed in GM factories, rather than at dealerships. It is tricky because OnStar now has to comply with the rigid requirements of production schedules. But it is worth it because OnStar has five million subscribers today. Further, "we made the decision a couple years ago that we'd go standard equipment on GM retail vehicles in the U.S. and Canada, which means we'll double in size in the next thirty months," says Huber, whose offices are now downtown at the Ren Cen. That means OnStar will soon have ten million active subscribers.

For Huber, OnStar is an example of how deeply cars touch Americans' daily lives. The system has been involved in responding to 80,000 accidents—in many cases, before the vehicle even comes to a stop. "Americans spend five hundred million hours a week in vehicles, and life happens while you're driving," says Huber. "That's 'I'm having a heart attack while I'm driving. My passenger's just had a stroke, my baby in the backseat just had a reaction to a prescription medication.' We are the lifeline for those people. Between ten thousand and fifteen thousand times a month, people press that button, and we get a chance to affect their life."

In December 2007, one call came from an eye surgeon in Michigan who was hunting in the remote northern portion of the state's Lower Peninsula. "He was way off of any road, and his firearm accidentally discharged," Huber says. "He had a muzzle loader, and a .52-caliber shell went through his chest and lodged two millimeters from his heart. He happened to have gone hunting in his Chevy Avalanche with OnStar.

"So he presses the button, but it was going to be a forty-minute wait until 911 could get anyone to this guy's scene. We had to describe the location by giving them approximate distances off of known roads and then precise latitude and longitude.

"The guy, as you would expect, just panicked. He's talking to the 911 guy and he was saying that he's going to get out of the car and start walking. He would have bled to death for sure, because his heart would have really started pumping and there was nowhere to go. And they're saying, 'No, stay in the car, stay in the car.'"

With the 911 operator still on the phone, the surgeon asked the OnStar adviser to get his wife on the phone. The 911 operator later said, "I was praying she wasn't home." From experience, he expected that the wife would panic and start screaming and crying, which would have had the effect of persuading the surgeon to get out of his truck and start walking, which would have meant certain death.

"We called the wife and she was like this unbelievable rock," Huber says. "She tells him, 'It'll be fine, honey, it'll be all right.' This guy's in tears, obviously, and she was amazing, and he's saying, 'I just want to let you know I love you and tell the kids that I love 'em and I hope they remember their dad.' It was like, this guy's *dying*. But she was amazingly calm." Local authorities dispatched a four-wheel-drive vehicle and OnStar guided it via satellite some three miles from the nearest two-track road. The surgeon survived.

Later, he was too distraught to talk about his experience, but his wife wanted to thank OnStar personally. Huber arranged for her to come to one of the monthly meetings where all six hundred OnStar employees get together to discuss the business. He also flew in the 911 operator from upstate Michigan as well as advisers from the call center who handled the episode (they are technically OnStar contractors, not employees). It was the last item on the agenda.

The wife told the people at the meeting, "You gave me my husband back. More importantly, you gave my kids their dad back."

It was an intensely emotional moment. "I got six hundred people who are incredibly analytical," Huber recounts. "They're a bunch of engineers. But after she talks, nobody's looking at each other. Everybody's looking down at their shoes" to avoid showing that their eyes had teared.

"So you look at that and you ask, Did GM ever expect to be in that business? We sure as heck had no clue we were going to be in that business."

Now that OnStar has achieved scale, the rate at which new services are being layered on seems to be accelerating. One of the newest is the ability to track and recover stolen vehicles equipped with OnStar and its GPS capability. OnStar is currently receiving requests to recover seven hundred stolen vehicles a month. "We're learning that your vehicle is most likely going to get stolen at a self-service gas station," Huber explains. "It's a crime of opportunity. People just find you vulnerable and take your car. If you're standing there, they'll push you aside, or if you're on the other side of the car pumping gas, they'll take your car."

To build this service, the OnStar people went to Tom Stevens's power train engineers and persuaded them to tweak the software inside the power train module, the computerized brain that controls the engine and transmission. That quickly allowed OnStar to equip half of the vehicles that GM started selling in the fall of 2008, or about 1.7 million cars and trucks, with the stolen car recovery service.

If a car is stolen, OnStar knows where it is because of the satellite tracking system. It then calls the local police department to report the stolen vehicle. The police can find it quickly because OnStar has told them precisely where it is. Many times, the stolen vehicle is being driven. "So the police are in visual surveillance of the vehicle and they're on the phone with us. They say, 'All right, it is now safe to initiate the slow-down.' We send a digital message. It lodges in the engine control module and takes the horsepower away from the vehicle. So the engine goes to idle mode. The power steering still works, the power brake still works. We put the flashers on outside the car so people around the car know something's going on. And now this car just coasts to a stop. Inside, a nice woman's voice says, 'This vehicle is being slowed at the request of law enforcement. Please pull quietly to the side of the road. They'll be with you shortly.'"

Police departments are thrilled with the service because it helps them avoid high-speed chases. One million vehicles are stolen each year, and the effort to recover them results in thirty thousand high-speed chases. About a quarter of those chases end in accidents, which kill three hundred people, according to OnStar statistics.

OnStar is also working on ways to help emergency response units, whether from fire departments or ambulance corps, know more about what kind of crash they're being asked to respond to. Huber got the idea from Dr. Rick Hunt, who was president of a national association of emergency physicians and head of emergency medicine at the State University of New York in Syracuse. At a conference, he thanked Huber for how OnStar had improved responses of accidents. But then he said, "Just one more thing—tell me about the crash. Tell me how bad the crash was, tell me the angles of the forces, tell me whether the vehicle rolled over or not." Hunt said he needed that information for two reasons. The first was to know what services to dispatch to the scene; if the crash is severe, perhaps an air ambulance should respond, or perhaps an ambulance should bypass a regular hospital and head for a trauma center.

Second, Hunt said, injuries in auto accidents have become more difficult to detect because air bags and other padding and insulation can conceal certain internal injuries from visual inspection. As Huber recalls Hunt saying, "You got no scratches. You got no bruises. You look pretty good. But guess what? Your kidney still ran into your spleen. If I don't test you and you needed it, you bleed to death internally."

So Hunt asked OnStar to create a "digital crash signature" that will be transmitted to emergency response workers from a vehicle that crashes. This signature will reveal whether the vehicle was hit from the side, which makes the human body more susceptible to internal injuries, and disclose other information about the severity of the crash, like whether the vehicle rolled over or not.

Huber went back to GM's vehicle engineers to see what could be done. The company already had installed many sensors in each vehicle to keep track of many functions such as oil level and the stability of the vehicle, so it turned out to be relatively simple to respond to what Hunt was asking for. The engineers said, "We can repurpose all these sensors we're building into these vehicles, and we can read out different data that we would otherwise not use for anything [to] create digital crash signatures." Almost every GM vehicle now has that capability. OnStar is now working with the six thousand different 911 jurisdictions to create a standard based on GM vehicle data that everyone will understand—a necessary step before the service can actually be used on a widespread basis.

One of the gains Wagoner sees from OnStar is its onboard vehicle diagnostics system. OnStar can monitor oil life and other key variables and send e-mails to owners when it is time for service. "That is a huge breakthrough," Wagoner says. "The whole issue is, How do we talk to our customer? They drive off the car lot, and you don't see 'em until they need warranty service or maybe when they need a new car. Now they sign up and every month they get an e-mail telling them the condition of their car. So we get a chance to talk to them monthly. That's a huge deal." It also provides GM with a way to understand how all its vehicles are performing on the road. "We get a chance to monitor the vehicle in a different way for quality reasons," Wagoner explains. "I suspect eventually we'll find different services we'll be able to sell and apply to the vehicle, electronically, without the consumer coming into the showroom. So there are a lot of opportunities there."

GM's R&D arm also has some long-term plans for OnStar. What excites them is the prospect of cars on the road "knowing" where they are because of GPS. This is the dream of having "intelligent highways," where the number of accidents is dramatically reduced.

One vision calls for cars on the road to communicate with a centralized computer network, using technologies like the ones now used in EZ Pass and other toll-paying systems. Each city or state would have to have a standardized system. The rival view, and the one that GM embraces, is this: if two cars both know where they are, they could be engineered to automatically apply brakes or make adjustments in steering to avoid a collision with each other. GM is testing that system at its proving grounds in Milford, Michigan. The test car goes around the track and comes up over a rise and suddenly confronts a stopped vehicle in front of it. It automatically slams on the brakes.

The GM approach to intelligent highways would not require a computer system to be built and would sidestep the thorny issue of making the New York City system work with, say, the New Jersey system. Of course, there are two big caveats here. First, the system would work only if both cars communicate with each other using OnStar's wireless system, and not every car on American roads is likely to have OnStar. Second, there are issues of privacy and driver concern. Many drivers fear and resent having any system that impedes their ability to control their vehicle, even if it is headed into an accident.

"OnStar is essentially a platform of wireless telemetry that is becoming increasingly sophisticated with processing power and memory," Wagoner says. "What we've used it for is this evolution of services that started with an air-bag crash and the door unlocking feature and with the diagnostics and then with the diagnostic e-mails and went to stolen vehicle tracking and then stolen vehicle slowdown."

He also is hopeful that intelligent highways can be built but cautions that it's going to take years to achieve. "One idea is built around putting hardware and sensors in the road," Wagoner says. "What you eventually conclude is that we ain't gonna live long enough for that to happen. The reliability of it has been mixed. But if we begin to build cars that are loaded with sensors for other reasons anyway, then all of a sudden you have the opportunity for the vehicles to govern the intelligence of the system and the feedback to each other."

OnStar is not the only example of technological innovation occurring at GM. Its major R&D efforts these days are directed at alternate propulsion systems, with results still to be determined. But in the meantime, the company has been in the lead with heads-up displays (which show a driver how fast he or she is going by looking at a projected image in the windshield); with keyless ignition systems; with rear-vision cameras to help larger vehicles avoid backing into objects; and with XM satellite radio. (Huber is on the board of the radio unit, which also was set up as a separate subsidiary. It has now merged with Sirius Radio, creating one profitable provider of satellite radio in the place of two struggling ones.)

The OnStar story is now the subject of two Harvard Business School case studies by one of the school's best-regarded professors, Clayton Christensen, author of both *The Innovator's Dilemma* and *The Innovator's Solution.* One of his core notions is about how new technologies and business models "disrupt" older ones. Christensen has long argued that very few established companies can allow disruptive change to occur because they find it threatening to their existing business. "His point of view is that you can count on one hand the number of big companies that have innovated outside of their core business and not killed it," Huber says. "The thing he loves about OnStar as an example is that this would probably have been from one of the least likely corporations you would expect could have done it."

Christensen, in a conversation with me, said he considers OnStar "an extraordinary success by any measure." He says there were several keys to how GM got it right. The first was that Wagoner allowed Huber time to experiment a little and find the right strategy, rather than dictating the strategy from the outset. He let Huber identify what customers really wanted—peace of mind—and then construct a way to give it to them.

"In an established business, it's usually a top-down process," Christensen says. "You get a bunch of smart people, they may be consultants or a top management team, and you develop a plan. You implement a plan." That rarely works, because start-up companies need time to sense what the market really wants. The strategy has to emerge over time. "If

Harry Pearce and Rick Wagoner had said, 'Chet, here's the strategy. Go implement it,' when things went wrong, they would have cut his head off and scuttled the venture," Christensen argues.

A second major factor was the way that Wagoner "stood astride the interface between OnStar and the standard operating procedures of General Motors and was able to make judgment calls about which of GM's processes and standards and ways of working would be imposed on OnStar and which ones it would be allowed to break." Without that intervention by Wagoner, OnStar could not have survived. Third, GM allowed OnStar to be organizationally independent rather than wrapping it into an existing division.

The first couple of years that Christensen used the OnStar case study, Huber would come into the classroom and sit there without being introduced. "I'd just be sitting there," Huber recalls, "and then Professor Christensen would reach the end of the class and he'd say, 'All right, now how many of you guys would have ever put this guy, a locomotive salesman, in his job? Shouldn't he be fired? Let's vote on it—should Chet be fired?' And I'd get fired by all these guys. And then Professor Christensen would say, 'Oh, by the way, I've got an old friend of mine—Chet's here.' "

After years of GM people studying at universities where they were held up as examples of failure, now they're in classrooms where OnStar is being held up as an example of successful innovation. And Christensen himself recently purchased a Saturn Vue equipped with OnStar. Cambridge may never be the same.

CHAPTER 12

China

Where Buick Is King

In 1994, some fifteen years after Deng Xiaoping started opening the country up to the world, GM was nowhere in China. Its only presence there was a small, failing joint venture called Jinbei GM. Other manufacturers, particularly Volkswagen and Chrysler's Jeep, had beaten GM to the market and were enjoying success. Even though the country's highway system was primitive and hundreds of millions of peasants could never buy vehicles, it was becoming clear that an emerging Chinese middle class of perhaps three hundred million people—more than the size of the entire U.S. population—had the money and the desire to purchase cars. For them, cars symbolized independence and the good life. China was shaping up as a critical battleground market. The U.S. and European markets were mature and therefore slow-growing; Japan's market, also mature, was essentially off-limits to the Americans. So whoever could prevail in China would have a leg up in the global car wars.

The GM board, which had several directors with Chinese experience in their own business lives, was questioning whether GM could be truly a global player if it wasn't successful in China in particular and in Asia as a whole. So Jack Smith turned to Rudy Schlais to get GM rolling in China.

Schlais was a highly improbable candidate. He had been working in Warren, Ohio, as a senior executive in charge of Packard Electric (which was later subsumed in the parts company today called Delphi). Typically, parts suppliers, whether company-owned or not, are not where the CEO of General Motors finds executives for high-profile international car assignments. Warren, located just north of Lordstown and northwest of Youngstown, Ohio, was a far cry from China. And Schlais did not speak Chinese or have any ethnic affinity with the East. His grandfather was Swabish, or ethnic German.

But what Schlais had done to attract Smith's attention was to help Packard Electric create a series of three joint ventures and one wholly owned subsidiary in remote towns of China, far outside the major cities. Beginning in 1992, Schlais had started commuting to China to set up those ventures and learned how to drink *maotai*, China's fiery sorghum-based whiskey, and *shaoxing*, a gold-colored rice wine. Being able to drink with Chinese officials had been essential to his success, but obviously Schlais also understood auto parts and international business. The four ventures started blossoming. Schlais's division of Packard had sixty thousand employees, and as a result of his efforts, two thousand of these were in China.

Smith called Schlais and asked him to represent General Motors in China, and he accepted. He opened a small GM office in Beijing in October 1994 with two other professionals and one secretary. "Our support was a portable computer with a fax card," Schlais recalls. "And that was it."

What made it possible for Schlais to be effective was that Smith, Wagoner (then CFO), and others were united in their support. "They wanted China to happen," Schlais explains. "There was no division at the top. What I did was organize a steering committee of people and sit down and say, 'Okay, guys, we need to figure out how to implement this.'"

One of the first things Schlais needed to figure out was the politics at the Ministry of Machinery Industry in Beijing. He knew he was competing against both Ford Motor and Toyota to be the foreign automaker assigned to a joint venture with Shanghai Automotive Industry Corporation (SAIC), which was owned by the Shanghai municipal government, and it was the ministry that would ultimately make the decision. To bring more Chinese expertise onto the GM team, Schlais tapped Bob Rice, who had experience with Alcoa setting up joint ventures in China, and Rick Swando, who had been part of the Jeep project in Beijing.

The ministry had concluded that it wanted a midsize luxury car project allocated to SAIC, which already had a joint venture with Volkswagen. "They didn't want Chevrolet," Schlais recalls. "They perceived it as at the low end of the brands. So we focused [their proposals] on Cadillac and Buick. The Chinese preferred Buick because of the historical associations it had. General Motors did not want Cadillac to go to China. By default, Buick ended up being the brand that we offered."

Although the Buick brand name is not at the top of the popularity charts in the United States, the Chinese attach great value to it, partly because leaders of dramatically different political stripes have owned or used Buicks. Sun Yat-sen, China's first provisional president, who Taiwan claims as the inspiration for its democracy, was once photographed in a 1912 Buick. Pu Yi, the last emperor of China, bought a Buick in 1926. And Chou En-lai, a Communist who became China's premier, also favored Buicks.

To his credit, Schlais proved to be very culturally adept in dealing with the Chinese, says Joseph Tan, a Chinese national who is now manager of Powertrain Planning for GM China. He was an early interpreter for Schlais. "Rudy knew how to make his Chinese counterparts feel that he respected them," Tan explains. "That was essential to building trust. He also knew how to say no to the Chinese in a very Chinese way. He understood how to maneuver within the cultural framework."

Schlais also understood that the Chinese wanted a brand-new car. All the previous foreign joint venture cars, like Volkswagen's Santana, were eight- to ten-year-old vehicles. Those manufacturers obviously were defending their latest designs against the epidemic of copycatting that was raging in China.

So even before a deal was signed, Schlais made it clear that he was willing to engage deeply with its prospective Chinese partner on sensitive issues of design. What GM did was to take a Buick Regal and work with SAIC to implement six hundred changes to make it a Chinese car, which would be manufactured by Shanghai General Motors (SGM), a fifty-fifty joint venture with SAIC. Schlais reasoned correctly that many buyers would have chauffeurs and would want to sit in the backseat. So the designers expanded legroom in the backseat and added more controls for air conditioning and the radio. They also modified the vehicle's suspension so that it could handle China's rougher road conditions. And the engines were modified to be able to run on the higher-sulfur fuels available in China at the time.

More controversial was GM's offer to bring advanced technology to China. The plan was to make electronically controlled automatic transmissions and other sophisticated parts, and also to create an engineering joint venture called the Pan Asia Technical Automotive Center (PATAC), which would, in effect, teach the Chinese how to design vehicles and power trains. The American media scolded GM for even considering transferring the technology to the joint venture. "The foreign concept had been, 'Don't give them anything,'" Schlais explains. "But we thought the market was going to be so huge that you had to have world-class technology to compete."

Jack Smith supported Schlais, in part by going to China six times in 1996 to meet Chinese president Jiang Zemin and other top leaders. As Schlais explains it, "I would call up Mr. Smith and say, 'Jack, we got an issue, and we need to get over this issue, and the only way we're going to do it is if you personally come.' He would grumble and moan about his schedule, then he'd say, 'I'm coming.' That was extremely impressive to the Chinese."

For his part, Wagoner supported allocating the funds that Schlais was seeking, even though Schlais said some of his proposals were "very sketchy" by GM standards in terms of the rate of return on investment. "Without Rick's support, I don't think the General Motors finance organization would have been as supportive of this type of a gamble, a speculative venture," Schlais says. "Hell, you didn't know whether anybody in China would change their mind, or whether the world economy would go south."

But the strategy mapped out by Schlais worked. In 1996, GM was chosen as the partner to continue on the project. Even before the central government formally signed off, contractors started work on clearing property for a plant in the Pudong section of Shanghai. This area is across the Huangpu River from the Bund, the series of buildings built by European colonizers. Up until about 1990, Pudong was just a swath of marsh with a few fishing villages. But the Chinese have transformed it into a huge residential, financial, and industrial complex. To build the GM joint venture plant, the residents of Shanghai cleared out six towns that were on the property and started driving pilings to erect the new factory by January 1997. Formal approval came in late March. GM and SAIC each put up $375 million to fund Shanghai GM and PATAC, the engineering joint venture.

Commercial production of the first Buicks started in April 1999, with three models called the GL, GLX, and Xin Shi Ji rolling off the line. The joint venture quickly became profitable. Schlais had left China in 1998 to take responsibility for the whole Asia-Pacific theater for GM but remained chairman of Shanghai GM until he retired in 2002. The seeds he sowed in China obviously bore fruit: China is GM's second largest market after the United States. The company's technology has been protected. And the story of how GM established itself in China, and the broader Asia-Pacific region outside of Japan, is revealing of how quickly the company can move when it is able to focus its strengths on a common objective.

It wasn't always a smooth path. Philip Murtaugh, who took over from Schlais, managed GM's operations in China for five years of solid growth and then quit in 2005 for what were called "personal reasons." He worked for SAIC for a period of time before jumping to Chrysler's international operations. Obviously, something went wrong in his relationship with GM; most likely, he chafed at having to report to GM's Asia-Pacific headquarters, also based in Shanghai, rather than straight to headquarters. He was replaced by Kevin Wale, an Australian with many years of experience in GM's international operations.

No matter who is in charge now, GM's relationship with SAIC has blossomed into its most important such venture in the world; the China market could one day be bigger than the U.S. market. "What they've done here is pretty remarkable," says Michael Dunne, managing director of J.D. Power's China operations.

Dunne notes that every foreign automaker has been obliged by the government to enter joint ventures with Chinese entities and that most of them suffer from the syndrome that the Chinese describe as "sleeping in the same bed, but dreaming different dreams." Chinese automakers want to learn how to make cars that they can sell in international markets; the foreign automakers want to use the relationships to expand sales in China while preventing the emergence of Chinese competitors. Because of that inherent conflict, Dunne says, many of the joint ventures are "knock-down, drag-out affairs." But the GM-SAIC relationship has been "the most amicable" of them.

GM, having invested roughly $4 billion, is on track to sell 500,000 passenger vehicles through SGM this year and another 500,000 small commercial vehicles through another joint venture with SAIC called SAIC-GM-Wuling, located in a remote southern part of the country. J.D. Power, which tracks automotive sales, counts only GM's sales through the Shanghai joint venture and excludes the output of the Wuling joint venture, because GM owns only 34 percent of that. But Dunne acknowledges that if commercial sales are included, GM is the largest foreign seller of vehicles in China, and almost all those vehicles are assembled there. Partly because of historical associations, GM is selling more Buicks in China today than in the United States. GM is putting down very deep roots in China.

From GM China headquarters in the towering Jin Mao Building, you travel about forty-five minutes to get to the Shangai GM plant in Pudong, past huge apartment complexes and sprawling industrial parks. Flags representing the United States, China, and Shanghai GM fly from flagpoles in front of a fountain with jets of spraying water. In the lobby showroom are the Chevy Lova and Chevy Aveo (both based on models from GM's Korean affiliate, GM Daewoo Auto & Technology Unit). Also there are three Buicks—the Excelle, the LaCrosse Eco-Hybrid, and the Park Avenue—and a big Cadillac called the SLS that is an extended version of the Cadillac STS, made especially for the bling-bling end of the Chinese market.

There are some hints that different standards apply here than at GM plants in North America or Europe; after all, it is a joint venture, and GM can't dictate policies. The grass outside is uncut and safety standards for visitors are relaxed. Visitors do not have to watch safety videos, nor don safety glasses or protective covering for watches and belt buckles. The discipline of walking inside painted lines on the factory floor so that pedestrians avoid getting hit by parts trolleys is loose; I dodge the vehicles and they dodge me. And the area where finished cars go through a water check is wet; I slip and nearly take a tumble.

But the essential manufacturing process is a blend of what I've seen at GM in North America and Europe. The plant is shaped like a T, just like the Brazilian plant and U.S. plants like Delta Township. Workers are organized in teams and are urged to embrace kaizen, or continuous improvement. The same andon cords with the scoreboard-style screen are overhead. What clearly come from Opel plants are the German-made automated guided vehicles delivering engines and transmissions to the line. The car bodies are on an overhead line, and the AGVs line up their cargo precisely and then push upward to perform the "marriage." That's much simpler than the method of lifting the engine into the car that I saw at Fairfax.

One other variation on a theme is that the parts resupply vehicles don't automatically and wirelessly receive information about materials that are needed; at this plant, workers push a green button that wirelessly communicates the information. And unlike American factories, here it is exclusively men on the factory floor. The average age is about thirty, and all the workers wear white shirts and blue pants. Women are present in the plant but only on the quality inspection line.

I'm walking the trim line in General Assembly with Jin Zheng, forty, a group leader who has thirty people reporting to him in three groups. He's likable, a jokester; he says his English name is Money King, a play on the translation of his name. Jin has been with GM Shanghai for ten years and has visited the Tech Center in Warren on four occasions. He understands some English, but we communicate mostly through an interpreter. Jin understands the origins of what he's doing with lean manufacturing. "America learned it from Toyota and China learned it from America," he says in Chinese. "But the source is the same."

He believes he and his colleagues are making cars better than anyone else in China. "We learned the thinking. That's the reason the Japanese have been a success." Like most Chinese, he realizes the Japanese have a huge advantage at the moment, but it is an article of faith among the Chinese that one day they will overcome Japan. That's highly debatable, but it's what most Chinese believe. "In the future, we can get as much success as Toyota," says Jin. Ironically, he does not have a driver's license and therefore does not own a car, preferring to take a shuttle bus to work.

Jin was born in 1969, at the height of the Cultural Revolution. How does he trace the arc of his life, from the Maoist purges to working for a joint venture that's related to one of the world's largest capitalistic companies? "People are now focused on economics, not politics," he answers. That is, in fact, what the whole country seems to be doing; its economy has been growing at 9 to 10 percent for many years.

One worker with a particularly dramatic story is Zhao Qingjie, a big, beefy forty-five-year-old group leader with a thin mustache. He's carrying a walkie-talkie as he sits down at a table in a conference room just off the entrance to the plant. He has thirty-four people reporting to him in four teams. They have responsibilities in the Chassis, Engines, and Interiors departments. He's making a base salary of about 3,500 RMB a month, or more than $500 U.S., average for his position.

Zhao was born in Pudong when it was nothing more than agricultural land with a few fishing villages. There was no mass transit, nor were there bridges or tunnels to Shanghai proper, on the other side of the Huangpu River. "If you wanted to buy anything, you needed to get coupons from the government," he recalls, speaking in Chinese. "You had to stand in long lines to get those, and then you could bike to the markets and get vegetables or eggs." It was a life filled with *kun nan*—hardships—with difficulty in getting enough food to eat and securing adequate shelter.

But after having worked for Shanghai GM for eleven years, including some time at a supplier in Shenyang in northern China, Zhao has been able to make strides in his lifestyle that once would have been unimaginable. He bought a Buick Excelle station wagon, which cost him 89,000 RMB or about $13,000 after a 25 percent discount. (Interestingly, Buicks Excelles are equipped with manual transmissions because those are cheaper than automatic transmissions and Chinese prefer to save the money.) He was also able to afford a license plate, which is very expensive in a crowded city like Shanghai, with some fifteen million residents. The plates cost anywhere from 30,000 to 50,000 RMB, or roughly $4,200 to $7,000.

Plus, Zhao and his wife were able to buy a thousand-square-foot apartment with two bedrooms, and his wife no longer has to work. This is a great luxury in a country where the vast majority of women have had to find jobs to help sustain their families. Being a housewife is a statement of success. To top it off, the Zhaos recently purchased a golden retriever, which involves another stiff fee for a license.

The old days of getting ration coupons and then riding his bike to buy food are a distant memory. "Now it's dramatically changed," Zhao remarks. "It used to take me an hour to get from one place to another by bike. Now it's twenty minutes by car."

It's one thing to assemble cars. It's quite another to design and engineer them. But the Chinese are trying to master these functions at the second joint venture between GM and SAIC, called PATAC, which is also located in a brand-spanking-new building in Pudong. Of the 1,600 people who work there, just 35 of them are American, German, or other foreign nationals.

After having spent so much time with designers in Detroit, I'm intrigued to meet Burt Wong, who is thirty-five. He's from Guangzhou, the capital of the southern province of Guangdong, and he lights up when I say hello to him in his native Cantonese. (Regional identifications are very strong in China, perhaps stronger than in the United States. Americans may have different accents but they speak the same English; the Chinese speak different languages that are mutually unintelligible.)

There aren't many Cantonese speakers living in Shanghai, but Wong came north to go to college and started his automotive career in 1998. Aside from his native tongue, he speaks English and Mandarin, the national language.

Wong, a small, bespectacled man with a wisp of a beard, did not have to rebel against his family's wishes to become an automotive designer, as so many others did. "In my family, there was no one who had any relationship with designers or artists," Wong says in a conference room on the first floor. His father, now retired, was a worker and his mother an accountant. "They did not believe I could achieve it." Still, he says, "My family gave me the freedom of choice to find what I wanted to do."

Wong says that designing cars in China is just the same as anywhere else. "You create from your feeling of the culture and your knowledge of people's lives," he says. "Chinese designers don't lack creativity." This seems to be a sore point—Chinese designers feel they are struggling for respect in the international design community because they haven't had much experience and lack conspicuous hit designs in world markets.

Wong was the chief designer for adapting the Buick LaCrosse to the Chinese market. His team took the existing architecture and amended both the interior and exterior. The Chinese market wanted a "grand and elegant" car that was as sophisticated as a Lexus and as sleek as a Jaguar. They wanted more "fullness," Wong says. They wanted a grander statement on the front and rear ends of the vehicle. So Wong and his fellow designers accentuated the waterfall grille on the front of the car (vertical strips of chrome that resemble water falling) to make it look wider. Wong calls this "the jewelry effect."

Making the backseat more spacious and luxurious was important for the Chinese market, and there is a slightly different aesthetic regarding interior designs and colors. "Material harmony is important for the Asian customer," Wong explains. "The Asian customer is more sensitive to the harmony of the tones and to the touches. You want a peaceful environment." The differences between a Western interior and a Chinese one are subtle. The key difference seems to be that the colors inside a Chinese car are in a narrower range than those in an American car, meaning that the colors blend together better. The sense of harmony and peace inside the car may be more important to the Chinese because of the intense traffic and urban chaos that exists just outside the car.

Wong uses the same design vocabulary as GM designers I've met in the States and Europe; whatever their cultural differences, they have a common language. Much in the way an American or European designer would discuss his or her market, Wong says the Chinese like more sophisticated cars that are Lexus-like; other times they want the fullness that a Jaguar communicates; they also want grander front ends and rear ends. Their "perception of quality" is important, he adds.

Wong has met and shaken hands with Wagoner during the CEO's seven visits to PATAC. "He spends an hour in the studio and wants to see all the future products," Wong explains. And it's clear that Wong wants to move from adapting designs for China to creating designs for world markets. Chinese movies and drama are beginning to win viewers all over the world, so Wong thinks it's only a matter of time before Chinese auto designs will win acceptance too. "The opportunity is open," he says.

Elsewhere in PATAC, a sprawling building complex that is separate from SGM, rooms are filled with young Chinese staring at the screens of high-speed computers showing parts intended for the Chinese version of the Buick Epsilon II, scheduled to go to market in late 2008. They may not be full GM employees, but they are plugged into the company's global design and engineering systems. This is a sensitive area of collaboration. The Chinese want the latest technology and engineering know-how. And, like the designers, the engineers have big ambitions. Lu Xiao, thirty-six, a graduate of Shanghai University of Engineering Science, is putting in sixteen-hour days working on the Buick Epsilon II launch because the Chinese market is so important for GM and for this particular model.

The Chinese have an abundance of young engineering and mathematical talent, and they have a knack for analyzing three-dimensional images of parts, possibly because their minds are trained to recognize shapes as they memorize thousands of Chinese characters. So Lu sees it as just a matter of time before PATAC gains stature inside GM. "We have to acknowledge that Warren and Rüsselsheim are one step beyond us," Lu says. "But PATAC is moving up, and we are just one step behind them. I think we'll be catching up with them very quickly. We'll be there in five years."

GM's relationship with SAIC has brought another major benefit: it helped the joint venture establish a retail network of 1,600 dealers in all thirty-one provinces for the Buick, Chevy, Cadillac, and Saab brand names. In the early days, the market was for bigger Buicks, which were bought by businesses for the use of their senior officials and executives. But now more individual Chinese families are buying cars, and the demand seems to be shifting toward cars for the masses: smaller Buicks like the Excelle and smaller, more affordable vehicles from Chevrolet. GM has adapted Chevy's advertising tagline from "An American Revolution," which would make absolutely no sense in China, to "Advancing with You."

As for Cadillac, I'm surprised to see a brand-new CTS on Nanjing Lu, the major shopping avenue that runs from the Bund into the heart of Shanghai. This car was made in the United States, and the price tag in China would be well over fifty thousand dollars, including import duties. The Caddy marketing tagline "Life, Liberty, and the Pursuit" again would make no sense in China, so GM has devised this one: "Believe, Create, Possess."

Cadillacs have not taken off, though. Their designs have a masculine quality to them, and Chinese women are deeply involved in family decisions about car-buying, maybe more so than in the United States. The vast majority of families have only one car, so it has to be something that women feel comfortable driving. Cadillac is also up against entrenched competition from BMW, Mercedes, and Audi, which have big positions in the Chinese market. Saab is still quite small.

To get a taste of the retail end of GM's operations, I paid a visit to Hanson Yang, the co-owner and board chairman of Shanghai Pacific HongQiao Auto Trade, which owns two Buick dealerships as well as a variety of BMW, Audi, VW, Toyota, Honda, and Nissan dealerships. The dealer networks in China appear to be more dominated by bigger players than in the United States, and the players tend to control multiple brands more often than their American counterparts.

As I enter the dealership on Wuzhong Road, two young women bow and say "Good morning" in English. I'm escorted past a plush customer waiting area, where a young lady in a short skirt will prepare any of a variety of teas for waiting customers, then past an area where customers can use personal computers and a room where customers can play pool. It's plush beyond belief, but all the amenities suggest that customers spend a fair amount of time at the dealership having their cars serviced.

Yang is waiting for me in a fancy conference room with dark wood and pictures of Rick Wagoner on the walls. Wagoner was present for the official inauguration of the dealership, and Yang proudly shows a video clip of Wagoner cutting a red ribbon in a ceremony that included a dragon dance. It's lunchtime, so Yang serves me pizza from Pizza Hut.

Yang, forty-seven, is one of the private-sector entrepreneurs who are making millions of dollars in China today. He was an official in the Education Bureau in the Shanghai Municipality but in the late 1980s made his *xia hai*, or "descent into the sea," a uniquely Chinese expression for leaving the state-owned sector and going into business for oneself. His brother had gotten a head start selling trucks, and the two of them together were able to secure a dealership for VW Santanas. Yang actually rode his bike to the dealership to sell cars. Now they are wealthy men.

I ask him what Chinese consumers think about the differences between foreign brands. "The Japanese and Germans are more focused on details," he explains in Chinese. "The Japanese are more focused on fuel efficiency. Their territory is so small that they have to be conscious of their resources."

But his customers obviously have a soft spot for American cars. "When people first came out to buy an American car like Buick, they saw a connection to the American culture—the country on wheels," he says. "A lot of Chinese people are chasing the American dream."

Sales at his Buick dealership are down about 10 percent from last year, but Yang says that is typical of what is happening throughout the Chinese car industry, with the exception of Toyota, which is doing well this year. The Chinese are encountering some shock waves from the American financial collapse, and their exporters are worried that the Americans will not be able to continue buying an avalanche of Chinese-made televisions, computers, shoes, clothing, and other goods. Car and housing sales began to encounter some headwinds in late 2008.

But the country has huge momentum and is still expecting 8 percent growth in its gross national product this year, partly because the Chinese government is sitting on $2 trillion in foreign exchange reserves and clearly can spend some of that to prop up growth. The Chinese may have to adapt to new economic realities, but it's widely assumed that they'll be able to do it and that auto sales will continue on their long-term upward trajectory.

There are other industry-specific reasons why Buick sales were soft. VW was an official sponsor of the Olympics and gained some sales momentum from that. Because of rising fuel prices, Toyota and Honda have gained ground with vehicles that got better mileage. Toyota, in fact, passed GM in passenger vehicles sold but still lags in total sales. Buick also was caught in a trough in the cycle of product introductions, and that costs sales in any market. It started to fix that in late 2008 by introducing the new Buick based on the Epsilon architecture. And it was planning two new models for 2009. "Right now is a critical time," says Michael Dunne of J.D. Power. But Yang is not worried. "I'm pretty sure the market will continue developing," he says.

Sharing that view is a customer. Shuanghui Liao, vice president of East Money Information, a start-up company that is the biggest online provider of financial information to individual Chinese investors. He bought a black Buick GL seven years ago and has put about ninety thousand miles on it. Liao, who is now thirty-two, is wearing a knit shirt, and his cell phone and other devices keep erupting. He's a young man in a hurry, another representative of China's private sector entrepreneurs. He's pleased with his Buick. "The car is still in very good condition," he explains. "I don't want to get a new one."

Having owned a Nissan previously, Liao says he is "kind of frustrated" with Japanese cars but feels that "the brand perception of Buick is growing rapidly." One of the Buick marketing lines that worked for him was "Be confident and still stay humble." He would never buy a Cadillac because he feels that would make him a "show-off." So the Buick is just right. "I can feel a sense of generous proportions and the quality is reliable because it comes from a big company like GM," he explains. "I don't need to worry about technology from GM because I really trust the technical ability of GM." He's irritated that his car doesn't have a cup holder, and he'd like to find a car eventually that has a device to heat water so that he can make tea while in the car. But for now, he's sticking with Buick. Hundreds of thousands of other Chinese are, too.

One sign of the depth of GM's commitment to China is its creation of a whole network of Chinese suppliers. Bo Andersson, the former Swedish military officer in charge of GM's purchasing, is the mastermind of this effort. GM China has 685 people, including 200 expatriates. But Andersson has another 250 people spread around the country, who "piggyback" on GM China but largely operate separately and report to him.

Andersson and his people are reaching deep into the provinces to try to find and develop entrepreneurs who can build parts for GM, in China and around the world. "We now have a third of our people in Beijing, a third in Shanghai, and a third in Guangzhou," he explains. "But now we are moving a lot of people into the countryside to find local entrepreneurs, help them develop a business model, and give them scale."

The scale already is significant. "Last year, we bought one million components in China for our domestic [American] needs," he explains. And Andersson's network exported roughly $2 billion worth of parts from China to GM's global operations, including its plants elsewhere in Asia. "I've been working extremely hard in China," Andersson says.

The top three categories of parts coming from China are aluminum wheels (some 50 percent of GM's global supply of these wheels is coming from China), chromed parts, and electronics and radios. "If you take twenty-two-inch wheels, they cost a hundred bucks each, and the transportation is seventeen dollars," Andersson explains. "Radios also cost a hundred bucks, but the transportation costs are two dollars. The first time we shipped a radio from Shanghai, it was five dollars. What I said to my people is that the best way to get good at something is to do a lot of it. When you ship a lot of radios from China, you figure how to do it a smarter way."

Of course, part of the reason Andersson wants to buy from local entrepreneurs is price. If he buys parts from Bosch or Lear or Johnson

Controls, large companies that manufacture parts in China, he has to pay them a standard global price. But if he can work directly with Chinese suppliers, he gets them for less.

But he also seems to be building up the suppliers for long-term strategic reasons. One example is GM's work with Yintai Jiang, president and owner of Shanghai Daimay, which makes more than five million sun visors for GM a year. "It's a great business for them," says Andersson. "It's a privately held company, and he loves our business. He helped us to reduce a hundred-plus categories of sun visors to four families. Secondly, he's now doing steering wheels for us and doing the same type of transformation. When I go there, it's a very well run company, and he as an entrepreneur is extremely proud."

Andersson says he is building "future leaders." "It may take us ten years to develop them, but we'd rather do that and have loyal suppliers for the rest of our life," he says. "Our strategy is based on the fact that we are willing to do a lot of work with people who have the right mindset and the right culture and the right cost structure, versus just sourcing from China. What we're doing is much more difficult, but the payoff is much better, and the loyalty from these suppliers is very different." He also seems to be laying the groundwork for more ambitious plans than merely cracking the Chinese market.

GM faces many challenges in China. One is the cultural challenge inside GM China itself, which is a mix of different cultures. Some Chinese working there have had education or work experience in the United States; these returnees are jokingly called *hai gui*, or sea turtles, after the ones that come in from the sea to lay their eggs. Having absorbed American styles of management and conflict resolution, to varying degrees they feel a cultural gap with Chinese who have never left the country. The local Chinese, meanwhile, feel that there is a glass ceiling inside GM China. But the fact is that, in general, the dramatic gap in experience and culture leaves them without the skills and experience to move up.

Many of the Americans who work there are on their first overseas assignments and speak little or no Chinese. These Americans tend to want yes or no answers to many questions, whereas the Chinese are willing to tolerate greater ambiguity. There's also a sprinkling of Australians, Brits, and people of other nationalities. Wale, the president of GM China, is an Australian who has been posted to Australia, Detroit, Canada, New York, Singapore, Britain, and now China for the past three and a half years. Even though the cultures are complex, GM China's makeup is broadly consistent with all the major multinationals operating in China, and it appears to work.

A second challenge is dealing with the joint venture partner, SAIC. Some of GM China's people are assigned to Shanghai GM or PATAC in an attempt to influence the decision making in those ventures. But they cannot seek to control them outright because that would irritate SAIC, which owns a 50 percent stake in each. Neither GM nor SAIC is a majority owner, so they are condemned to cooperate.

Altogether, SAIC has fifty to sixty different joint ventures with different foreign partners. The essential Chinese strategy has been to draw in major multinationals and attempt to absorb technology, management know-how, and all the ingredients of global business success. In the automotive sector, the government has been leaning on SAIC and other domestic manufacturers to innovate and come out with their own products. So SAIC has been mining its joint ventures for talent and ideas; it hired some Chinese employees away from its joint ventures with GM, and that has been sensitive. At the end of the day, technology is in the minds of people, and when those people change jobs, some technology goes with them.

GM does not appear to be naive about SAIC's intentions to launch its own products that might compete against GM's. "GM has its eyes wide open," says Dunne of J.D. Power. "They are not babes wandering in the woods." Adds Wale: "SAIC wants to be a very successful global automotive company. They've got products on the streets. They're doing it already. We've known that from day one."

The essential game that GM must play is transferring enough technology and training enough engineers so that SAIC feels it is advancing, but doing that without giving away any crown jewels. And at the same time, GM itself has to keep moving ahead. "Our task is to continue to innovate faster than all our competitors, whether foreign or Chinese," says Wale.

Dunne believes that China's state-owned auto companies may never be able to achieve their dream of designing and engineering their own products for global markets. There are too many car brands in China— fifty-one—and the Chinese manufacturers all operate at the provincial or municipal level. That means the central government in Beijing cannot consolidate them into a handful of national champions that have greater bargaining power with the foreign automakers like GM. "The hoped-for transfer of technology from the globals to the locals hasn't happened," Dunne says.

Another possible competitive to GM threat comes from privately held Chinese companies that are announcing big plans to go into the auto business. The best-known is Chery, which settled an intellectual property case with GM out of court. Neither side will discuss it, but it appears that Chery misappropriated some of GM's designs. Other private companies that have announced automotive ambitions include Geely, Brilliance, and BYD, the maker of batteries. But the cost of entry into the automotive business, and the sheer sophistication that is required, means that any Chinese company is five to ten years away from being able to compete outside China, if indeed any of these Chinese companies can get the formula right. So for now, it appears that GM will be able to continue expanding in China without giving rise to direct competitors.

A bigger question perhaps is whether GM can stay ahead of Toyota in the Chinese market, which is now emerging as a hot battleground between them. The way J.D. Power measures it, Toyota sold 327,536 vehicles from January through July 2008, compared to the 300,509 Shanghai GM sold. Toyota, which has two joint venture partners, does not do as much design and engineering in China, which will be essential to its long-term success. It does not have as big a distribution network as GM has. It also suffers from a liability of history—at least some Chinese have negative attitudes toward the Japanese because of Japan's occupation of China and brutalities in Nanking and elsewhere.

But Toyota has vast resources and could pour more of them into China. Everyone involved in GM's China operations, from Wagoner on down, is aware of what Toyota is doing in China, and they seem determined to maintain their lead. That's why the product introductions scheduled for late 2008 and 2009 are so important.

The question that seems most intriguing is, How extensively will GM use its China operations to compete in North America? Right now, it is exporting parts to other GM plants in Asia and some to the United States. But there is the potential for many more components and much more designing and engineering. The Chinese working at GM's joint ventures feel that one day they will be able to design and engineer cars for the U.S. market and manufacture them as well.

Harvard's Clayton Christensen, who says he has regular conversations with Wagoner, argues that GM should use its Chinese and Korean operations to "disrupt" Toyota in North America, by introducing products that are cheaper than anything Toyota can make. "Finally now they recognize, 'Oh, my gosh, This is what Toyota did to us,'" Christensen argues. "They came in it at the bottom of the market with these rusty little vehicles and then they went upmarket. The next disruptors were the Koreans, Hyundai and Kia. They already have stolen the bottom of the market from Toyota. It's not that Toyota was asleep at the switch. Why would they ever invest to defend the bottom end when they have the privilege to invest against Mercedes with their Lexus? The Koreans are now what Toyota was in 1980."

GM's operations in China could be "the next wave of disruptors," Christensen argues. "Right now, they frame those businesses as serving the Chinese market. But within three or four years, they'll come back into the United States. It's exactly the right thing for them to do." Company spokesmen are cautious about any such plans because they would have explosive implications for remaining UAW workers at U.S. plants. The spokesmen note that GM has its hands full keeping up with the demand for its products in China and that Chinese-made vehicles would have to rise to a higher level of quality to compete in the United States.

It seems unlikely that GM would simply shut down all its American plants unless it were undergoing extreme trauma. But the economic logic of relying more heavily on China to compete against Toyota in North America is compelling. To do that, Chinese designers and engineers would have to keep improving their skills, and the SGM joint venture would have to improve the level of its manufacturing, which is not quite at U.S. or European or Japanese levels. But clearly, the Chinese have the ambition to become global players. They just might do it through General Motors.

However GM ultimately uses its China platform, the fact of the matter is that China has emerged as a source of profit for GM at a time when it has lost spectacular amounts of money in the United States. Had it not been for the profitability of its China operations, GM would have felt its profit and cash crunch in North America much more acutely.

GM's China operations thus have emerged as a kind of Rorschach test of who and what GM really is. Is it still an American company? Or has it become untethered from its American roots and truly gone global?

CHAPTER 13

The Global GM

In many ways, GM has been on the receiving end of globalization. Free trade has allowed foreign companies—from Japan and Germany in particular—to sell their automobiles in the United States. Meanwhile, Detroit's Big Three have been specifically disinvited from the Japanese market. In the 1950s, the State Department asked American automakers to leave the country to allow Japan's own automakers to grow and expand so that Japan's economy would be strong enough to support the political system the Americans hoped would take root. That market has remained substantially closed to American automakers, despite years of trade negotiations. As late as 2007, Daimler AG, the most successful importer of cars to Japan, had just 1.4 percent of the market. (The German market is much more open—both GM and Ford have significant presences there.)

In the mid-1980s, amid tensions in Washington over the lopsided trade deficit with Japan, American state governors started to entertain the notion of inviting the Japanese automakers to locate factories in their states; to them, it seemed like a way to ease the trade gap and create jobs at home. Many in the auto industry acquiesced, thinking that if the Japanese opened factories in the United States, they would have the same cost structures and the same problems with organized labor. Governors threw hundreds of millions of dollars in tax incentives at the Japanese to persuade them to locate plants in their states.

Obviously, Honda, Nissan, Toyota, and others surprised those who believed they would not be able to operate at a lower cost structure than Detroit's Big Three could. They located in mostly southern states—like Kentucky, Tennessee, South Carolina, Mississippi, and Texas—that didn't embrace unionism. They hired younger workers who required fewer benefits, and proceeded to use those transplants to increase the competitive pressure on Detroit, not lessen it. At the same time, GM was making only incremental moves to expand internationally. The playing field was decidedly lopsided.

GM did place some bets on the global game starting in the 1920s, such as the acquisition of Opel in Germany, but the far-flung acquisitions were never integrated into a coherent whole. Following the Sloan model, they continued to operate as essentially separate national and regional companies. GM's intense global push of the past ten years has come late in the game. Yet when a company of GM's size wholeheartedly embraces a vision of globalization, it has huge power and impact. Hundreds of thousands of people, perhaps millions, are feeling the shock waves, for better or worse. Certainly the Chinese are feeling it for the better.

The story of how GM has globalized, and continues to globalize, is part and parcel of one of the most complete reorganizations of a major corporation in modern history. Consider four examples explored earlier in this book. First was manufacturing know-how. It took a Canadian, Tom LaSorda, to work with colleagues of many nationalities to test and roll out GMS, a philosophy borrowed from the Japanese; the successful dry run was accomplished in East Germany with East German workers. Then the techniques were refined in Brazil and Argentina before they were rolled into the American plants. Many Germans were involved, as were many Japanese advisers. GM's adoption of the Toyota system, and improvement upon it, is a textbook example of globalization. It's hard to say whether that process has been good or bad; it created dramatically better quality and reliability for American consumers and at the same time forced huge disruptions for GM management and labor, resulting in dozens of factories being closed.

Second was design. The Camaro was designed by a Korean, engineered in Australia, and manufactured in Canada. It was a Nigerian who came up with the winning design for the Chevy Volt. Third, many non-Americans are in senior positions at GM—Andersson of Sweden and Weber of Germany—and many first- or second-generation Americans, like Posawatz and Manoogian, have been involved in GM's transformation drive. And last, GM's expansion in China, and potential use of that country as a platform for other markets, is also important. Yet these four examples are just one piece of the equation. Globalization is at work inside GM at almost every level.

Ed Welburn, from the outskirts of Philly, has led GM's charge toward globalization of design. All the design for the Corvette and Cadillac brand names is still done in North America, as it is for larger trucks, such as pickups and SUVs. But for the rest of the models, design has become a truly international process, with projects and designers assigned almost everywhere GM operates. "We tell designers, 'Come work for GM—you can see the world,'" Welburn says. "We move people around to get just the right group of people, the right knowledge, and then we share that knowledge."

Welburn had his first international living experience when he worked for about a year in GM's design studio in Rüsselsheim, some ten years ago. "It was interesting because it was during the World Cup, and there were twenty-nine nations represented in that design studio," he recalls. "There was always somebody to cheer for, whatever team was playing."

In that era, it was a small studio, concentrating on Opel designs for Europe. Welburn has now turned it into GM's global design center for midsize and compact cars, as well as for all of GM's interior designs. Why choose the Germans for this? "I think all of the teams are good, but in a different way," Welburn explains, sitting at Cipriani's in New York. "I think when we were really struggling on the interior design, the team in Rüsselsheim had the lead in doing good interiors. We learned a lot from them [about attention to detail and materials]," he says. "The interiors in North America were pretty good, but it was not the priority. We didn't put our best people on it. We didn't have a real good understanding of doing quality interiors."

Germans also are strong on midsize cars because the European market, where gasoline costs as much as nine dollars a gallon, is dominated by vehicles much smaller than those in the United States. Simply put, the Germans are better at midsize cars because that's what their affluent, highly discriminating drivers buy.

Korea is even better at the smallest cars, and that's why GM's design "homeroom" for those vehicles is located there. GM had a long, tortured history with Daewoo and its legendary founder Kim Woo-Choong, the former shirt salesman who created one of South Korea's largest industrial groups. But after Kim was disgraced in a financial scandal and lost control of his empire, GM was able to buy key parts of the bankrupt Daewoo Automotive Unit, giving birth to GM Daewoo Automotive. In North America, "designers could sketch small cars all day long, but frankly, we have not done a good job designing small cars in North America, ever," Welburn says. "The team in Korea, that's what they do. That's what they understand. You let the experts do what they do best." The Chevy Aveo, now in the U.S. market, is one of the best examples of what GM Daewoo has created.

Australia is the homeroom for modestly priced rear-wheel-drive sedans, because its automotive culture is very similar to America's, owing to its wide-open spaces and scant population. "They've got a great history of doing that work," says Welburn. "We transferred the [Camaro] project to Australia, and they engineered it with great passion and enthusiasm down there." In his words, the Australian team did the "productionizing" of the vehicle, turning it from a design into something that could be physically assembled. Small trucks are designed in Brazil, where vehicles of that size are widely used in agriculture and business.

What Welburn's reorganization means is that there are fewer Americans working at GM design jobs in America than there were ten years ago. But much energy has been injected into GM's overall design program, because designers from all over the world are competing to win—and the fruits of that competition are tasted by American consumers. After the market fell so precipitously in the second quarter of 2008, for example, the company was able to turn to its overseas operations to find the Cruze, a compact car with a two-tier grille, which was developed in Europe and Asia. It will be manufactured in Lordstown, Ohio. This is a case in which consumers and workers both will benefit from GM's global design reach.

GM's globalization effort is complicated by the fact that much of the company's design and engineering work is "distributed," meaning that design and engineering centers around the world can see what other teams are doing courtesy of the information technology system that Ralph Szygenda has built.

The logistics are astounding. A complete vehicle, including specifications, consumes approximately two hundred gigabytes of memory, the equivalent of two full library floors of academic journals, or ten thousand trees made into paper and printed. According to Szygenda, this data is transmitted at speeds up to fifty times as fast as the standard U.S. home connection. The initial transmission of a complete vehicle from the United States to Europe takes twelve hours. After different GM design and engineering sites get the models, any changes are synchronized overnight so that all the people working on a vehicle can see the latest version. Approximately 125,000 files are shipped around the world each night.

That's what allows the kind of cooperation that is taking place on the new Buick Epsilon, which was expected to launch in late 2008. The Koreans were in charge of the interior, the Americans were designing the exterior, and Germans were doing the power train. Germans such as Sylke Rosenplaenter had the ultimate responsibility because Rüsselsheim is the homeroom for midsize cars. Shanghai GM and PATAC were also involved, because getting the product right for China was critically important. Americans from Fairfax will be manufacturing the car in the United States, so they are also in the loop.

But there is a human challenge in persuading people of different nationalities in different time zones to cooperate smoothly. For Rosenplaenter, *balance* is a very important word, both at home and at work. She has two sons, Max, five, and Tom, three, so in the afternoon, she tries to get home at five P.M. "When I'm with my children, I'm there one hundred percent." After the kids go to bed, though, she goes back to her Lotus Notes e-mail and works late into the evening, catching up on work-related correspondence from different time zones.

Part of her job is reconcile differences among people in different countries who are fighting for their particular power train, say, versus people who are fighting for a particular exterior design that may not be fully compatible. "Someone has to balance," she says.

The cross-cultural experimentation, in her case, started around 2002, when staffers across the globe began holding "net meetings" on the GM intranet. Participants would share computer screens, meaning they could look at the same images or pictures even though they were not in face-to-face contact. "It was very uncomfortable at first," she recalls. "If you can't see someone, you can't tell if he is hesitating."

Over time, the tools have become more sophisticated, and different players have been able to travel to each other's design and engineering centers to begin establishing personal relationships, an essential lubricant. The most intense part of Rosenplaenter's day is between eleven A.M. and two P.M., because that's when she can be on the phone in conference calls with engineers and designers in Asia, Europe, and North America at the same time. It's end of day in Asia, and early morning in North America. "In Germany," she says, "we miss our lunch very often."

Part of the challenge, as noted, is that the English skills of Koreans and Chinese might not be as strong as those of Germans. There are also big differences between the cultures about resolving inevitable conflicts, compounded by the fact that Chinese and Korean men are not used to women who assert themselves as forcefully as some American and European women do.

Compared to other auto companies, Rosenplaenter thinks GM is way ahead in creating true cross-cultural collaboration. One key is the internal IT systems that allow the robust sharing of so much data. "This is a real cultural thing we have to learn within GM," Rosenplaenter says. "We have to trust each other. Otherwise, we will not survive."

I could see how difficult the process is after visiting China and speaking with engineer Lu Xiao, who also is working around the clock on the Buick Epsilon project. He has been arguing for years that the new Buick had to have a particular exterior part, which he won't identify, that is customized to conform to Chinese legal requirements. "It's not an issue in Europe, but it's a no-go issue in China," he explains at PATAC.

It is noon in Germany and six P.M. in China when the conference calls start. "Every night we have a conference call," Lu explains in excellent English. "We have a debate or conversation or whatever you want to call it. The Germans talk to the Americans, and the other guys are quiet. Because of the language, we don't say too much. Usually on the conference calls, we are good listeners."

But it's clear that he does not think too highly of his Western counterparts. "The Americans are talking, talking, talking," Lu says. "That's their culture. They don't have any ideas, but they keep talking. And the Germans made many stupid mistakes," such as refusing to adapt the one part for the Chinese market. "But they are very stubborn. They just don't want to change."

Lu says the conference calls can last well into the evening, and he doesn't have much sympathy for the Germans having to work through their lunch hours. "The Germans are the luckiest guys in GM," he says. "They don't have to stay up too late."

Such is the cultural kaleidoscope that GM is attempting to bring into focus. It's not easy for anyone involved. That's another reality of GM's globalization: it's not just Americans who are feeling its impact.

The function that GM has most thoroughly globalized is arguably the procurement of parts, and the senior official who is the most globalized personally is Bo Andersson. He sits in his first-floor office in the Cadillac Building at the GM Technical Center in Warren. The walls are filled with encyclopedic diagrams and data: glass, interiors, power train, electrical components, and other categories of components. He's known for his photographic memory, for being able to retain amazing amounts of data and detail about the $121 billion a year in parts and logistical services that allows GM to function.

In short, this is the man who knows where all the parts are. In addition to having global responsibilities, he also runs North American purchasing with military precision. Every evening at six P.M., with the exception of Saturday, he calls his key lieutenants. He requests perfect attendance—no excuses. "It should be a two-minute call," Andersson says. "We supply parts to eighty-seven plants in North America. What I would like the call to be is twenty-eight vehicle assembly plants, no issues; twenty-five power train plants, no issues; twenty-six metal plants, no issues."

If someone is having a problem getting the right parts to the right plant, the logic from Andersson is simple. As he explains it, "If you have an issue, frame the issue. Frame the root cause. Frame the near fix. Frame the long-term fix."

When there's a crisis, he may swing into action personally. When I met with him, he explained that he had flown to Mexico the previous Sunday morning to work on a problem: a supplier of a 300-volt electrical motor to a GM hybrid SUV, which had been advertised on television during the Super Bowl, was having troubles getting the components to Baltimore, where they would be assembled into a power train and then provided to GM for final assembly. That could have been disastrous if the advertising increased demand for the vehicles precisely at the moment that they couldn't be produced because of the absence of a single part.

"The supplier was struggling," he explains. "First, I got them on the phone last week and said, 'This is what I expect.' Secondly, I wanted to see and understand and feel this myself. I wanted to meet with the people on the floor. Typically, when I go to visit a supplier, I never go to the conference room. I want to go to the machines. I want to talk to the operators. I want to see the flow. I want them to point out the bottlenecks. I want to understand it."

Bo told his procurement people to work with the supplier around the clock to help him improve his processes with his existing equipment, and put in an order for new equipment. He obtained four hundred motors and scheduled daily charters to fly them to Baltimore. Then it was time for a brief meeting in the conference room: "You are a key player," he told the supplier. "I have three expectations. First, I need 90 a day. I need perfect quality. And effective March 24, I need 510 a week. So that's it. I told my team members to stay there and help them get this done." Total elapsed time at the supplier: two hours. Then he flew back to Detroit.

But how can he possibly be aware of where every part is? "In today's environment, I have three issues," he explains. "Number one is complexity, number two is complexity, and number three is complexity. We buy one hundred sixty thousand part numbers for GM globally every day. Most of them are not interchangeable."

Beginning five years ago, he started to simplify the complexity by locating "clusters of responsibility" for each part or group of parts. "We moved all the seat belt buying for the world to Mexico," he says. "Today we have a team in Mexico buying 9.3 million seat belt sets," ranging from two to seventeen belts per vehicle, "for all the usage worldwide. I hold them accountable. They wake up every morning and ask, 'Did we have any issues with seat belt shipments yesterday?' That does not mean [the team] buys the stuff from Mexico. But it's single-stop shopping. Another reason why we picked Mexico was because we had the best people and the best engineers, and it's the largest manufacturing base for suppliers globally."

So, in other words, even if a car is being assembled in the United States or Europe or China, the people in charge of buying the seat belts for that car are in Mexico. Similar clusters have been established around the world for other components. "With the global programs, I get more scale and I get my synergies in the supply base," Andersson explains. "The second thing is I get much better flexibility. We don't know where demand is going to be. Now I can use my logistics network that we've built up over the past two years, and it's a very strong one, to really get better flexibility."

Andersson's method puts very tough pressure on many stay-at-home suppliers. Some of them go out of business, which costs jobs. But Andersson's tough bargains keep down GM's costs, and some of that savings is passed on to consumers in the form of lower car prices. Are U.S. factories sourcing globally? "For our North American needs, we still supply ninety-five percent of what we use in North America inside NAFTA," he says. "You're seeing a trend going much more into Mexico and Canada," he adds. "If we had a better logistics system, north-south, we would have seen much more [manufacturing] going into Mexico."

Surprisingly, relatively few parts are coming directly from Korea or China, at least not yet. "Our lowest cost country is not China," Andersson says. "It's the state of Alabama, where about twenty Korean-based suppliers bring in components and assemble them there."

The next phase in attacking complexity centers on the new Buick the company is launching. It will be built in Europe, Asia, and North America. Andersson is expecting that he will need five thousand parts apiece for a million of these vehicles. "In most cases, we have one supplier [per part]. In some cases, we have two suppliers," he explains. "But in all cases, the parts are the same" from country to country. "If I need to, I can ship parts from Romania to Mexico or from Mexico to Romania or from China to Mexico, because they all fit." If Andersson can pull that off, it will drive down or hold down the costs of all those vehicles. It is a job of gargantuan proportions.

Aside from being a parts maven, Andersson has a unique view of GM's globalization effort, courtesy of his upbringing. The Swedes, like the Dutch and the Danes, are passionate believers in globalization because that's the way their smaller countries have amassed and maintained their wealth. Some nationalities are able to operate better across cultural barriers than others, and he thinks GM's ability to adopt a globalized model is an advantage over other companies. "It's a strength compared to Toyota but also the Germans," he says. "Having lived in Germany and speaking German, I know that they have a lot of strengths, but they have a lot of weaknesses," one of which he thinks is their difficulty in absorbing people of different cultures.

Some of Andersson's philosophy appears to have rubbed off on Wagoner. "I think it's very clear if you are a forty-five-year-old American white male, you're somewhat handicapped if you're not embracing this global environment," Wagoner says. "The majority of people working for me have worked in two countries or more out of their own country."

The idea that someone is global simply because he travels a great deal does not cut it with Andersson. "It's important that people move with their families," he insists. "If I take my former experience in the Swedish military, we never let people go overseas without taking their families. In the selection process, they typically interview the wife as deeply as they do you as an officer. So I say to my people, they need to move with families. They need to go through the hassles of getting into schools, learning the language, and understanding living there. Every given day we have two hundred people who are working and living outside their home countries, and we have people in forty countries." The new GM increasingly demands that its people live and work abroad at some point in their careers.

Ultimately, it is Rick Wagoner who has been pushing GM to become a more global company. The origins of his thinking date back to the first time he was in Brazil. The operation stood largely alone; parts were acquired locally, and the manufacturing operation ran with very little supervision from Detroit. High tariffs encouraged that independence because imported parts were too expensive. "To play in Brazil, you had to be a very local company," Wagoner recalls. As long as GM do Brasil made its sales and profit numbers, it was largely left alone.

But in Europe, Wagoner could see how procuring parts across national boundaries was hugely effective. Rather than having one parts supplier for German plants and one for Spanish plants and one for British plants, it was far more cost-effective to have a single supplier for all of them. In Brazil, where the economy had opened up somewhat by the time he returned for his second posting, Wagoner pushed for the introduction of GM Europe vehicles and parts, and also pushed the GMS system. He saw again how breaking down the barriers among GM's different international operations could lead to big financial gains.

So what is his ultimate vision of what a global GM should look like? He first outlined his thinking in a speech entitled "The Race to the Middle," which he gave in Japan in October 2003. "I thought it was a good speech," he jokes today. "But everyone fell asleep while I was reading it.

"My thesis was, we had started in the industry at a time when we were completely decentralized, because that was the way the business was then," Wagoner explains. "Brazil was Brazil, Germany was Germany, the UK was the UK, and the U.S. was the U.S."

Sitting in his office now, he's drawing on a legal pad. At one end of a spectrum he puts GM, and at the opposite end he places Volkswagen and Toyota. "They started later and with a completely centralized model," he explains. "They basically built in their home countries and exported globally."

The central idea of his speech was that GM had to race toward the middle from being an overly decentralized company, while VW and Toyota had to race to the same middle space from being overly centralized. "The winning company is the one that gets the best balance between decentralized and centralized, or local and global," he says. "Centralized is great, because you can build expertise and apply it consistently. Decentralized is great, because you get the value of understanding local customers and markets. My thesis was that getting that right balance was critical. And I think it's truer than ever."

Of course, it doesn't work if every decision is made at the center in Detroit. How, for example, will a U.S. engineer know what kind of suspension Brazilian or Chinese buyers want or what size cars fit in their garages? There has to be a delicate balance. "We said we are not going to centralize all of our engineering to get functional excellence," Wagoner says. "We're going to knit together a network of engineering centers around the world. Sure, we've got a guy who runs them. Bob Lutz happens to sit in the U.S. But we're going to knit these together. Because of our electronics and systems and communications capabilities, it can be like these people are in the same place, but they don't all have to move there. And so we can get the advantage of having engineers in local markets living, understanding customers every day. They can represent the voice of the customer. But they can do work that's global. That's what we've been driving in product development. To a greater or lesser extent, we do that somewhat differently in each of the functions."

So Australia Holden may engineer the Camaro, even though Ed Welburn and Jim Queen sit in Detroit. GM Mexico may order all the company's seat belts, even though Andersson also sits in Detroit. After having spoken with Rosenplaenter in Rüsselsheim and Lu in Shanghai, and hearing about the cultural complexities they face, I asked Wagoner whether an organization the size of GM can be globalized without becoming confused.

"The answer is yes, we have to," he replies. One of the company's top priorities is changing its culture to accommodate globalization. "I preached those priorities myself for about five years until people were sick of hearing me talk about it," he continues. "And these were specifically things that we needed to change if we were going to be successful in these new [organizational] models. And the simple words were 'one company," meaning rather than being focused on just being a division or GM Brasil, we needed one global company, we needed GM integration."

The automotive world seen through Wagoner's eyes is like the board game Risk: when you try to invade the Middle East and hold the continent, someone else invades your territory in Brazil, threatening your grip on South America.

Wagoner does not see expanding in other markets as walking away from the United States. Just the opposite, in fact. Revenue from booming global markets has helped keep GM afloat and fund future product programs, even in the midst of the long painful restructuring in North America. And aggressive growth outside the United States also keeps pressure on GM's global competitors because if one of them has a protected home market, or if GM doesn't compete in a market where that competitor is strong, then the competition can use profits from its safe harbors to come after GM in the United States. Expanding elsewhere, Wagoner says, "strengthens our ability to compete here." The conversation is getting hot. He's passionate about this.

"We were not allowed to compete in Japan for a long time," he continues. "We had higher market share in Japan in the forties" than the company has today. After the U.S. government asked GM and other automakers to leave Japan in the 1950s, they never truly got back in. "Here we are fifty years later. How well did that [pullout] serve us? Are we glad we did that?"

GM was also "in Korea a little bit and not very well," Wagoner says. That market as well has been largely closed to U.S. manufacturers and is now dominated by Hyundai. "So we essentially didn't compete in Korea for a long time, and they've got a foothold here," Wagoner says.

"Does anybody seriously think that that's a better way to handle China—act like it's not there? These other countries have their own models, which enable them to attack our home market, and it's weakened us. We got a lot of feedback early on, concern in some quarters, when we made the push into China—about investing in China rather than the U.S. We did invest a lot of money initially in China. But we basically are reinvesting our profits, and we're sending dividends back to the U.S. So, ironically, we're investing in China but we're sending money back from China, which, to take a little poetic license, could be going to the restructuring of the U.S. business. Or investments in fuel cells. So it's crystal clear to me that a strong global presence will support a stronger GM presence in the U.S. And certainly the opposite has proven to be true, that if you're relatively weaker in key overseas markets, it actually hurts us here because those competitors can use that to come and attack our market. A couple of our competitors have done a wonderful job of that."

In the global game of Risk, Wagoner sees the emerging markets such as China as essential to competing against Toyota and others. Simply put, that's where the growth is going to occur over the next five to ten years, even if it is slightly less than the 10 or 11 percent annual growth China has experienced for many years. Europe, Japan, and the United States are in recession. "Look," he says, "the way the company's shaping is that sixty-four percent of our sales in the first quarter of 2008 were outside the U.S. Three years ago, we never thought that we'd never sell more than fifty percent outside. You look at our production statistics—they're astounding. This year, we will produce almost as many units in all of Asia Pacific as we will in the U.S."

He estimates that 80 percent of the growth in demand for vehicles over the next five years will be in emerging markets. "There are eight hundred twenty-one vehicles per one thousand inhabitants in the U.S. In China, it's something like twenty-six. So it's just math. India's the same, and Brazil's the same. Russia's vehicle penetration is higher than you would think, and the population base isn't so huge. But still, it's a huge amount of growth versus here. So it's just basic demographics, and as the rest of the world gets wealthier, they're all gonna buy more cars. That's our greatest opportunity for growth. If we're not global, we'll lose."

Who ultimately wins and who loses from GM's global drive? GM's globalization means that many design and engineering jobs that used to be in the United States will be in Seoul or Shanghai or Rüsselsheim. That's a challenge for some American designers and engineers, but an opportunity for those American employees who are willing to travel or live internationally. There is a cultural fault line; designers and engineers who cannot or do not choose to embrace the globalized model face limited career prospects; but others can actually enhance their professional lives, partly because they have a chance to work for a company that's winning in the global game, not losing.

GM's global procurement practices put pressure on American parts suppliers who keep their manufacturing in the United States, but they create new opportunities for those willing to go global. The knife cuts both ways.

The American consumer is a net winner, as almost every car that GM sells, with the possible exception of large trucks, SUVs, Cadillacs, and Corvettes, feels the impact of globalized design, engineering, or purchasing. GM as a company is stronger competitively and financially, which should ultimately benefit its long-suffering shareholders. And it means that the GM employees of all stripes who remain face brighter, more secure futures. In geographic terms, however, the city of Detroit will never again see massive GM hiring because the GM that emerges from this period of reorganization will never be as Detroit-centered as the old one was. But many other areas, from Kansas City to Silicon Valley, will benefit from a GM that endures.

Is it still true that what's good for GM is good for America and vice versa? It's not clear that was true even in 1953. There was some overlap of interest between GM as a company and the broader nation. Both benefited from the spread of the automobile. Both benefited from the rise of the middle class. But on other issues, they clearly diverged. It was in the company's interest to have lax environmental regulations of the waste from its plants; but it was in the national interest to clean up the environment. It was in the company's interest to produce big cars that consumed lots of gasoline; but (now we know) it would have been in the national interest to encourage more fuel-efficient vehicles.

Today there may be less overlap in interests if more than half of GM's sales and employees are outside of the United States, but GM is still essential to maintaining the U.S. manufacturing and technology base. Knowledge about the entire chain of designing, engineering, manufacturing, and retailing cars remains in American hands; crucial sets of skills and capabilities are preserved. And there are still huge economic ripple effects. The decision by many political leaders of both parties to embrace globalization, and to actively recruit and financially support the arrival of the foreign transplants, means that GM has little choice but to be a global player. If it isn't, Wagoner is right that it cannot compete in its home market. A stronger, more globalized GM offers more sustainable economic benefits than a domestically-focused GM that loses ground year after year. Even if its geographic footprint is very different from what it was in 1953, GM still matters to the health of the U.S. economy.

PART III

The Future

CHAPTER 14

The Battle of Perception

No matter how sweeping the changes GM has embraced, the fact remains that it still faces a perception problem in the American market. For decades, GM did not offer the most attractive, reliable cars—and anyone who was stung by owning a bad car will be reluctant to go back to a GM dealership. GM essentially missed the baby boom generation, and is not doing very well with their children either. The company has to learn anew how to project an image of quality as vehicles leave the plants and head for dealerships.

Moreover, GM has to persuade automotive publications and auto industry followers that its vehicles have closed the gap with Toyota and Honda. The environmental issue looms large; at one point, opinion research showed that 75 percent of Americans thought Toyota was part of the solution to the nation's energy and environmental concerns, and the same measure, 75 percent, thought GM was part of the problem. Shareholders and Wall Street analysts are skeptical, having seen the GM stock get hammered down from a recent high of about $40 to below $10, then to below $3.

The mainstream media looms as a particularly key constituency to win over. At the moment, the speculation is feverish: GM is going bankrupt. It can't possibly make it. Wagoner is about to be fired. As one executive at a rival company put it, "The media call you up and say, 'Are you prepared for the sky to fall?' If you say, 'No, maybe not,' they say, 'Well, then aren't you being irresponsible? Don't you need a plan in case the sky falls?'"

So quite apart from anything that the Obama administration does, the key to how the GM drama plays out over the long term truly lies in the hearts and minds—and pocketbooks—of several American constituencies. As with so many other aspects of the GM transformation effort, this is a story of people. From a vice president at headquarters to a struggling Chevy dealer in upstate New York, a small army of people is trying to convince the American public that buying GM's cars is smart. Others are waiting to be persuaded.

If GM's management team were a basketball squad, Jamie Hresko would be point guard. Wagoner appointed him as the chief apostle for quality at GM in March 2006, putting him in charge of changing public perception about GM products—of instilling what he calls "perceptual quality."

In the language of GM, perception has three dimensions. Initial quality reflects customer satisfaction after three months of ownership. Long-term quality covers the reliability and durability of the vehicle over time. Perceptual quality—the most elusive and perhaps the most crucial to sales—touches on the customer's feelings. What a customer sees, hears, touches, and experiences in the vehicle affects his or her perception. So too does what the customer reads or hears in the media, and hears from friends and associates. Perceptual quality is the form of quality that GM needs most.

Hresko, forty-four, has seen the worst of what happened at GM over the years. He was born in Flint and worked at a plant there that closed. "All those people lost their jobs and they were good people, too," he says. Hresko is a manufacturing guy and worked his way up through the plants, including a stint at NUMMI in 1998, to his current position, vice president, GM quality. When we meet, he is wearing a black polo shirt and is chewing gum. He's obviously not a headquarters kind of guy. We're in a tiny conference room in the Vehicle Engineering Center at the Tech Center in Warren. Organizational charts of the 160 people who report to him line one wall.

Wagoner knew Hresko in an earlier position and turned to him when the Malibu was being launched. The fact that Hresko has seen plants closed out from under his feet and also has seen how Toyota works at NUMMI gives him powerful motivation, and Wagoner seems to recognize that. After hiring him as quality chief, Wagoner said to him on the phone, "I gotta talk to ya for fifteen minutes. You need to know your priorities."

The message from Wagoner was that the launch of the new Malibu had to be perfect, and Hresko accepted the challenge. "If the Malibu doesn't win," Hresko says, "I'll take the blame, because that's my job, to make sure the Malibu wins. The Malibu must win. It must beat the Accord, it must beat the Camry, it must beat everything in its segment, which is twenty vehicles."

There are two major new tools that Hresko is using in the fight for perceptual quality. The first is that the company has tied its largest dealers into its plants, using a system called the 24-Hour Concern Detection Process. In the past, dealers would report problems with cars to the Sales and Service Group, but the data didn't make it back to the factories or engineers in real time, and in many cases, the data did not make it at all. There were too many layers of bureaucracy.

But starting in 1998, as part of a warranty improvement program modeled after the Centers for Disease Control's rapid-response process to the outbreak of infectious diseases, dealers who participate in the program send e-mails alerting GM engineering and manufacturing people to any problems they spot in cars. Hresko can jump on quality concerns very early and get the factories to correct whatever the problem is. "We get real-time data before a customer ever gets a car," he says. "If the dealers see anything, we'll call an assembly place. We're taking the bureaucracy out. In engineering, we just completely bypass the bureaucracy."

After a problem has been spotted, Hresko insists on a response from the factory or from engineering within twenty-four hours. "It requires a certain level of leadership to correct each issue," he says. This means he's demanding that problems get fixed or he won't allow the vehicles to be sent out to market. "I won't ship 'em—that's one of the things I was given the authority to do," he says. "We will not ship a car unless it meets the new validations standards. They are designed not to fail, period. If the gaps in the exterior sheet metals aren't perfect, I won't ship 'em. If there's a problem on a new car program like the Malibu or the CTS, look at me, 'cause I shipped it. And if I don't get my job done, I expect them to get rid of me."

The second tool is OnStar's onboard Vehicle Diagnostics system, which is installed now in every vehicle. The system monitors 1,600 different aspects of a vehicle's performance, and that information can be downloaded from vehicle test fleets. "We can extract the performance of the vehicle whenever we want it," Hresko explains. "If we had sent ten cars to Mexico City for city driving in hot weather, which we did, we would check their engine performance, fuel economy, potential trouble codes, how the engine was running. We checked for emissions, calibrations. The technology is such that you can gather that information [while the car is still in the field]."

That information then goes back to the engineers who worked on that model. "So if I'm the engineer who's responsible for emission and power train, I don't have to sit there and call people," Hresko explains. "I just look at my e-mails. If an emission failure comes up on a car, I get an e-mail that says a vehicle with a certain VIN [vehicle identification number] in Mexico City has triggered an emissions code. [An engineer] can actually get on at OnStar and interrogate that car." No other competitor has that ability.

All that is well and good, but how can you persuade David Champion, the head of automotive testing at *Consumer Reports*, that your cars are the same quality as Toyota's and Honda's? "I talk to him," Hresko responds. "And I use whatever he tells me. I don't argue with him. I just say, 'Tell me what we need to do better.' "

Hresko thus is in charge of channeling insights from Champion back to GM. Champion warned him, for example, that GM would not be able to get a "recommended buy" rating for any vehicle after 2009 unless it had electronic stability control. So Hresko is pushing a plan to get that done. Champion also offered criticism of the zero-to-sixty acceleration, turning ratios, and braking distances on the Envoy and Trailblazer, which led Hresko to push the engineers to work on those issues. "Our strategy has been to aggressively remediate the issues as fast as we possibly can," Hresko says. The fact that he has Wagoner's ear gives him real clout.

The Aura, Malibu, Buick Enclave, Cadillac CTS, and other models are getting recommendations from Champion, so now the pressure is on to win more, particularly in the small-car segment. For example, the Opel Astra, which arrived in American showrooms in January 2008 as the Saturn Astra, was made to satisfy European tastes. "The cup holder design is terrible for the U.S.," Hresko acknowledges. "In Europe, they don't drink in the car. They have no use for it. No customer would ever complain about it. Here they want a cup holder. David will say, 'Hey, you don't have a cup holder in here that's workable for the U.S. market.'"

Hresko's engagement with Champion is critically important because, for years, GM simply ignored *Consumers Reports*, and that resulted in Japanese brands sweeping the ratings. But even if Champion is an important player, he is only one piece of the broader challenge of persuading more Americans to buy GM cars. "We have to win every car that we make," Hresko says. "Every car has to be better in fuel economy. It has to be better in quality execution.

"Toyota can come out today because of the public perception, deliver mediocre results, and do fairly well," he argues, a judgment that Toyota would certainly dispute. "But we have to deliver outstanding results because our perception's been damaged in the marketplace. So it's one customer at a time and there is no margin for competitive products anymore. Just take the word *competitive* out of your vocabulary. The word has got to be *win*. Be the best in everything—price, execution, fuel economy, and durability." In 2007, Buick tied Lexus for the top rating in durability in *Consumer Reports*. For Hresko, it was a triumph. Just as gratifying, Cadillac came in second.

"We've upped our game," Hresko says. The day of perceptual quality, "it's coming."

The marketing launch for the Cadillac CTS sedan in 2001 was a smashing success, but seen from the inside, it represented an amusing collision of personalities and cultures. Mark R. LaNeve, who had just returned from a stint running Volvo North America, was thrust into the position of general manager of Cadillac. LaNeve, from an Italian American family in Pennsylvania, had been an all-American football star at the University of Virginia, where he played middle linebacker as a six-feet-one 25-pounder. He personified clean-cut Middle America.

The Cadillac Escalade had been successfully introduced, but now it was time for Cadillac to make a statement about its new cars. LaNeve liked the theme "breakthrough," which was one of dozens of ideas submitted by an ad agency. "The agency set it to 'Break on Through to the Other Side' by the Doors," LaNeve recalls. "We negotiated with the Doors, but we couldn't buy the rights to the music. So we looked at fifty or a hundred alternatives. The one we liked best was 'Rock and Roll' by Led Zeppelin."

The song, originally performed in 1971, featured the line "Been a long time since I rock and rolled." "We liked the energy of the music, and it implied, 'Hey, Cadillac was asleep for a while. But now we're back,'" LaNeve says. He was able to negotiate rights to the music after the former all-American met with Robert Plant, the long-haired Led Zeppelin lead singer. "It was quite an experience," LaNeve deadpans.

Then Bob Lutz, the ramrod-straight former jet fighter pilot who had just joined GM, asked LaNeve how he intended to market the CTS. When LaNeve told him, Lutz said, "You're going to use Led Zeppelin music? Don't you think Cadillac should be set more to classical music?"

LaNeve says he told Lutz, " 'Bob, Led Zeppelin *is* classical music.' Bob loved that." So did customers; Cadillac car sales rebounded. Total sales were 172,000 units in 2001, and that number reached 235,000 by 2005.

Today LaNeve, forty-nine and relatively svelte at 195 pounds, is vice president of vehicle sales, service, and marketing for North America for all GM brands, which means the job of repairing GM's brand image belongs to him. Because GM put such an emphasis on trucks and sport-utility vehicles for many years, the truck brands are less of a challenge.

Chevy Trucks and the GMC division have strong market share and customer loyalty.

But the car brands now are where the company has what LaNeve calls "trailing perceptual gaps." That means he's working on Cadillac, Chevrolet, Saturn, Buick, and Pontiac. The Corvette brand name is largely sustained by enthusiastic driver groups and the specialized auto press. GM spends very little on promoting that brand.

LaNeve uses what he calls "brand health indicators" to measure how each of the company's brands compares. These indicators are aggregates of other statistics, and the company does not disclose just how they are compiled. But according to these numbers, GM's car brands had a 30 percent gap against leaders of each segment three to four years ago. These measurements would compare Chevy cars with Toyota cars, and Cadillac cars with BMW cars, for example. In recent years, "we've closed that gap by about half. We've taken it from a thirty percent gap to about a fifteen percent gap on brand health," LaNeve explains. "That's very significant. Their brand health stayed the same. Ours improved. The problem is there's still a gap."

What can LaNeve do about that? Advertising has only a limited impact. "Our brands, unlike a lot of other industries, are very dependent on the actual product execution and consistency over time," LaNeve says. "I like to say that in some of the packaged goods businesses, like toothpaste, you spend a dollar on product and ten on the marketing. In our business, you spend ten on the product and a dollar on the marketing. If you consistently execute a good product over a series of generations, you will have a good brand image almost despite the advertising."

So while a big part of selling the cars is simply making them better, LaNeve still has many aspects of branding to work on. One of the most important is called market presence. People in general, and particularly people in New York, Boston, South Florida, and California (GM's toughest car markets), need to see GM cars in actual use. "If you never see a GM product, if you never see a Chevy car, on the road, in your neighborhood, in your circle of friends, or among your peers at work, you're going to be less prone to want to buy one," LaNeve explains. "We've got great truck market presence and word of mouth almost everywhere in the country, but our car market presence in certain markets on the coasts is very weak. You don't rebuild that overnight."

In introducing the new Malibu, LaNeve is advertising (spreading the slogan "The car you can't ignore"), but he's also making an effort to expand the Malibu's market presence, getting it into demographic and geographic areas where GM cars have not been visible. "I told the dealers, it would be more important to sell one Malibu into a neighborhood full of Camrys and Accords than if every single customer saw every single ad," he says. "If somebody in your neighborhood has one, if somebody on your kid's soccer team has one, or if somebody in your church has one, then it's okay for you to get one. But if you never see one, people are creatures of habit. Nobody wants to have to explain what they bought."

One of GM's strategies for expanding market presence, although not aimed specifically at Camry or Accord, is called garage mates. The company can identify customers who own one GM product and another product from another company. It then sends direct mail or an e-mail to those customers giving them a cash incentive to replace the non-GM car in their garage with a GM product.

The reason it's so hard to change people's minds is that there's a certain inertia in their buying patterns; once they start in one direction, they often continue in that direction. "Our new Malibu is better than a Camry or Accord," LaNeve argues. "But those car customers are perfectly happy. There's no God-given right for us to go in and conquest them."

"Conquesting" or "getting conquest" refers to making the sale that converts a customer of another car company to a customer of GM. In the case of the Malibu, 43 percent of the buyers are new to GM products. They may be moving up from smaller cars. They may be moving down out of sport-utility vehicles. Some are coming from the Japanese competition. "There's some degree of direct conquest of the Honda Accord and Nissan Sentra," LaNeve says. Not so much from the Toyota Camry, but the Malibu is appealing to the same type of people who buy Camrys. "They're almost identical," says LaNeve. "We are getting a younger, higher educated, affluent customer for our new generation of products."

Saturn is also getting conquest in the marketplace, and the newly re-designed Cadillac CTS was the fastest growing luxury product in the market in 2008, gaining ground against BMW, Lexus, and Mercedes. So, clearly, GM feels it is making progress in changing minds and getting conquest. The problem, says LaNeve, is that "it never comes as fast as you want."

Tom Young looks like he's been sent from Central Casting to play the role of Chevrolet dealer in upstate New York. In his midfifties, he's a big beefy guy with ruddy cheeks and white hair that covers the tops of his ears. He's wearing a polo shirt with the name of his twenty-four-foot speedboat on it. He's not busy because there are no shoppers on the floor in the middle of the week.

Young isn't his real name, and he's asked that his identity not be revealed because he does not want General Motors to know what he has to say. He's not worried about Wagoner or anyone in senior management. In fact, Wagoner has been on a fact-finding mission to his region and met with dealers, though the CEO learned very little, Young says, because of the zone managers and other sales executives who stand between Wagoner and GM's dealers. (There are five zones in the United States: Northeast, Southeast, North Central, South Central, and Western.) Their presence in dealer meetings discouraged complete candor. That alone is revealing: it's possible that the GM sales bureaucracy is filtering some of what Wagoner hears.

It's a decidedly mixed picture for Young, and his story demonstrates that GM has serious work ahead of it. Young's showroom, stocked with a snazzy bright-yellow Corvette Z06, a cinnamon HHR LT crossover, and a cherry-red Impala SS, is where the rubber hits the proverbial road. "My frustration is that in the Northeast, we really have a perception problem," Young says.

The two coasts, east and west, have indeed been tough territory for Chevrolet, which prides itself on being a heartland kind of brand. Chevrolet's market share in New York is way below its national average of 12 percent. "They have not been able to stop the slide," Young adds. He lost money in 2007 and is on track to lose money again in 2008. He has personally owned his dealership for fifteen years. "I don't have a voice, and I'm getting killed," he complains.

It used to be that he parked his big pickup trucks next to the highway so that passersby would see them first, but as gasoline prices soared, it became clear that consumers weren't just waiting before buying trucks—they were engaged in a full-fledged flight from the larger vehicles. "Six or eight months ago, people felt that it was a temporary phenomenon," he says, referring to gasoline prices topping $3.50 a gallon. "They were not going to close down their spending. But now people think it's here to stay. That means we are competing for the food dollar and the energy dollar, and there's not a whole lot left after that. A lot of consumer spending has just stopped."

Now the pickups are in the back of his dealership, and he has moved his Chevy Equinoxes and a handful of Malibus to be most visible. "The Malibu is the greatest," Young says. "People come in and they road-test it. They buy it. They love it. We've got something to sell now."

He's getting conquest from Toyota, Nissan, and Honda; owners of Camrys, Sentras, and Accords are coming into his showroom, never having owned an American car, or at least not for several decades. "The Malibu is bringing people into the dealership. We sell Impalas to some of them. People who own foreign cars also rent Impalas on vacation and say, 'Hey, this is a pretty nice car.' So they come in too."

So what's the problem with the Malibu? "I can't get more than six or seven or eight at a time. I should have fifty or sixty or seventy on my lot at any one time. I don't know where the disconnect is." One part of the disconnect is that the company simply hasn't been making enough Malibus at Fairfax and in Lake Orion, Michigan. The strike at Fairfax didn't help matters, but the decision in May to add third shifts at some factories should help ease that problem.

Young says he faces other deep-seated challenges. One is that there are simply too many other Chevrolet dealers in his region, which is known as an industrial, working-class area. Chevrolet still has 4,000 dealers across the country compared to only 370 for Lexus. "So people come in here after they've been to three other Chevy dealerships," he says. Obviously, they try to drive down the price by making the dealers compete. "We're banging our heads against each other," Young says. "I ought to be competing against Toyota, not against other Chevy dealers."

The heart of the problem, of course, is that GM has a much larger sales infrastructure than it has actual sales. "GM is at twenty percent market share, and they probably have [dealer] capacity for forty percent," says Young. "We're over-dealered." Many weaker dealerships are failing, but the shakeout is not occurring fast enough to suit Young.

This is one reason it's very sensitive for him to be talking about what he really thinks. If he wants to be in line to consolidate his presence in the market, and possibly take over another dealership or force a Chevy competitor to close, the GM sales hierarchy might punish him if it felt he was being disloyal.

And there are too many models. He likes the company's decision in early 2008 to put the suddenly moribund Hummer division up for sale. "Get rid of it," he says. "Just cut the cord." And he wants the company to reduce the overlaps among Chevrolet, GM, Pontiac, and Cadillac. "The Trailblazer was a huge-volume vehicle for Chevrolet," the dealer explains. "People were four-wheel-drive crazy, SUV crazy. So I've got all these customers, and they've already leased a Trailblazer three times. They're not going to do it again. They want something new. I need something else to put them into."

But he suffered a delay in getting a logical step-up from the Trailblazer. Buick got the Enclave and GMC got the same vehicle, badged as the Acadia. This is a luxury crossover vehicle, meaning it has the handling characteristics of a car but the size of a SUV. It starts around $33,000. Only later did Young get the Chevrolet equivalent—the Traverse. Not having the right vehicle at the right moment hurts. "Trying to get a customer back is really hard," he says.

The last challenge for Young is found in the particular economics of used cars. Used Toyota and Honda vehicles retain their value better than GM cars have, at least in recent years. Their residual value is higher. That means the competition can be more aggressive in offering leasing deals. Most of the business in this region of New York is leasing, as opposed to selling. People "buy payments," meaning they shop for vehicles based on how much they can afford to pay each month. If Toyota and Honda can beat his lease price by even a few dollars a month, that gives them another edge.

Having said all that, Young does see progress in the cars that GM is making, and he has hopes for the future. "I don't want to come across as being negative," he says. One positive sign he points to is in "dealer prep." It used to be that his mechanics had to go through each new car with a fine-tooth comb, inspecting for problems. They would add grease or fluids, tighten nuts, and generally fix manufacturing defects. "But I don't have to do that anymore. The guy who washes my cars, I just promoted him to be in charge of dealer prep. He doesn't even own a toolbox."

Repairs are also way down. It used to be that GM offered only twelve-month/12,000-mile warranties. "After that, if you had problems, you were on your own." But now the company offers five-year/100,000-mile warranties, and cars are not coming back into the service bay like they used to. "This is not something that happened overnight, but the quality is there."

GM's bet on technology also is paying off, in his view. The video camera on the back of his Chevy Avalanche shows startlingly clear images of objects behind him as he backs up. And both OnStar and XM Radio are winners. "Once people start using these things, they can't live without them," Young says.

Walking the lot, he points out the vehicles he feels confident about. He likes the new hybrid versions of the big vehicles, such as the Chevy Tahoe. The Silverado pickup truck is a lifestyle vehicle for people with boats or horses, and he regards it as the best in its class. He drives the Avalanche because he needs to pull his boat to lakes, but even it gets twenty miles per gallon on the highway, thanks to improved engine technology, as opposed to the seven or eight miles per gallon that he used to get with comparable vehicles. There's not much sales action for his smallest vehicles, he says, such as the Aveo and Cobalt.

He clearly likes the Malibu and is looking forward to the Volt. He's already getting customer inquiries about it. "I think it's going to be a great car," he says. "But am I going to sell a hundred of them a month? That's what I'm looking for, something with big volume."

So he sees enough positive trends at General Motors that he is going to tough out the current money-losing period. He's obviously made enough money in previous years to subsidize the dealership through this difficult period. "I'm willing to hang in there and make the investment," he says as he shows a visitor to the parking lot. "I'm ready for the next wave."

I asked LaNeve about Young's comments, without revealing his identity. The brand czar says GM has reduced the number of dealers by 25 percent in the past decade to 6,600 today, and several high-profile bankruptcies hit in late 2008. "It's a very personal decision for dealers to consolidate or exit the business," says LaNeve. "Many of them have been in the business for generations."

Yes, it's true that GM has more dealers than its competitors. "In some ways, that's an advantage," he says. "We have more places where customers can go purchase vehicles. We have dealers in rural areas where we have great market share. If you look at the most recent J.D. Power sales and satisfaction scores, our dealers are all above industry average."

But there's a downside: Because GM has more dealers, individually they don't achieve the same sales per store as Toyota and Honda dealers. The company is trying to improve its dealerships through its "channel strategy." Rather than having a stand-alone Cadillac dealer, a Hummer dealer, and a Saab dealer, it is trying to combine them into a single dealership that will offer broader choices to customers. The same with Buick, Pontiac, and GMC.

But LaNeve acknowledges that much work remains to be done. "Our dealer system was put in during the 1950s," he explains. "Anywhere there was a little town or hamlet, we put in a dealer. But shopping patterns have changed. You've got auto parks and auto malls and interstate highway systems. Suburbs have sprouted around the little towns. We've got to adjust on the run."

Are your dealers frustrated? "Dealers are always frustrated," LaNeve says. "Even when business is good, they're frustrated. They're competitive and entrepreneurial. They've got their personal lives at stake."

David Champion, a fifty-two-year-old silver-haired Brit, is the king of American automotive testing. Operating from a 327-acre testing facility in the backwaters of rural eastern Connecticut, Champion is director of the automotive test division of *Consumer Reports*. We take the tour of his facility, a former drag strip, with Champion at the wheel of a BMW 535i. Even though the compound has seven miles of paved roads, it's not a racetrack, sadly; we're not going to hit high speeds on the straightaways. But Champion does put the BMW through some of the handling tests that his testers inflict on every vehicle. He shows me the skid circle, where testers measure how well cars grip a curve, and also a new hydroplaning facility, which is covered with precisely ten millimeters of water to see how well tires perform in very wet conditions. Champion handles the car expertly, as one would expect.

Champion has been testing cars for thirty years, including previous stints at Land Rover and Nissan, and clearly relishes his role as the arbiter of what's good and what's bad in the automotive world. Has the proverbial lightbulb been switched on at GM? "In many ways, it has," he says.

He thinks Wagoner and Lutz have permanently altered the psychology of making substandard products and spending massively on advertising and incentives to move the metal. "They never really looked at what the consumer wanted or at the other products," he says. "They had an attitude that 'If we build it, they will come.' "

But now, he says, the Malibu is "very competitive" and is "close" in quality to the Toyota Camry. He's very positive about the Outlook, Acadia, and Enclave, as well as the CTS. All have good value and meet customers' expectations, he says.

Where he faults GM is that they haven't got every model to that same level of quality. On some vehicles, he finds that GM's attention to detail hasn't been as good, and Champion and his testers are very detail oriented. They tested one Pontiac, for example, in which the struts in the trunk didn't keep the trunk open as they were supposed to. "Today," says Champion, "it's the small stuff that comes back to haunt you."

GM, though, is listening to him "rather than saying, 'You don't know what you're talking about.' They're more willing to listen and implement changes." Champion says that Hresko "seems to be a very straightshooting person" with the "right attitude and determination."

At the same time, Toyota hasn't been perfect as it has expanded in the United States, now with plants in eight states. It had three models that dropped to "below average" reliability for 2008. "The bigger you get, the more difficult to continue the day-to-day work," Champion explains.

Aside from talking to Hresko, Champion also meets Wagoner once a year at the Detroit Auto Show. He's been doing that since 2002, and Champion gives Wagoner high marks for wanting to hear the story straight from one of the company's toughest critics. "He wanted to cut through the yes-men," who were trying to tell him the company's products were better than they really were, Champion says.

Aside from quality, there are at least two other factors that shape customer buying decisions. One is resale value, where Toyota has had better results than GM. "Are you going to put your money on a Camry or drop it on a Malibu and say, 'I hope it holds its value'?" Champion asks. In coming years, this will be a critical indicator.

A second battleground is design, and Champion thinks GM may have the advantage here. "GM has much more heritage behind them," he says, referring to the Cadillacs of the 1930s and 1940s, when the company was "the king of desire," in his words. He estimates that 50 percent of the buying decision is based on the style of the vehicle.

Bottom line, is GM as good as Toyota? "No," Champion says, "but they're getting there." Can GM match the Japanese attention to detail? "They've got to."

Jerry Flint, at seventy-seven, has earned the right to be called a curmudgeon. He has been covering automobiles for more than fifty years and says he is past the point of doing any reporting. He reckons that he doesn't have to speak with auto company executives who don't understand their own business. What's the point of that? He writes the "Backseat Driver" column for *Forbes* magazine and is one of the deans of the automotive press corps. Normally given to wearing ascots in public, he's wearing a knit shirt with a collar when we have breakfast at a diner on the Upper West Side of Manhattan, close to where we both live. His mustache is white, as is the fringe of hair that surrounds his bald pate.

Flint is one of the gatekeepers of perception toward General Motors, and he is implacably hostile to Wagoner and his management team. Having been born in Detroit, Flint remembers the Detroit of his youth and is obviously angry about what he believes GM has done to his hometown. In a well-known speech that he delivered to GM's engineers in 2000, he explained his background this way: "I was born in Detroit in 1931. We lived on Willis between Second and Third, a few blocks south of Wayne University, which was a city university back then. I went to the neighborhood schools, tough schools; it was a workers' hillbilly neighborhood.

"As a boy, my father and I would walk miles from our apartment to the Fisher Theater to see the movies—and we walked to save the nickel bus fare. We would always stop at the General Motors building to look at the cars and the models. They used to have a contest. Young people would enter futuristic car designs, or make a copy of a Louis XIV carriage. I loved that GM display and dreamed of the day we would have a car."

But, obviously, over time, GM didn't live up to the promise of Flint's youth. Much of downtown Detroit is a ghetto. Though the Fisher Theater still exists, scenes of urban devastation are not far away. GM's travails have obviously played a major role in causing that. As Flint told the engineers in his speech: "You are badly led, with an organization that just doesn't work."

The past eight years have not changed his thinking. His most recent *Forbes* column, which he hands to me, is entitled "Abandon Ship." In it he suggests that GM is in the process of abandoning the difficult American market. "Sixty percent of its 9 million vehicles are abroad, and profits are robust there," he writes. "Can or should the sickly U.S. operations be cut away to save the company?"

In conversation, Flint argues that Wagoner and his team are incompetent. "I see no reason to think this management can turn around General Motors," he says over a hearty breakfast of scrambled eggs and hash browns. "They haven't turned around the business in sixteen years, since 1992. They've lost market share in most of these sixteen years. The amount of money they've lost in these sixteen years is beyond comprehension."

Flint loves making analogies and offers this one: "I have a saying: if your wife hasn't cooked you a good meal in sixteen years, she's not going to. If they haven't been able to turn around this company in sixteen years, there's no reason to think that they're going to."

He's just getting warmed up. What about how Wagoner has transformed the company's management structure? "I could give the same speech about Mussolini," Flint says. "He had to destroy all that democracy and set up a structure to get the trains running on time. I think what you say is absolutely untrue. What they did was to destroy a workable structure. What Jack Smith did was turn General Motors management into a Boston political clubhouse because Jack was from Massachusetts. He set up a management system in which the only people could get a job came out of the Treasury Department. But the people who knew the product, who knew cars, were completely cut off from rising high in the company." There's a measure of truth to this; the company has traditionally been run by a finance man, and that person had a president, or a number two, who was the product person.

But surely you agree that the company has made major design strides in the Lutz era? "Lutz is the ultimate proof that no car guy can rise," Flint says. "When Rick Wagoner decided he needed someone who knew cars, he, the CEO of the largest car company in the world, didn't know one person in his own company who he felt knew cars. So he had to hire a retired near-seventy-year-old man to be his car guy."

Flint saw Wagoner's choice of Lutz not as a demonstration of his own confidence but as a calculated move to avoid creating a rival for the CEO's job. "The thing about him that was attractive was that he was old," Flint argues. "Even if he walked on water, he was never going to be CEO."

Flint believes that Wagoner was the wrong person for the job of running North America because much of his experience had been outside the United States. "When Rick took over North American auto operations, it was incredible awfulness," Flint says. "He knew nothing about the business. He should never have been given that position. It's not that he's not smart. Maybe he should have been put in a position where he could learn something about the business. If you look at Rick's résumé, he knew nothing about the American auto business. Nothing. And the results have proved it. He's led General Motors to destruction, to the point that many people think they're bankrupt, where the stock is selling at ten dollars a share. So don't tell me he's been in the auto business all his life. He's been screwing up this car company since he got there."

Flint does acknowledge that GM is hitting the market with attractive cars, as opposed to just trucks and SUVs. "Thanks to Lutz, they're still in business," Flint acknowledges. "They have some nice products now. That's absolutely true. Their trucks and big SUVs are the best in the world. The cars really are getting pretty decent." Then he adds, "But so what? Nobody's buying them. Why is that? Customers left General Motors and Ford because they hated them. They felt betrayed. Their cars broke down. Their dealers didn't help them. They're never coming back. Why should they? Do you think all those people who own a Toyota are saying, 'I hate my Toyota. I can't wait to buy one of these better General Motors cars?' No, they're happy with their Toyota. They're happy with their Nissans. They like their Mercedes and BMWs.

"When you're behind, it's really not enough to have just a good product. You say, 'Hey, mine is just as good as the other guys.' That doesn't get you anywhere. You have to blow them out of the water with your looks and your design. You can't have middle-of-the-road boring. You have to have cars that when they go by, people turn their heads and say, 'Jesus Christ, what was that?' "

But what about the CTS and the Camaro and the Volt? Have you driven a Volt? he asks. No. Have you seen a Volt? No. "Oh," he says, dripping sarcasm, "it's something you haven't seen or driven and yet you know it's going to be terrific."

Flint fundamentally rejects the notion that the old lumbering GM can be succeeded by a leaner, more globalized GM with better products. "None of the things you say are important," Flint says. "What's important is building products that people want and will pay top dollar for. And we aren't there."

Rebecca A. Lindland is a specialist on generational attitudes toward cars, partly because of her own family background. Now about age forty, she had seven older siblings who all were born before 1964. She is considered a Gen Xer but obviously had close contact with baby boomers and their attitudes. Growing up in Connecticut's affluent Fairfield County, she had extensive exposure to autos from a very young age. "From the time I was a kid, I've always loved vehicles," she says. "My neighbor down street had a fleet of Ferraris and Porsches and Lamborghinis. It was a candy store of cars."

As a girl, she was fascinated by automotive metal. "My Hot Wheels collection was just as big as my Barbie collection," she jokes, "so apparently I was very well balanced."

After a stint with Allied Signal, she joined the economic consulting firm DRI, then a part of Standard & Poor's, which has since been renamed Global Insight. It's one of the hottest economic research firms in the country. Now based in Lexington, Massachusetts, Lindland is director of industry research for the Americas.

She notes that baby boomers started turning fifteen in 1962, the same year that GM reached its high-water mark of 50.7 percent of the American market. Millions of new drivers started entering the market, and they rebelled against their parents, who were devout loyalists to the Big Three. "The automakers didn't give the baby boomers a lot of reasons to buy their products," Lindland explains. "Honda and Toyota and Nissan did."

Japanese quality at that time wasn't always great, but that didn't matter. "There were a lot of rust buckets, but they were very different," she adds. That's what the boomers were looking for—something to differentiate themselves from their parents. "The baby boomers did change everything," she says. "The problem was, that happened when Detroit was resting on its laurels. They did not respond quickly or appropriately."

So the boomer attitude toward GM cars is rooted deeply in the culture of the 1960s. "It is also rooted in the characteristics of baby boomers, which is that they say, 'I'm not wrong,'" she argues. "They don't want anybody to say that maybe things have changed and they should take a second look at GM, Ford, or Chrysler. It's very difficult to change your views of something if they were instilled when you were young.

The other issue GM has with demographics is that, unlike previous generations, Generation Y is not rebelling. In fact, their parents are their friends. As Lindland sees it, "When a Gen Y daughter says to her mother, 'I'm getting a tattoo,' the mother says, 'Oh, I'll drive you and get one too.'"

So even though boomers rejected their parents' choices, they are having an influence on their own children, she says. "When you have a Gen Y kid who comes in and says, 'Hey, I really like that Pontiac Solstice,' the parent says, 'You're not buying a Pontiac. Here's a Toyota Corolla for you.'"

Thus, GM is having difficulty overcoming negative perceptions of their vehicles, even among people who have never owned one. "People continue to think that the only thing they produce are gas-guzzling SUVs, that their vehicles are poor quality, that they're unreliable, that they're not aspirational vehicles," Lindland says. "You don't really aspire to one day own a Chevrolet or a Pontiac or a Buick."

Are the perceptions of bad-quality gas-guzzling SUVs still true? "No, I don't think it's true anymore at all," Lindland replies. "It was eight to ten years ago. But they have made tremendous improvement in their fit and finish, in how carefully they craft the vehicle, how carefully they build it. The allowance of error in terms of the fit, how a front and a side panel may meet, all those parameters have been tightened dramatically. In part, they weren't doing that before because nobody asked the workers to build a better vehicle."

Yet the message of bad-quality gas-guzzling SUVs gets pounded in the media over and over. And in Lindland's view, that's because many auto reporters and editors are boomers themselves. "Baby boomers don't like to be proven wrong, and they are against the Big Three in large part," she says.

"Look at what Toyota did," she argues. "Look at the last plant they built, which was their full-sized Tundra pickup truck plant. They didn't build a Prius plant. Well, the baby boomer media doesn't want to hear that. That means that Toyota did something a little bit close to incorrect. The message that the media sends—just continuously pounds—is that GM is inferior and they rarely give credit for the positive changes [GM is] making. The media certainly plays a huge part in this misperception."

Can it be overcome or is it permanent? She believes that Cadillac, in particular, has overcome the wall of negative perception, earning a very high approval rating for both its cars and trucks. Now GM has to do the same with its other brands. "I think they can continue to make progress," she says. "It can be a very fickle market. Small, stupid things can alienate people. Vehicle purchases are based on an emotional connection to a vehicle. That's something that Cadillac has done exceptionally well. They have products and a marketing campaign that resonate with people, including younger people. People say, 'I want to own that vehicle.'"

That kind of outreach is expensive and requires constant focus at a time when the company is being pulled in many different directions. "Certainly the CAFE [corporate average fuel economy] requirements that are coming up are putting a lot of pressure on them as a company," Lindland explains. "They're having to spend billions and billions of dollars to improve their fuel economy. From a financial standpoint, the stock market doesn't think it is a particularly sexy industry. It doesn't move fast enough for them. Wall Street is very much a 'what have you done for us this quarter?' environment." That, in turn, makes it more difficult to raise capital.

Lindland herself is an example of the work GM has cut out for it. She owned a Chevy Blazer in the late 1990s but then moved to a BMW X3 sport-utility. When the lease was up this past May, she looked at the possibility of leasing a Saturn Vue. "It was such a nice vehicle," she recalls. "It handled so nicely." But she was irritated that the Saturn didn't have an onboard computer that would calculate her fuel economy and tell her how many more miles she had before she ran out of gas. Plus, BMW offered her a "great deal." So she went with the BMW. The baby boomer attitude rubbed off on her after all.

Changing perception is tricky, laborious work that needs to be done at several different levels on a sustained basis. GM not only has to build better cars but has to improve perceptual quality—to be *seen* as building better cars. As the debate that erupted late in 2008 over federal loans for the auto industry revealed, there is still an absolute wall of hostility toward GM in many quarters. The truisms about the old GM were all trotted out: GM doesn't make cars that Americans want to drive. GM hasn't changed from its fundamental strategy of making gas-guzzling SUVs. GM hasn't begun trying to respond to Toyota's higher quality levels; its cars just aren't as good. The constant din of headlines about

GM being on the brink of declaring bankruptcy, despite repeated de-
nials, further compounded the battle of persuading Americans that it is
wise to buy its cars. As much as Wagoner and his company have done,
it's not yet enough—because buying a car in the end is an emotional
decision as much as it is a financial one. And the emotional currents
were certainly not all running in GM's favor.

CHAPTER 15

Toyota

"Human After All"

One of the major issues in contemplating GM's future is how well Toyota will fare over the next five years, during and after the deep U.S. economic downturn. In late 2008, both companies were suffering from the overall plunge in vehicle sales. (Car sales tumbled to an annual rate of slightly more than ten million, way below the sixteen or seventeen million the industry considers healthy.) No matter how that economic cycle plays out, GM doesn't ever have to "beat Toyota," in the sense that it forces Toyota out of the American market; such a thing is inconceivable. Toyota did, in fact, become the biggest-selling carmaker in the world for a brief time in 2007, much to the excitement of the automotive press. And depending on exactly how the economic crisis plays out, it could once again consolidate its hold on the top spot.

Toyota is one of the most remarkable success stories in international business history, particularly in view of its feudal, inward-looking origins. Toyota City was once called Komoro, a castle town where Ieyasu Tokugawa, the shogun of James Clavell's well-known novel, was born. It was Larry Armstrong, the Tokyo bureau chief of *BusinessWeek*, who educated me about Toyota's origins when I was editing the magazine's first cover story on Toyota in 1985.

The area's workers are descended from the Mikaswa bushi, the fierce

warriors who fought under Shogun Tokugawa. The saying is that Toyota drives its workers as hard as the shogun did his army, through a
mixture of stern discipline and generous patronage. It is much the same
approach Toyota takes to driving for the best price from its suppliers.
As the shogun used to say about his subjects, "Don't let them live, but
don't let them die."

The Toyodas are an intensely private clan, and their contact with
outsiders has been minimal, at least until recently. As Armstrong described it, "Inquiries are met with polite but deliberately vague responses.
Japanese newspapers, for example, have dubbed the president [Shoichiro
Toyoda] as president 'Otoboke,' a nickname that implies feigned innocence or playing dumb."

The family's code of silence extended to employees, Armstrong added.
"Sons of employees are given jobs at Toyota companies, making it hard
for their fathers to quit or even complain. A local farmer says friends
have been denied promotions at Toyota because they associated with
'outsiders.'"

The company (which originally made sewing looms) first tested the
American auto market in 1957 with its Toyopets, which were laughed
out of showrooms because of their odd design, small size, and poor
quality. But the company learned. Toyota withdrew from the market to
fix the product before reentering the United States in 1959. And from
that point on, for many decades, the company didn't miss a beat. It
used its joint venture with GM at NUMMI to learn how to set up a network of plants and just-in-time suppliers in the United States. Overall,
it executed brilliantly, even launching a new luxury division, Lexus, that
challenged Audi, BMW, Mercedes-Benz, and Cadillac, the world's finest
carmakers. The launch of the Prius hybrid was also brilliant.

One of its strengths has been its management talent. The Toyoda
family has been able to promote such talented executives as Hiroshi
Okuda, who in the mid-1990s, when I met him, was executive vice president with responsibilities that included North America. Okuda, fluent
in English and savvy about American ways, ultimately became CEO
and guided the company's expansion before being replaced by another
seasoned professional. Being family-dominated has not meant that

Toyota was family-managed, a critical shortcoming for 1
companies.

But beginning in late 2004, stress points started appear
Toyota, even as it pursued its 15/15 dream—that is, to hold 15
the world's auto market by 2015. In the annals of business I
company has been able to grow at Toyota's speed for four (
cades without developing excesses. They become overconfic
structures get out of control. Blind spots develop.

Some of the first signs that Toyota was having growing pain
ported in the fall of 2004 by Toshio Aritake in *Chief Executive* 1
which I edited at the time. After a period of rapid expansion,
tionally inward-looking company suddenly had 260,000 emp
twenty-six countries. Toyota was wrestling with how to mai
growth and how to balance decision making between headqua
various foreign geographies. The balance between Japan and th
States was particularly sensitive because the U.S. market was
Aritake wrote that Toyota's CEO at the time, Fujio Cho, was wor
the drive to expand internationally, adapting products to loc:
could start hurting Toyota's quality. Toyota had a human capit
lem, particularly in the ranks of its middle management. "Ever
becoming extremely busy," Cho told a small group of correspo
That comment has to be interpreted: Of course, everybody inside
was obviously busy. Cho's point was that they might be so busy tl
take their eyes off crucial priorities.

Toyota's first stumble was in the U.S. truck market. Driven
15/15 vision, the company charged into the heavy-duty pickup se
to compete against the GMC Silverado. It introduced one genera
heavy-duty Tundra trucks, then another, then another. But they
sell well, even with rebates.

Part of the explanation is that General Motors had long pl:
much greater emphasis on trucks than it had on cars. The design,
ity, and utility of its trucks proved to be a much tougher nut for 1
to crack. But another part of the explanation is that Toyota's Jap
management didn't listen adequately to what their American engi
were telling them. The story that emerged in the automotive pr

that when the American engineers said the Tundra needed extra-rugged features, Japanese management couldn't believe anyone would actually want those; no one in a Japanese cultural context could *imagine* needing them. So they vetoed those suggestions. But, of course, the American engineers were closer to the American truck-buying pulse than the executives back in Japan.

In 2006, Toyota reported double the number of recalls it had in 2005. This was unprecedented—Toyota issuing recalls? This pattern started in Japan but extended to the United States. Something obviously was going wrong someplace with the flawless Toyota method.

Another stress point that reemerged in 2007—at the very moment that Toyota temporarily became the world's number one automaker— was the balance between decision making in Japan and in the United States. When Toyota opened its first American plant, in Georgetown, Kentucky, its manufacturing operations reported straight to Japan; its sales operation in Torrance, California, also reported straight to Japan through different channels. The two units did not have a management structure in North America that governed their activities. A reporter who called the plant in Georgetown in the early 1990s often had to wait for the personnel there to send a fax (yes, a fax in that era) to Japan asking for instructions on how to respond to a question. It was the same for the sales division. Decision making was concentrated in Toyota City and Tokyo. There was an entity called Toyota North America headquartered in New York City, but it had very little authority.

The person who largely solved this issue was Jim Press, a native of Prairie Village, Kansas, who emerged from Toyota's sales division in Torrance. He built Toyota North America into a much more powerful decision-making body, allowing Toyota's operations in the United States to run almost as if they were an American company. On his watch, Toyota continued to expand sales and build new factories. In early 2007, having spent thirty-seven years at Toyota, Press was elected to the company's board, which was then all-Japanese.

At the time, he said he would be able to improve communications between the company's Japanese headquarters and its operations in America. His nomination to the board "allows us to operate more as a single entity," Press said at the time. That is a very revealing statement.

Getting the right balance in decision making was a real issue even in 2007, but Press would have enough power to mitigate it by representing the interests of American customers and other constituencies directly with top management and the board. At the same time, he served the function of being "the face of Toyota," in his words, to American consumers, politicians, and others.

But by the end of the year, Press was gone. Apparently frustrated that he could not move up within a Japanese-dominated company and sensing a better opportunity to lead, he left Toyota to join the ruling triumvirate at Chrysler, then newly independent from Daimler.

Toyota did not replace him with an American. Instead, it tapped Shigeru Hayakawa, who had been in charge of public relations in Tokyo and is known for being close to the Toyoda family. The departure of Press was more than the departure of one executive; it meant that Toyota's sensibilities in the United States would not be as keen. The balance in decision making almost certainly will shift back toward Japan. Indeed, the company was in some ways pleased to replace Press precisely because he had become so powerful. Toyota headquarters was worried that it was losing control of its North American operations, which were becoming "a Jim Press company," as one source put it.

At the same time Press was leaving, Toyota's breakneck expansion emerged as an even hotter issue within the company. Members of the Toyoda family, most notably Shoichiro Toyoda and former CEO Okuda, began expressing concern that the company had raised too many factories too quickly in the United States. It had built or started construction of eight plants in eight states, which was done for partly political reasons. Toyota wanted to have those states' senators and representatives on its side if ever it faced a showdown with the domestic auto manufacturers in Washington, which proved to be a powerful political strategy.

But that strategy created logistical problems; unlike in Japan, where Toyota's plants are more concentrated geographically, shipping parts between, say, Kentucky and Texas creates the possibility of delay. Toyota also faced the reality that its cost of operating in North America was increasing, due to a growing and aging labor force and expected increases in wages and benefits. Quality problems also were manifesting themselves. Toyota was running so hard to achieve its target of displacing

GM and selling 10.4 million vehicles in 2009 (the first time it would sell more than 10 million) that its growing pains were becoming more evident.

By November, the *New York Times* proclaimed that 2007 had been "a difficult year" for Toyota. "Its reputation for building high-quality vehicles has been tarnished, most recently by the decision by *Consumer Reports* to stop automatically giving a 'recommended' label to all its cars and trucks," wrote reporter Micheline Maynard. "Toyota's sales growth, which has been in the double-digit range in recent years, has slowed more in the United States than the company expected, causing it to lose its grip on the biggest-automaker title it took from General Motors last spring."

Even though GM's problems obviously were more severe, Toyota's challenges became more evident in 2008. Toyota president Katsuaki Watanabe came to the Detroit Auto Show in January and made a highly unusual appeal to his employees to take personal responsibility for the quality of Toyota cars and trucks. "Responsibility" is a loaded word in Japanese. If you take responsibility for an error, you may have to resign your job—the modern equivalent of falling on your sword. So it was remarkable that Watanabe said, "each individual must carry the responsibility" for fixing the company's quality problems. At the time, Toyota had recently recalled 470,000 vehicles in Japan, its fifth recall during 2007. Watanabe said his dictate was "something that's really shameful for us to share with you." By Japanese standards, this is strident language, implying deep frustration.

The fact that consumer demand shifted so suddenly in the second quarter of 2008 when gasoline prices shot above $3.60 a gallon did not help matters, for any car maker. As sales of bigger vehicles slumped, Toyota, for its part, suddenly had excess capacity at its truck plant in San Antonio, Texas. That means the factory was not running full steam, which is anathema to any car maker but particularly to hyperefficient Toyota.

Moreover, by the spring it was reported that Detroit's massive job cuts and restructurings had all but eliminated the labor-cost advantage that Japanese rivals such as Toyota had once enjoyed. *The Harbour Report*, the bible of car-making statistics, said Toyota's transplant factories needed just over thirty hours to assemble a vehicle and GM needed only two additional hours, meaning the difference now in labor cost per vehicle was a mere $260. "From a productivity standpoint, there is almost near-parity," said Ron Harbour, now a partner at Oliver Wyman. The Big Three "have never seen that before," he said.

Incredibly, *BusinessWeek* reported that sources close to Toyota said its assembly plant in Georgetown, where most workers are at the top end of the pay scale, could soon have the highest labor costs of any auto factory in the United States. Toyota's cost advantage per vehicle could start becoming a disadvantage.

Even though it has burnished its reputation with the expansion of the Prius hybrid brand, the more important commercial push for Toyota was into SUVs and pickups, which accounted for 20 percent of its lineup in 2008. After the surprises of the second quarter, Toyota said in July that it would shut down truck production at two U.S. plants for three months and consolidate its pickups into the San Antonio factory next year. "It shows that Toyota is just as fallible as anybody else," said auto analyst Joseph Phillippi. "They're human after all."

By August, Toyota started backpedaling on its sales projections, another startling admission of doubt by the standards of Toyota, which for years has been in expansion mode. It cut its 2009 sales outlook by 700,000 units to 9.7 million cars and trucks, and more startling, announced in the summer of 2008 that it is slowing down the pace of new product introductions. "We have been going at top speed up to now," Watanabe said. "It is time to set more cautious targets." In short, even if it has not officially said as much, the company appears to be retreating from its goal of 15/15.

Two other competitive issues bear mention here because GM is obviously trying to exploit them. In the absence of Press, Toyota's top management and board consist exclusively of Japanese men in their fifties and sixties, all wearing dark suits. They are culturally monolithic compared to GM, which although clearly dominated by white American men in their fifties and sixties still boasts a much higher percentage of American women and minorities, and non-American nationals, at the board and management levels, and indeed throughout the organization. GM's profile represents a cross section of the American populace;

one important piece of its market research is right in the building. To a much greater extent, Toyota has to rely on outside research, translated and communicated through channels to the leadership in Japan.

Toyota also was at risk of losing some glitter to GM's new designs, which have become both more aggressively forward-looking and more evocative of America's design history. Toyota's designs for the Camry and Corolla were still very workmanlike compared to that of the Malibu, which was enjoying increased sales despite a deteriorating market. With the possible exception of its Lexus SC 430 sports car, Toyota simply was not able to, or did not choose to, design vehicles as sexy as the Camaro or CTS Coupe.

To be sure, Toyota is not going away, not by any stretch of the imagination. It still sets the world standard in automotive manufacturing, and its brand equity remains higher than GM's by a wide margin. Further, its cash hoard of $40 billion means that it has enormous spending power. But it has entered a period of consolidation, or pause, in the badly damaged U.S. market.

The world financial crisis also could hurt Toyota, which has benefited from a stable exchange rate (about 105 yen to the dollar). Wagoner has complained for years that this rate was not based on the economic fundamentals of trade between the two nations. But major U.S. investors such as hedge funds and pension funds helped keep the Japanese currency stable by borrowing yen at low interest rates in Japan, converting them to other currencies, and then investing the money. This practice was called the carry trade. Unlike the Chinese government, the Japanese government did not have to intervene massively in currency markets to keep the yen at what Wagoner regarded as an unfairly low value.

But under pressure from mounting losses into 2008, U.S. investors were unwinding the carry trade, and this caused the yen to increase in value to 91 to the dollar. That swing is significant because Toyota makes 74 percent of its sales outside of Japan. Every time the dollar's value slips by one yen, Toyota's profit is cut by about $400 million. "It's tough," Yoichiro Ichimaru, a senior managing director, told the *Wall Street Journal*. "We really feel it." The yen could strengthen further, which makes it more expensive for Japanese companies to export from Japan to the United States.

Any student of Toyota would assume that the company will come back, perhaps stronger than ever. But temporarily, at least, the competition that GM feels from Toyota could be softening. The company appears to have expanded too fast in the United States and must consolidate. It also must wrestle once again with devising the right balance in decision making between the United States and Japan, in view of Press's departure. And the company cannot be immune to economic turmoil, particularly the threat of a continued surge in the value of the yen. "I think they have a lot of strength to build off of," says Wagoner. "They also have some challenges, like us. I shouldn't have this job if I wouldn't say this, but I like our odds."

The Economic Crisis and GM's Future

Even before the full weight of the economic crisis had landed, Wagoner understood what the stakes were for General Motors. "This is a company with a hundred years of history," he said. "It's a massive transformation. Just look at the changes in the way we've interacted with our unions and the structure there. It's a massive move from a traditional approach to 'how do we be successful in a new world order of globalization?' It's the whole ball game for the company."

By Wagoner's metaphor, the home team may have been winning for three and a half quarters, but the visiting team has suddenly grabbed the lead. The obvious response from the coach is "We win or lose the whole game in the next few minutes. We can't win part of the game."

So even in mid-2008, it was clear to Wagoner that "If we get it right, we get a hundred years of success in front of us. And if we don't, we're not gonna make it. I'm sure every generation of leaders at GM felt similarly challenged. But this is as big a set of changes as I've seen in my history with GM."

Those stakes rose abruptly during the meltdown of the financial markets in the fall of 2008. Auto sales, already in bad shape, fell off the proverbial cliff in October, plunging by about a third, as many potential buyers simply stayed out of showrooms. Taking into account adjustments for population, it was GM's worst month since World War II, during the era when food and other commodities were being rationed. In October, GM sold only 170,585 vehicles, a decline of 45 percent from the same month a year earlier. "It was like somebody turned the lights off," said sales chief Mark LaNeve.

Inside GM, the plummeting sales set off a series of management meetings and conference calls. As the company planned a response, it was critical for Wagoner to bring his board along. "They are with us every step of the way, providing their counsel and advice as we make the decisions we have to make," Wagoner said.

The essential issue was cash flow. GM had been holding $16 billion in reserves, enough to allow it to cover continued losses of about $1 billion per month until the benefits of cost savings and new models kicked in by 2010. This was the core strategy—essentially gutting it out until the company could turn a profit. But with dealers unable to get credit to loan money to customers, and with customers unable to make separate arrangements to buy cars, the industry was suddenly frozen. As a result, GM had burned a terrifying $4.2 billion in the third quarter. The company faced the very real prospect of dipping below the sum it needed—$11 billion in cash—to finance its global operations until 2010.

So it was in early November, just days after the United States elected a young African American senator to be its next president, that GM issued an astonishing statement. In a filing to the Securities and Exchange Commission, the company said its "ability to continue as a going concern" was in doubt. It had no choice but to turn to the government for a loan.

Amid an explosion of media coverage, most of which termed the loan a "bailout," like the $700 billion that had been set aside for the reeling finance industry, a date was set for the Big Three automakers to appear before Congress and plead their case. The first session before the Senate Banking Committee was called for November 18, and a second for the following day before the House Financial Services Committee.

After all the years of pushing to transform his company, Wagoner must have been deeply disappointed to have to turn to the federal government for help. But Wagoner couched the decision mostly in business terms: "It wasn't my preference to go and ask for funding," he told me.

"But to make sure the company and the domestic industry would survive this crisis, which was brought on by the global financial crisis, it was the option we had left, so we had to do it. It wasn't what I wanted to be doing. But I had a clear conscience—these were the circumstances that arose and we had to do what was right for the business."

At the same time that he faced a political process in Washington, Wagoner was facing a parallel challenge on Wall Street. GM's drop in sales was compounded by a troublesome move by Cerberus, the private equity group that owned 51 percent of GMAC (with GM holding the other 49 percent). Prior to the outright financial meltdown, Cerberus had announced that it would raise the creditworthiness standards of applicants for new GM car loans. For GM, this was an awful development; if its own financing arm was making it more difficult to buy cars, how could the company attract the customers it needed?

Cerberus may have made the decision purely for reasons of its own profitability. But there was a darker possibility. Cerberus also owned Chrysler and was trying to cajole GM to take the ailing automaker off its hands. Reports of a prospective merger dominated the auto news for several days in October. Many of the leaks in these articles came not from Detroit, but from New York. To many knowledgeable observers, that implied that the private equity crowd, and other investors who had lent money to Cerberus, were attempting to pressure GM into taking over Chrysler. For years it had been standard practice to use the media in this way during a possible merger or acquisition. It was never confirmed publicly, but many speculated that GM's "partner" in GMAC may have raised credit requirements—at a very tenuous moment—to force Wagoner to either accept the Chrysler merger or be squeezed out of business. In the end, the gambit didn't work because the industry quickly realized it had to turn to the federal government for help, but it did succeed in choking off financing to many people who might have purchased GM cars.

Much of Wall Street, including investment banks, hedge funds, and private equity funds, seemed to be campaigning for GM's destruction. In July 2008, Merrill Lynch had put out a report saying that GM's bankruptcy was "not impossible," which was completely unsubstantiated at that time because GM's cash reserves were in fine shape. But the report attracted wide media coverage—then Merrill Lynch proceeded to go out of business by selling itself to Bank of America at a bargain basement price.

In the fall, Deutsche Bank issued a report saying, "We are lowering our target on GM equity to zero dollars." It went on to suggest that the people who owned GM shares were "unlikely to get anything," meaning that any prospective bankruptcy or bailout would require wiping out the assets of shareholders. It's possible that Deutsche Bank, like others of the investors trash-talking GM in public, may have hoped to profit from "shorting" GM shares. With investors facing losses on so many other fronts, shorting was a desperately needed source of profits. Shorting involves selling "borrowed" shares at a given price in hopes that the value of the shares will decline, so that the investor with the short position can buy the stocks for less than they've already sold them for, thereby earning a profit. The shorts often make public statements (on blogs and websites or in traditional media) that they hope will help them achieve their objective.

Some firms were shorting GM in a big way. According to the financial weekly *Barron's*, GM was the company with the fourth largest number of shares shorted as of November—some 102 million, less than only Ford, Wells Fargo, and American International Group. And there was no way to know if Deutsche Bank was shorting GM shares. But how else was there to explain its estimate of zero dollars for the share price?

Convulsed with their own huge losses on highly leveraged positions and faced with the need to pay back money to angry investors in "redemptions" by year's end, hedge fund managers also were trying to push GM's shares south. All of which helped explain why GM's market capitalization (that is, the total value of all GM shares outstanding) was less than $4 billion, when the company had reported $178 billion in automotive sales last year, an absurdly low price-to-earnings ratio. (Wagoner wouldn't comment on the practice of shorting: "I don't think any money will be made if I go into some tirade on it.")

It was against this punishing backdrop that Wagoner, Ford Motor CEO Alan Mulally, Chrysler CEO Robert Nardelli, and UAW chief Ron Gettelfinger appeared before the Senate Banking Committee to seek

$25 billion in loans to their companies. Wagoner's testimony did not present him at his best; he was on the defensive and was more irritated than I had ever seen him. He was out of his element; he was communicating with numbers and strategic concepts, but the senators were playing for the cameras.

As Wagoner had long argued, Chapter 11 bankruptcy might have been an option for an airline or an investment bank, but not for a car company. Why would anyone have the confidence to buy a car from a company that was in bankruptcy proceedings? In his testimony, Wagoner cited an independent study from CNW Research that showed 80 percent of prospective car buyers would not purchase a vehicle from a bankrupt company. The report was entitled, "File for Bankruptcy? Kiss Buyers Bye, Bye." For Wagoner, a figure like 80 percent is overwhelmingly clear. He repeated it emphatically. But the senators did not seem to be listening to figures.

One of the most implacable was Senator Richard C. Shelby of Alabama. "The financial straits that the Big Three find themselves in is not the product of our current economic downturn, but instead is the legacy of the uncompetitive structure of its manufacturing and labor force," said Shelby, the senior Republican on the committee. He called GM and the other two domestic manufacturers "dinosaurs" and added: "The financial situation facing the Big Three is not a national problem but their problem."

Shelby's rhetoric was shockingly off the mark. The survival of the U.S. auto industry was certainly a national issue, and GM in particular had made major strides in improving its cost structure, nearly eliminating the cost gap with Toyota's Georgetown, Kentucky, facility.

If it wasn't the facts that were supporting Shelby's views, there seemed to be several factors contributing to the bitter resistance that he and other southern Republican senators displayed. One was free market ideology. Free marketeers had felt obliged to go along with the $700 billion for Wall Street because Treasury Secretary Henry Paulson (the CEO of Goldman Sachs at the very moment that it had become embroiled in Wall Street's love affair with mega-leverage) had convinced them the entire financial system would shut down if they did not.

But when it came to the auto industry and the UAW, they wanted to

slam the brakes on. Part of it also was sheer spite: Republicans were reeling after one of their most devastating electoral losses in history. The
auto industry, and particularly the United Auto Workers, had helped get
the Democratic vote out and deliver the crucial swing states of Michigan and Ohio to Barack Obama. Moreover, the UAW was an old adver-
sary of lawmakers from right-to-work states, which have long resisted
unionization. The hearing was an opportunity to settle old scores.

And the presence of so many transplant factories in southern states
was a major new variable. Shelby had four auto plants—Honda,
Hyundai, Mercedes, and Toyota—in his native Alabama, whose government had provided hundreds of millions of dollars' worth of financial assistance to persuade those manufacturers to locate there. It was
no small irony that he was fighting government loans to auto manufacturers located elsewhere in the country. If the Big Three were to go out
of business, the transplants would inevitably pick up more business. Alabama would receive more jobs—never a bad thing for a senator who's
looking toward the next campaign.

It was in this political environment that the second day of testimony
began in the House. The issue that quickly dominated the headlines and
the talk shows was how the three CEOs had traveled to Washington—
they all had arrived in their company jets. Late-night comedy shows
and op-ed writers crowed that "beggars" with "tin cups" had come to
Washington—on their fancy jets. A vital debate was reduced to a sound
bite.

Of course, most CEOs of large companies travel on corporate jets,
partly because of security concerns but also because their time is under
such pressure—particularly when they're preparing to face Congress.
But in a climate of economic fear, it was clearly a miscue.

Temporarily at least, GM and the domestic auto industry were left
twisting in the wind. Gerald F. Seib, writing in the *Wall Street Journal*,
explained how the increased political power of the southern transplants had helped turn the political tide against the Big Three. That
factor helped explain "why AIG—a company that doesn't even make
anything shiny a lawmaker can lay a hand upon—is getting more than
$100 billion in bailout money from Washington, and Citigroup has just
got $306 billion of its troubled assets guaranteed by the feds, while an

effort to provide a simple $25 billion bridge loan to America's iconic Big Three auto makers collapsed," Seib wrote. "It is, in many ways, a bizarre anomaly."

At a minimum, the first round of the political debate helped clarify the economic stakes. As the experts contemplated what would happen if one Big Three manufacturer declared Chapter 11 bankruptcy, they discovered that all three supply bases were interlocking. Which meant that if Chrysler, say, went into bankruptcy, that would throw many of its tier 1, tier 2 and possibly tier 3 suppliers into bankruptcy as well. That would in turn prevent those suppliers from sending parts to GM, Ford, and even some of the transplants. The latest figures to emerge showed that the Big Three employed 240,000 workers and their suppliers an additional 2.3 million, amounting to nearly 2 percent of the nation's workforce. That didn't include dealers, trucking companies, or any other company that depended on the domestic auto industry.

Current jobs weren't the only jobs at risk; future prospects were on the line too. The United States' hope of obtaining a piece of the $150 billion lithium-ion battery business would be dashed if GM didn't create a market for the batteries by building the Volt. If GM were crippled or forced into bankruptcy, "the foreign companies would develop the batteries, but not here," said Sean McAlinden, chief economist at the Center for Automotive Research in Ann Arbor. "We would lose all the additional development connected to that technology. It would be a technology opportunity lost."

One explanation for why the political circus prevailed over the economic stakes seemed to be that Americans were so scared for their own prospects. Unemployment was increasing, and hundreds of thousands of Americans were losing their homes to foreclosure. Health care insurance costs kept escalating and some forty-five million Americans were living with no health insurance at all; gasoline prices had declined to around $2 a gallon, but few believed it was an enduring trend. Retail sales, which represented nearly 70 percent of the American economy, were cratering; credit card companies that had helped fuel consumption were experiencing mounting losses and were tightening credit conditions. Millions of Americans who had borrowed against their home equity to sustain their household spending now found that resource disappearing. The stock market was suffering sickening downward lurches on a regular basis.

Americans seemed to be hungry for someone to blame, and Wagoner became a prime candidate for that rage. Unlike Ford's Mulally and Chrysler's Nardelli, who had been at their jobs for only short periods and had come from outside the industry, Wagoner had been in the auto industry for his entire career. The national zeitgeist seemed to be: If somehow Congress could tear down Wagoner and force GM into bankruptcy, it would represent a long-awaited act of justice. Of course, he was in an entirely different category from the CEOs of Merrill Lynch or Citigroup who had run their financial institutions into the ground and then walked away with multimillion-dollar golden parachutes. They were invisible as they headed into wealthy retirements. Wagoner, struggling to transform and save an American icon, was clearly in the sights of the American people.

The toxic climate meant that the automotive CEOs had to come back a second time, in early December, but this time they and the UAW were better prepared as they sought $34 billion in loans, admittedly an increase from the prior round of testimony. This time Wagoner, like his two counterparts, drove to Washington, an image of which was displayed on the front page of the *New York Times*. A different, humbler tone was on display. "We're here today because we made mistakes," Wagoner said.

GM had devised a plan under which it would take steps that critics had long urged. With Fritz Henderson's fingerprints clearly on its proposal, GM said it would revamp its product lineup by concentrating on four brands: Chevrolet, Cadillac, Buick, and GMC. Pontiac would become a specialty brand. Hummer was already up for sale, and Saab would almost certainly go on the block. Further, the company would talk to Saturn dealers to explore alternatives for that brand. Wagoner had long resisted this drastically strong medicine, but Henderson was quoted a couple of years earlier as saying, "no brand has a God-given right to exist." In effect, the preparation of GM's survival plan represented Henderson's continued ascent toward running GM's day-to-day operations.

For his part, Wagoner announced he would accept a salary of $1 for 2009, which defused the important issue of his $4 million in compensation in 2007.

The UAW also threw in its set of sweeteners, saying it would reopen its 2007 contract with the manufacturers to eliminate the Job Banks program. Although the program had been whittled back in recent years to cover only a few thousand workers, it was still a target of ire for lawmakers on both sides of the political aisle. Gettelfinger promised other steps to allow the domestic industry to close the cost gap with the foreign transplants.

Thanks to the fresh approach—combined with massive lobbying efforts by dealers and other constituencies that would be hurt by bankruptcy—the political climate shifted enough that the Bush administration decided in late December 2008 to grant $17.4 billion in loans to GM and Chrysler as part of massive continued restructuring plans. The money came with the condition that the manufacturers prove their financial viability by the end of March 2009. But in any case, the loan would be enough to allow them to survive to see Barack Obama take office in January 2009. The president-elect's sentiments were clear. Obama had said in an interview with *60 Minutes* that the collapse of the auto industry "would be a disaster in this kind of environment, not just for individual families, but the repercussions across the economy would be dire." He wanted a solution that involved compromise by labor, management, suppliers, lenders, and other stakeholders, which is precisely what the industry was offering.

No matter what action Obama takes, GM still faced the long-term task of righting its businesses and returning to profitability in North America. Barring an extraordinary recovery in the American economy, no one would know for sure whether or not that was possible until 2010 or later.

In attempting to assess the future of General Motors, I'm aware that seemingly infinite cynicism toward the company has at times been appropriate. Over the course of the past three decades, many of the things that GM management promised didn't happen—or happened incredibly slowly. And yes, it appears that everyone who held out hope for GM finally turning the financial corner in 2005 or 2006 or 2007 was disappointed. The events of 2008, most of them beyond the control of GM or anyone else, delivered to the company and the country what can only be described as an annus horribilis.

In the darkest possible interpretation, the weight of history is so great that nothing Wagoner does can work, no matter how well organized and executed. GM's efforts to spin off its parts supplier Delphi could remain bogged down in bankruptcy court. It still owns a hefty piece of GMAC, which could condemn it to further losses because of that entity's exposure to bad real estate loans. Wagoner, the skeptics say, is not the right man to lead a company in crisis. Rather than being too bloody-minded, he is too soft, too much of a southern gentleman. He didn't shut down factories and fire layers of management bureaucracy fast enough. He didn't attack the UAW outright. In the second quarter of 2008, when GM and the rest of the industry were surprised by the rapid shift in the market, he didn't fire John Smith, who, as head of planning, should have seen it coming. Nor did he fire Gary Cowger, head of manufacturing, for allowing strikes to happen at Delta Township and Fairfax.

On the basis of hundreds of interviews and thousands of miles of travel on three continents, I believe that GM, with the benefit of federal loan guarantees, will reach a point at which it is very competitive. GM's transformation should be allowed to play out because the company has made enormous strides. The federal assistance will not be wasted (as it may be in the case of AIG, whose losses appear to be a bottomless pit). Given assistance through the most difficult economic patch most Americans have ever seen, GM can rebound. The federal investment will pay off in many ways.

As this book has established, the very structure of GM has changed. The transformation effort has in fact taken a long time, sometimes far too long. But that doesn't mean that nothing has been accomplished. Powerful forces already have been unleashed inside GM. Wagoner didn't start them all; he inherited momentum from Jack Smith toward getting the right management model in place. But he pushed the reorganization, and in 2008 his management team demonstrated how fast it could move. Confronted by rapid shifts in the marketplace, management made a staccato series of decisions to close plants that made the wrong products and bring on new plants and new shifts for the right ones. Even during a collapse of sales, the traces of an accelerated decision-making ability were clearly visible.

Wagoner also has put the right cost structure in place, taking $5,000 out of the cost of each car. He inherited the push toward lean manufacturing from Smith, but saw it through to the point that GM has for all intents and purposes eliminated the quality gap with Toyota products.

Critically important was a steady stream of new products hitting American and world markets. (Ford and Chrysler are not nearly as well-endowed.) The oft-repeated argument that "GM just doesn't make cars that Americans want to drive" is simply out of date. GM has secured a design lead over Toyota, which simply could not compete with the appearance and performance of the new CTS or Camaro, for example.

The company's technology profile is also robust, thanks in part to the success of OnStar and the strides it is making with alternate propulsion systems, as with the Volt. And the global GM is now able to marshal its human resources, design and engineering resources, and purchasing power in ways that the company never could before.

To be sure, the months of uncertainty about GM's survival and the damage that its reputation has suffered at the hands of Congress and the media will make it harder. "The base of jumping off into the future is lower" than it was six months earlier, Wagoner told me. But because of a new round of belt-tightening measures that would involve shedding several brands, coming after years of restructuring and downsizing, Wagoner has argued that GM will be "very lean and mean" when world economies start to recover.

Moreover, he should be able to overcome the argument that GM offers nothing but gas-guzzlers, as many pundits have suggested. Aside from the Volt, the company has eight other vehicles on the market with either hybrid power systems or hydrogen-based engines (even though hydrogen is a distinct long shot because the infrastructure to support it would be so expensive to build).

Cynics may argue that the company was promoting the Volt so heavily in 2008, a full two years before it was to become available commercially, because it wanted to enhance its bid for federal loan guarantees or to push for tax credits for consumers who wish to buy a Volt. Undoubtedly there is some truth to that. But the deeper point is that GM will no longer be sidelined in the race toward alternative propulsion systems. Toyota might also be introducing a lithium-ion battery plug-in product in 2010; it might even beat GM to the market. But it won't be a repeat of the situation in which Toyota introduced the Prius and GM was not able to respond for years. In this case, "GM will be on the field," says Stephen Girsky.

When the economic crisis eases, where will GM's U.S. market share stabilize? Eighteen percent? Seventeen and a half? No one knows, and it is useless to speculate. At some point, the company will reach a defensible size, an equilibrium point, particularly if it shrinks to four brands. Overall U.S. sales will increase at some point, perhaps sharply, as buyers have money in their pockets again. And at some point, GM will start gaining market share, making more conquest sales not only against Toyota but also against Ford and Chrysler (particularly if Chrysler sells itself; of the three American automakers, it was least well equipped to survive intact). By suggesting that it was committed to only four of its eight brands, GM seemed to be acknowledging that it would shrink and no longer strive to be number one in the world.

The new GM is going to be much more global, with as much as 75 percent of sales outside the United States. Michigan and Ohio are not likely to ever see a surge in General Motors' employment. In these areas, GM's transformation does not presage a return to the good old days.

The new GM is going to make a much higher percentage of cars and fuel-efficient vehicles than the old GM; it's going to be a technology leader and design leader, thanks to a globalized, diverse group of people. "We will survive," lead director Fisher says. "I think General Motors will still be one of the largest automotive companies in the world."

Although many thousands of GM people have either left the company or been forced out over the years, Wagoner has kept the company's morale up. Those who remain believe they have a future. The company also appears connected to reality. GMers know what the marketplace is saying and are striving to prove that they have responded. It's a far cry from the GM of Roger Smith's day, when denial and arrogance dominated.

As a result, it does not feel like a defeated organization. A pattern of dysfunction usually sets in inside organizations that know they're failing. They lock up. They don't invest in new products. They don't invest in grooming talent. GM has put some product programs on hold to conserve cash; in one sensible case, they stalled work on a big new SUV because clearly the market doesn't want SUVs at this time. But in general, GM is not anywhere close to being in the condition of Lehman Brothers in its final days, when stunned young investment bankers walked into their offices and carried their possessions out in cardboard boxes. Nor is it like Enron or Worldcom. Or Merrill Lynch or Washington Mutual or Fannie Mae or Freddie Mac. GM is not an organization showing signs of a breakdown in confidence.

Wagoner doesn't give off the air of a man who has been defeated. One of his strengths has been an ability to project confidence throughout the organization. Some photos of him have captured a sense of unease on his face, and he was certainly uncomfortable during his congressional testimony. That's hardly surprising—the game is down to the final sixty seconds, and he's got his best team on the floor. The whole game is still to be won or lost.

As for the cries for Wagoner's scalp, I asked him about a report in the *Wall Street Journal* suggesting that support for him on his board was cracking. Does the board still support you? "I guess the answer to that is yes—until it's no," Wagoner joked. No CEO can know the precise moment at which he or she loses support from a board. They learn about it after the fact.

But then Wagoner became serious and described a conversation with George Fisher: "I just got off the phone with our lead director, and I assure you I get nothing but recognition and support and thanks for putting up with all this stuff," he said.

To be sure, there is a feeling in the air that Wagoner, at fifty-five, is beginning to imagine a life after the CEO's chair. Before the economic crisis erupted in a full blaze, he told me about having bought a Pontiac Solstice sports car just before Christmas 2007. "It's got a fancy paint job on it," he said. "It's pretty cool. It has not been out of the garage yet. I told the boys it's not to be driven until the snow is gone. I think the next add will be a sixty-nine Camaro. Then I'd like to get a new Camaro. People ask me, 'Is that all you're going to buy? GM products?' The answer is that I would actually like to get an early-sixties Jag," like the one the Navy guy used to drive up to Richmond from Norfolk.

But it seems unlikely the GM board is going to push Wagoner into full retirement to tend to his car collection until he's ready. The reason they haven't fired him, despite billions of dollars in losses and the need to appeal for federal help, is that they agree with his long-term strategy and believe that it was working until it was interrupted by an international economic crisis.

That could change if the Obama administration and its new "car czar" insist that Wagoner step aside in exchange for federal support. In that case, Wagoner would likely be made just chairman of the board and Henderson elevated to the CEO role. Henderson is seen as more aggressive about making painful changes. He has credibility with Wall Street, which could be crucial. Henderson also appears to have a strong working relationship with the UAW, which could be equally as important. In a soft transition of this sort, Wagoner could still set the company's strategic direction with Henderson growing into the role of a full-fledged CEO. And GM could announce to the world that Wagoner had, in fact, left the job of CEO; but his influence would endure for some time longer.

Bob Lutz will clearly be leaving the scene at some point. He likes to joke that he'll have an accident on one of his motorcycles or in one of his airplanes, but the more likely scenario is that he will retire peacefully by the time he turns eighty years old in 2011. But the impact of what he has done will last for many years.

Whoever occupies the CEO's chair, the fundamental strategy will remain the same for the foreseeable future. The idea that an outsider with fresh ideas could parachute into the top job at GM and introduce sweeping change in one or two years is preposterous. The scale and complexity of managing a company of GM's size is simply too great.

Ultimately, the GM transformation effort is a test of the resiliency of the American economy and of what role America plays in the world. Does it choose to maintain a vibrant technological and manufacturing base, or does it place all its bets on services and finance? Does it make the right decisions to maintain high standards of living? Or in an alternative scenario, does America head down the path toward something approaching Third World status with others controlling its manufacturing base? Does it support its ability to project military power in places such as Iraq and Afghanistan, as former general Wesley Clark argued it should?

Now that the economic crisis has struck, many of the jobs created in finance, whether in mortgage finance, investment banking, or hedge funds, were built on the concept of leverage. They were not involved in creating genuine wealth. They have proven ephemeral, as have jobs in construction and tourism. The fact that 70 percent of the American economy was based on consumer spending, and much of that spending was based on borrowing money from abroad, was almost certainly not realistic for sustaining the economy. The consumer is going to have to deleverage, just like Wall Street is.

In a time of crisis, when traditional forms of credit are simply not available, I predict that a percentage of Americans are going to ask themselves, "Where does wealth come from? And what kind of wealth creation is sustainable?"

Washington alone cannot turn the economy around with stimulus packages; the very structure of the economy must change to begin reversing a thirty-year cycle of borrowing too much money from the rest of the world. Consumer spending must decline as a percentage of the total. To help fill the gap, I'm convinced that the industrial sector, of which GM is a major part, will prove to be a source of sustainable wealth creation for America in the world. As this book has established, manufacturing is amazingly intricate. It offers the very sort of high-end jobs in design and engineering that Americans want and the country needs. And it extends its nerve endings in many different directions throughout the economy, including the high-tech sector. It's hard to imagine a healthy technology industry without an auto industry to buy from it.

Seen in that light, GM is not a dinosaur left over from the previous century. It is a crucial piece of America's effort to revitalize its economy and sustain its position in the world for the next century.

Acknowledgments

Some old friends provided great moral and intellectual support. Fred Mackerodt, who manages General Motors' press fleet in the New York area, provided deep insight into the company and suggested several key interviews. Herb Shuldiner, one of the deans of the automotive press corps, with many decades of experience at *Ward's*, read parts of the manuscript and prodded me to ask tough questions. Alex Taylor, the automotive correspondent for *Fortune* magazine and the most respected auto writer in the land, read and critiqued the manuscript.

Outside the auto world, Leah Nathans Spiro, a colleague from *BusinessWeek* many years ago, helped me develop the concept of the book. My friend William Lang argued with me for hours about the future of the Detroit automakers, which was always stimulating. And Toshio Aritake, in Tokyo, whom I've known for nearly thirty years, helped me with the chapter on Toyota.

My agent, Paul Bresnick, was a source of wisdom, and my editor Nick Trautwein's meticulous editing style was a pleasure. At General Motors, Steve Harris, the senior vice president in charge of corporate communications, saw the wisdom of cooperating with me in this endeavor, and Tom Wilkinson, also in the public relations department, played the day-to-day role of opening up channels inside GM and fielding a steady stream of inquiries from me.

My children, Jason and Ali, endured growing up in a home in which global economics were the subject of dinner conversation. And my fiancée, Rita Sevell, endured being alone or being shortchanged of my affection because of all the time and travel I invested in this book. Most important to any author involved in the intensely lonely task of writing a book, Rita believed in me.

Index

A Note on the Author

William J. Holstein has written for *BusinessWeek, U.S. News & World Report*, the *New York Times*, and *Fortune*, among other publications, and is the author of the books *Manage the Media* and *The Japanese Power Game*. He graduated from Michigan State University in East Lansing, Michigan, the heart of auto country, in 1973. After starting his career with United Press International, he became a UPI foreign correspondent in 1979 in Hong Kong, where his reports on Deng Xiaoping's economic modernizations won an award from the Overseas Press Club for best economic reporting from abroad. From 1985 to 1996, he worked as an editor at *BusinessWeek*, where he managed much of the magazine's Asian coverage and orchestrated its first cover story on Toyota, along with many stories on the auto industry. In 1989, he spent months in Japan, researching and writing *The Japanese Power Game*, which appeared the following year. At *U.S. News*, which he joined in 1996, he covered the American economy with a specialization in autos (and also began a serious love affair with cars, driving Cadillacs, Corvettes, Ferraris, Maseratis, and Porsches, among many others). He interviewed Rick Wagoner first in 2003 for *Chief Executive* magazine, and then again for the *New York Times* in 2005. In this same period, he joined the board of the International Motor Press Association in New York. His favorite recent test drives include the new Cadillac CTS-V and the Mercedes CL 63 AMG.